Aspects of
Early Childhood Education
THEORY TO RESEARCH TO PRACTICE

EDUCATIONAL PSYCHOLOGY

Allen J. Edwards, Series Editor
Department of Psychology
Southwest Missouri State University
Springfield, Missouri

In preparation:

Merlin C. Wittrock (eds.). The Brain and Psychology
Marvin J. Fine (ed.). Handbook on Parent Education
James H. McMillan (ed.). The Social Psychology of School
Learning

Published

Dale G. Range, James R. Layton, and Darrell L. Roubinek (eds.).
Aspects of Early Childhood Education: Theory to Research
to Practice
Jean Stockard, Patricia A. Schmuck, Ken Kempner, Peg Wil-
liams, Sakre K. Edson, and Mary Ann Smith. Sex Equity in
Education
James R. Layton. The Psychology of Learning to Read
Thomas E. Jordan. Development in the Preschool Years: Birth
to Age Five
Gary D. Phye and Daniel J. Reschly (eds.). School Psychology:
Perspectives and Issues
Norman Steinaker and M. Robert Bell. The Experiential Tax-
onomy: A New Approach to Teaching and Learning
J. P. Das, John R. Kirby, and Ronald F. Jarman. Simultaneous and
Successive Cognitive Processes
Herbert J. Klausmeier and Patricia S. Allen. Cognitive Develop-
ment of Children and Youth: A Longitudinal Study
Victor M. Agruso, Jr. Learning in the Later Years: Principles of
Educational Gerontology
Thomas R. Kratochwill (ed.). Single Subject Research: Strategies
for Evaluating Change
Kay Pomerance Torshen. The Mastery Approach to Compe-
tency-Based Education
Harvey Lesser. Television and the Preschool Child: A Psycho-
logical Theory of Instruction and Curriculum Development

The list of titles in this series continues on the last page of this volume

Aspects of
Early Childhood Education

THEORY TO RESEARCH TO PRACTICE

Edited by

Dale G. Range

Department of Elementary Education
Southwest Missouri State University
Springfield, Missouri

James R. Layton

Department of Educational Administration
and Special Programs
Southwest Missouri State University
Springfield, Missouri

Darrell L. Roubinek

Department of Elementary Education
Southwest Missouri State University
Springfield, Missouri

 1980

ACADEMIC PRESS
A Subsidiary of Harcourt Brace Jovanovich, Publishers
New York   London   Toronto   Sydney   San Francisco

ACADEMIC PRESS, INC.
111 Fifth Avenue, New York, New York 10003

United Kingdom Edition published by
ACADEMIC PRESS, INC. (LONDON) LTD.
24/28 Oval Road, London NW1   7DX

Library of Congress Cataloging in Publication Data
Main entry under title:

Aspects of early childhood education.

   (Educational psychology series)
   Includes bibliographies and index.
   1. Education, Preschool. 2. Education, Primary.
I. Range, Dale G. II. Layton, James R. III. Rou-
binek, Darrell L.
LB1140.2.A838   372'.21   79-28850
ISBN 0-12-580150-5

PRINTED IN THE UNITED STATES OF AMERICA

80 81 82 83   9 8 7 6 5 4 3 2 1

To Sandra, Bret, Chad, Waldo, and Helen

D. G. R.

To Barbara, Kent, and Dee

J. R. L.

To Jerri and Darren

D. L. R.

Contents

CHAPTER **6**

**Research and the Teacher: Teacher Effectiveness in Early
Childhood Education**   **143**

SYLVESTER KOHUT, JR.

CHAPTER **7**

**Implications for Early Childhood Education Practices
and Procedures**   **181**

DALE G. RANGE, JAMES R. LAYTON,
AND DARRELL L. ROUBINEK

List of Contributors

Numbers in parentheses indicate the pages on which the authors' contributions begin.

Barbara D. Day (39), Department of Curriculum and Instruction, University of North Carolina at Chapel Hill, Chapel Hill, North Carolina 27514

Susan L. Hom (87), Department of Psychology, Southwest Missouri State University, Springfield, Missouri 65802

Harry L. Hom, Jr. (87), Department of Psychology, Southwest Missouri State University, Springfield, Missouri 65802

Sylvester Kohut, Jr. (143), Department of Secondary Education and Foundations, Tennessee Technological University, Cookeville, Tennessee 38501

James R. Layton (1, 181), Department of Educational Administration and Special Programs, Southwest Missouri State University, Springfield, Missouri 65802

Dale G. Range (181), Department of Elementary Education, Southwest Missouri State University, Springfield, Missouri 65802

Paul A. Robinson (107, 119), Department of Psychology, Southwest Missouri State University, Springfield, Missouri 65802

Darrell L. Roubinek (181), Department of Elementary Education, Southwest Missouri State University, Springfield, Missouri 65802

Barbara Mathews Simmons (1), College of Education, Texas Tech University, Lubbock, Texas 79409

Eddie L. Whitfield (1), College of Education, Texas Tech University, Lubbock, Texas 79409

Preface

This book contains research-based information and expert opinion related to the development of effective practices for early childhood education. It can be used by faculty members in education and psychology, preservice and inservice teachers of young children, and by program designers in developing scientifically based programs to benefit young children and their parents.

The chapters are organized to allow the reader to move progressively through sections of information in which various authors, from allied fields of education and psychology, have isolated specific aspects of early childhood education. When viewed simultaneously, the chapters contain historical, empirical, and resultant practical procedures moving the reader from theory to research to practice.

In Chapter 1, Barbara Mathews Simmons, Eddie L. Whitfield, and James R. Layton trace the historical origins of early childhood education from Plato and Aristotle through contemporary practices. Emphasis is placed on the influences affecting teacher preparation as well as influences affecting the nature of programs for children.

In Chapter 2, Barbara D. Day presents relevant research findings related to the effects of Project Follow Through and the positive and negative effects of television, play, and formal reading instruction for young children. Both Chapters 1 and 2 contain information that can be used to develop goals and objectives, as well as specific activities, for early childhood programs in teacher education or for planning programs for young children.

Harry L. Hom, Jr. and Susan L. Hom, in Chapter 3, and Paul A. Robinson, in Chapter 4, detail specific methods that may be used by teachers and parents in modifying and controlling the behavior of young children. In Chapter 5, Robinson discusses parental influences and parent education programs. The chapter contains information that can be used in planning parent, preparent, and teacher inservice and pre-service programs.

In Chapter 6, Sylvester Kohut, Jr. presents research findings and expert opinion related to teacher effectiveness. The section contains specific practices or competencies as well as implied competencies for teacher education programs.

In the final chapter, Dale G. Range, James R. Layton, and Darrel L. Roubinek identify the major implications of the preceding chapters for three groups: (1) the family, (2) implementors of early childhood education programs, and (3) designers of teacher training programs.

ACKNOWLEDGMENTS

As editors, we are indebted to many persons who contributed to this book. The major part of the work was done by the authors of the individual chapters. We are also indebted to Debbie Berrier, Faith Clayton, Fran Sullivan, Jane Tracey, Beth Trickey, and Carol Zinn for their efforts in preparing parts of the manuscript. Special acknowledgment is given to Barbara Layton for typing portions of the manuscript and for verifying bibliographical references. Kent and Dee Layton were especially helpful in the final editing of the index. We wish to acknowledge the editor of this series, A. J. Edwards, for his patience and support in completing the project.

CHAPTER 1

The Preparation of
Early Childhood Teachers:
Philosophical and Empirical Foundations

BARBARA MATHEWS SIMMONS
EDDIE L. WHITFIELD
JAMES R. LAYTON

During the early 1960s interest was rekindled in the educational welfare of children between 3 and 5 years of age. Federal funds were allocated for the study of programs that existed, for program development for teachers, and for new and innovative programs for young children. By the mid-1960s a new phrase, *early childhood education,* came into prominence. The phrase was used to encompass and be synonymous with the terms *early education, preschool education,* and *kindergarten education.* The rebirth of interest in the young child resulted in a substantial increase of kindergarten programs being implemented in the public schools. To many observers, those programs are considered as important as the elementary and secondary programs that formerly dominated American education.

Further study and research into the nature of teacher education and young learners led to the current trend of a redefinition of early childhood education to include children from birth to age 8; that redefinition resulted in, and will continue to have, an impact upon the nature and design of teacher education programs. One significant result has been a shift in the responsibility for educating prospective early childhood education teachers. Programs that were conducted largely by child development specialists are now being shifted to educational psychologists and early childhood education specialists in schools or departments of psychology

1

ASPECTS OF EARLY CHILDHOOD EDUCATION
Theory to Research to Practice

and education. Another impact of the redefinition has been in the development and implementation of preschool, early education, and kindergarten programs. Once those programs were varied and relatively unrelated to one another. But as a result of researchers' attention to young children and federal legislation regarding the education of all children and youth, prospective early childhood education teachers will be well educated. As the teachers enter the 1980s, the programs they develop based on their education and preparation may not reflect the wide differences that formerly existed between lower elementary or primary grade programs and preschool or kindergarten programs (Range, 1978).

Hom and Robinson (1977) were among the first psychologists to question the degree to which early childhood educators, prior to the 1960s, attended to research findings when teacher education programs and schools for young children were designed and implemented. They stated, "Early education in the United States prior to the 1960s was not strongly influenced by research data and theory from child psychology [Hom & Robinson, 1977, pp. 23–24]." Earlier, Evans (1975) had discovered traces of Freudian psychology as well as Deweyian philosophy within the curricula of early childhood programs but concluded that the programs were void of any organized framework. Seemingly, the retrospective view may lead to the conclusion that prior to the 1960s, teacher educators and teachers of young children had no definitive philosophical or empirical research base for the programs implemented. However, that charge may not be altogether true.

Prior to the mid-1960s the designers of early education programs subscribed to or were noncognizant proponents of maturational theories of learning. Their beliefs were influenced by writings of Plato, Aristotle, Luther, Erasmus, Comenius, Rosseau, Pestalozzi, and Froebel. Later, Dewey, Hall, and other educators in the United States presented ideas that were interpreted by the proponents of maturational early education programs to be supportive of their philosophies and theories. Consequently, few changes or alterations in programs were made prior to the 1960s era.

The remaining portion of this chapter will contain a historical overview of the early philosophical thoughts and European influences that dominated early education in the United States. Next, views of early, prominent Americans will be presented as evidence to support the contention that the early education designers did view their programs as being based on reputable research findings as well as contemporary educational thought of the period. Finally, the early education movement will be traced to the 1960s and beyond to reveal the three major categories or psychological views of contemporary early childhood education: (a) behavioral; (b) maturational; and (c) cognitive. Each phase of the chapter contains information concerning the nature of early childhood education as it relates to young children which in turn must be viewed as foundations for programs developed for educating prospective teachers.

PHILOSOPHICAL FOUNDATIONS

The education of young children was deemed important by many early philosophers who are still credited with having identified and classified the values, mores, and attitudes that have guided and directed the thoughts and actions of human beings in the past and present. Many of their beliefs regarding young children were employed in the designs of European preschools, and as a result were transferred to preschool programs in the United States. The influence of those early thinkers is prevalent today and may never completely disappear from educational practices.

EARLY PHILOSOPHERS AND EUROPEAN INFLUENCES

Plato and Aristotle

Hutchins (1952) identified the specific contributions of Plato and Aristotle to the education of young children. Plato recognized the "young and tender thing" to be at a stage of development when character was being formed. He viewed that period as one in which impressions would be more readily accepted. Plato also believed in a coeducational system in which teachers would provide equal opportunities for both sexes. However, Plato was aware of the natural differences in human beings to learn, study, remember, discover, and make application of knowledge (Hutchins, 1952, p. 359).

Aristotle's concerns for young children were similar to Plato's in matters of intellectual discipline. However, Aristotle specified that prior to the age of 7, children's growth would be impeded if they were required to enter formal study or work. Aristotle recommended that parents assume the responsibility for children's education during the early years and that the children be provided with sufficient motion activities "to prevent the limbs from becoming inactive [Hutchins, 1952]."

Luther and Comenius

According to Braun and Edwards (1972, p. 541), by the sixteenth century religious leaders began to direct their attention toward educational practices.

Luther believed that parents were unqualified to educate their children and preferred the employment of trained public school teachers to conduct religious and moral lessons. Erasmus also desired to prepare teachers by training them in an orderly humanistic process. In turn the teachers would apply the same humanistic methods in teaching children (Braun & Edwards, 1972, p. 29).

Comenius wrote the first picture book for young children. However, the book was more specifically a guide to enable teachers to prepare humanistic, appealing lessons rather than the remote and austere lessons Comenius observed in practice. DeYoung (1950) indicated that Comenius viewed educational programs of that period (1657) to be a waste of children's time and a "slaughterhouse of the mind." Curtis and Boultwood (1961) wrote that Comenius contended that the acquisition of knowledge resulted from activities followed by reasoning. Therefore, Comenius believed strongly that the use of concrete objects and sensory training in educational activities was superior to verbalism if true learning and the acquisition of knowledge were to result.

Rousseau

In 1794 Rousseau's ideas were gaining prominence and being incorporated into educational schemes. Rousseau denounced theories that children were inherently evil and expressed his theory of naturalism. Lee (1953) wrote that Rousseau believed that children proceeded through natural stages of growth and that learning experiences should be shaped to fit those stages. According to Rousseau, only attempts by adults to force children into learning activities not commensurate with their growth patterns would predestine the children to failure.

Rousseau also recognized the variability in learning among children and stressed that all children should not be required to conform to one standard. Rousseau did not view children as miniature adults and advocated child-centered educational environments in which children could progress individually through natural stages of social, emotional, and intellectual growth. Educational environments, so designed, would be based upon Rousseau's naturalism theory which stated that individual children should be given the freedom to express interests and fulfill needs. Designers of teacher education programs, influenced by Rousseau's theories, stressed input and discouraged verbal instruction (Bloom, 1978).

Pestalozzi

Pestalozzi was another prominent educator who exerted a marked influence upon early childhood educators. He too viewed educational practices to be responsible for stifling children's growth. Pestalozzi (1892) viewed sensory learning and oral language development to be the basis or substructures for the later learning that would be required of children. Pestalozzi agreed with Rousseau's naturalism theory and suggested that children be provided opportunities for active involvement, object lessons, and oral language development. Pestalozzi also believed that the ideal educational institution was the home and that schools should reflect the characteristics of a good home. He believed that curriculum should be practical and designed to allow graduated subject matter to be presented that would be commensurate with stages of growth, always beginning with the simplest elements. To prepare teachers for those responsibilities, Pestalozzi recommended that experimental schools be provided (Cordasco, 1970).

Froebel

By 1889, recommendations for the education of teachers and children were abundant. However, Froebel (1889) is heralded as Father of the Kindergarten. His extensive work was in learning, teaching, curriculum, materials, experiences, teacher aides, cultural deprivation, and teacher training, all related to children below the age of 6. Froebel influenced not only European educational systems but also those in the United States. As late as 1969, Dowley (1969, p. 318) wrote, " . . .the curriculum of compensatory education which is emphasized today as an antidote for cultural deprivation draws heavily from the thinking of Pestalozzi and Froebel." Specifically, Froebel is credited with the following ideas:

1. Children should be allowed to play in school to provide them with the "germinal leaves of later life."
2. Children should be provided with natural materials and engage in creative activities (i.e., large blocks, live pets, etc.).
3. Mothers should be utilized as teachers' aides.
4. Teachers should be trained in apprenticeship programs.
5. All children, including the poor, should be included in kindergarten programs.

Froebel's influence, along with that of the earlier thinkers or philosophers may never entirely disappear from contemporary early childhood education programs. In fact, many of their ideas have been shown by contemporary researchers to be reputable ideas worthy of inclusion into programs for young children.

LEGACY FOR AMERICAN EDUCATORS

Perkinson (1968) wrote that when colonists first arrived in the new land, they depended more upon teachers and the schools they established than they had in Europe. The reason for that dependence, according to Perkinson, was threefold: (a) the parents spent many hours securing food, shelter, and clothing for their children, thus, ignoring their children; (b) there were no other civilized institutions in America; and (c) the parents supposed that their children would become savages if they were not educated. As early as 1642, the citizens of Massachusetts passed a law requiring parents to educate their children; by 1647 they enacted a second law requiring citizens in each town to provide teachers. Those schools were established to insure that children would become religious and God-fearing.

The ideas and beliefs of the early European thinkers were very much a part of the colonists' educational schemes (Demiashkevich, 1935). And although Smith (1965) did not find specific evidence that European and English reading materials were brought to America by the colonists, she did discover that books were shipped at later periods. By the 1790s the American citizens established a relationship between government and education (Perkinson, 1968; Smith, 1965). That relationship as well as the one with religion were both *essentialistic* in philosophy and directly traceable to the European thinkers (Demiashkevich, 1935). Demiashkevich also contended that the educational programs, the training of teachers, and other aspects of education during those periods could be traced to the same early and later European thinkers.

European philosophers and educators continued to influence American educators for many years. By the 1860s, early education or preschool programs were being studied in Europe and ideas were being brought to the United States for implementation (Layton & Phillips, 1978). The legacy from the earliest beginnings of philosophical thought in Europe to the first permanent, public kindergarten in the United States may be summarized as follows:

1. Early education of children is important.
2. Individual differences exist in children.
3. Natural stages occur in children's development.
4. Education of young children's bodies and characters is more important than intellect, per se.

5. Education of young children should be humanistic in nature.
6. Concrete materials and experiences should serve as the basis for learning rather than highly verbal experiences.
7. Education of young children should include activities in which they are free to express interests and fulfill needs.
8. Education of young children should include many varied opportunities for play.
9. Familiar influences are extremely important in the total development of young children.
10. Parents should be included in both formal and informal aspects of early childhood education.
11. Preservice and internship training of teachers is important and should include first-hand experiences with children.

In view of their simplicity, few persons would be able to provide strong arguments for the foregoing statements. Seemingly, each fits well within the theoretical bases upon which early education and preschool programs were established prior to 1964. Many of the practices still may be observed in contemporary traditional and innovative programs.

MAJOR INFLUENCES ON EARLY EDUCATION, c. 1839–1964

Early American educators sought to improve the learning opportunities for children by improving the quality of education for teachers. The ideas of Rousseau, Pestalozzi, and Froebel were broadly implemented by Mann, Blow, Hall, Parker, and Dewey. Each person influenced the educational programs designed for young children.

Mann, Peabody, and Schurz

Mann established the first normal school for educating teachers in 1839. He also established a system of public support and control of the school (Braun & Edwards, 1972). Mann is credited with initiating new educational policies that were adopted throughout the nation at every educational level. However, his wife and her sister, Elizabeth Peabody, wrote the first American kindergarten textbook and were leaders in the kindergarten movement. Their views paralleled Froebel's beliefs that teachers be friends to children and abstain from punishing them (Osborn, 1975).

Margarethe M. Schurz established the first American kindergarten in Watertown, Wisconsin (1856). She was also responsible for converting Elizabeth Peabody to Froebel's philosophy (Master, 1978). However, the

German language was used in Schurz's school. It was not until 1860 that the first English-speaking kindergarten was opened by Elizabeth Peabody and Mary Mann, in Boston. In 1868 a training school for kindergarten teachers was organized by Madame Kiege and her daughter. The first state normal school kindergarten was founded at Oshkosh, Wisconsin, in 1880. Other kindergartens were established in Los Angeles and San Francisco. However, it was not until 1873 in St. Louis that the first permanent public kindergarten was opened in the United States.

Blow, Harris, and Hill

Susan Blow (Layton & Phillips, 1978; Lundgren, 1976) was influenced by the works of Froebel when she resided in Germany. Blow returned to the United States in 1871 and received training from Maria Krause-Boelté who had studied with Froebel's wife, Louise, in Germany and later taught in England with Bertha Rongé, a student of Froebel's (Pyle, 1978). In 1873, Blow opened the first permanent, public kindergarten in the United States. Later, Blow was encouraged by William T. Harris, superintendent of St. Louis Schools, to implement an early teacher training program. Blow's influence spread rapidly across the United States. She lectured jointly with Patty Smith Hill at Teachers College, Columbia University, between 1905 and 1909.

Hill had formerly been director of the Louisville Kindergarten Training School in Kentucky and gained national recognition prior to going to Columbia (Wyckoff, 1978). Hill's work also was strongly, if not completely, influenced by Froebel (Elizabeth Peabody and Mary Mann were also disciples of Froebel's).

Parker, Dewey, and Kilpatrick

Parker, who served as superintendent of schools in Quincy, Massachusetts in 1875 and later at the Chicago Normal School (1896–1899), employed Froebel's principles in designing early education programs in Quincy and at the Cook County Normal School in Illinois. Earlier, in 1871, he too traveled to Europe to study the theories of Comenius, Pestalozzi, Herbart, and Froebel (Neff & Engle, 1978). Parker was hailed by Dewey as Father of Modern Education. In 1901, Parker became the first director of the School of Education at the University of Chicago and was responsible for founding the progressive education movement (Neff & Engle, 1978).

Dewey is considered to be the leading American educational philosopher and molder of teacher education policies in education. He joined the faculty at Teachers College, Columbia University, 2 years after the death of Parker and 1 year before Blow and Hill began their joint lecturing. Dewey was a critic of "sit and listen" schools. He inspired teachers to provide students with active involvement and experience learning. Dewey also advocated the establishment of an organic wholeness between the children's interests and the curriculum. The unquestioned success that John Dewey achieved in teacher training was responsible for drastic changes in schools and curriculum throughout the nation. Many of Dewey's ideas, like those of Parker, were developed directly from the teachings of Froebel.

Another key person in the progressive movement was Kilpatrick, a professor of education at Columbia University. He also indoctrinated thousands of elementary teachers who enrolled in his classes into the doctrines of progressive education. Kilpatrick encouraged teachers to design learning environments in which purposeful activities were constant with the children's goals (Cremin, 1964). As Dewey viewed education to be life itself rather than the preparation for life, Kilpatrick viewed education to be a set of purposes and plans for learners and not for teachers.

The geographical and chronological span of the Manns, Peabody, Blow, Harris, Schurtz, Smith, Parker, Dewey, and Kilpatrick enabled their beliefs to become solidly entrenched in educational practices in the United States. From the 1830s well into the 1930s and beyond, their views on educational matters were heard and their ideas implemented. The scholars were located in key cities and universities: St. Louis, Louisville, Chicago, Boston, and New York. As a group, they could be classified as proponents (cognizant or noncognizant) of the maturational theory, supportive of Froebel's philosophy.

THE EUROPEAN-AMERICAN LEGACY IN PRACTICE

Susan Blow's influence on William T. Harris was a strange phenomenon. Although Harris may be listed among those influential educators who supported the employment of the maturational theorists views in the kindergarten, his personal views toward educational philosophy and curriculum design for elementary and secondary schools were definitely *Hegelian*. Harris's strong belief in Hegel's philosophical views or *idealism* was reflected in his actions and recommendations for educational planning. Harris believed that the purpose for education was to take children safely through the world of theory (sense-perception and relativity doctrine) to the level of insight, and into the personal nature of the absolute. Harris believed that students should be punctual, exert self-control, and be industrious. Educational programs were designed to allow teachers to provide for those characteristics. However, Harris's writings reflected that he respected Froebel's beliefs and also the self-activity of students. But rather than free play or uncontrolled activity, Harris strongly believed that assigned tasks were of value regardless of the child's interests.

It may be hypothesized that Blow's success in influencing Harris was partly a result of the age group with which she worked. The children were, in Harris's terms, at the levels to be "taken safely" to the level of mature insight into the absolute nature of things. Kindergartens implemented by maturational theorists were a perfect environment for that development to occur. But beginning in the first grade, things would change for those children as they arrived at the age of reason or were ready to begin learning the absolute nature of things.

Mann and Parker also visited Europe to study and observe the educational systems. Mann observed that Prussian children were grouped according to ages that were relatively commensurate with the stages of growth that Rousseau and Pestalozzi had identified. During the 1840s and into the 1860s, schools in the United States were organized in the same manner. Also, books that were designed for reading instruction were written to be commensurate with the growth levels children would achieve as they advanced through the grades. That practice changed very little until the 1930s when teachers began to organize their instruction in accordance with the needs and interests of children (Smith, 1965). The *activity movement* as it was termed resulted largely from the influences of Dewey and Kilpatrick. However, the activity program required many books for the children to use as they pursued their interests. But few guidelines were written for teachers to follow; therefore, the impact of the activity movement was not long-lived (Smith, 1965).

It may be hypothesized that when graded schools evolved and teaching materials were written in graded editions, both of which were intended to be used to meet individual growth patterns, needs, and interests of students, that a decline began in the amount of attention teachers could devote to the maturational theorists' recommendations. Aspects of educational programs designed to provide children with reasonable learning tasks they could attain, as they became *ready*, were converted to hurdles for them to challenge, ready or not.

Dewey was a leading proponent of reading readiness. By 1925, the *preparatory period* (prior to first grade) was universally accepted as an important stage in the growth of children (Smith, 1965). Dewey stipulated that children should not be taught to read prior to the chronological age of 8. Morphett and Washburne (1931) indicated that children with mental ages beyond 6.5 years experienced fewer failures than children who were less mature. Those influences, in part, led to the belief and practice of teaching readiness in the first grade as a part of the reading program. Therefore, another task was delegated to primary grade teachers and not recommended for kindergarten teachers. Slowly, the materials that were designed for use in the elementary schools were developed with accompanying scope and sequence charts which teachers apparently misused. The teachers paced children through the material to be learned rather than allowing the children's success to set the pace. As a result of readiness programs being incorporated into the first grade, kindergarten teachers were left relatively free and unsupervised. Therefore, they were free to continue implementing programs that followed the guidelines established by maturational thinkers.

Another event that may have influenced teachers' misuse of graded, sequenced materials was the determination that supervisors were needed to insure that reading and other subjects were correctly taught (Smith, 1965, p. 262). Supervisors and building principals were given the responsibility for supervising classroom activities. Graded plans were established and materials were employed to teach children in a lock-step fashion. Additionally, the most efficient way for principals and supervisors to oversee the teaching processes was to devise plans for teachers in which they were required to complete certain units, achieve specific goals, and move groups, rather than individual children, through a progression of predesigned learning tasks.

The teaching procedures that were espoused during the progressive education movement, based largely upon the interpretations of the philosophy of Froebel, became inoperable as a result of attempts to transform the principles into mechanical systems. But, the kindergartens remained relatively untouched by the events as a result of the interpretations of research and the fact that kindergartens were either privately or parochially supported. Educational theory from the progressive movement was deeply entrenched in the kindergarten teachers' attitudes toward learning and children. Those attitudes and resultant practices remained until the early 1960s. Today, the application of those ideas has not completely disappeared from early childhood education programs for children between 3 and 5 years of age.

The only notable dissenter to the protagonists of Froebel's philosophy and leaders of the progressive education movement was G. Stanley Hall. The studies Hall conducted led him to believe that a multidisciplinary approach to early childhood program development was superior to the recommended procedures of the maturationalists. Hall studied experimental psychology with Wundt in Germany. Wundt was instrumental in the movement to make psychology as scientifically reputable as physics. Hall introduced scientific psychology into the United States and also the idea that schools should be child-centered. According to Cremin (1964), Hall believed that civilization could be judged by the way children grew and that school personnel should adapt themselves to providing programs commensurate with the natural growth of children. Hall believed that heredity placed limits on the child's ability to learn and that educators were powerless to change or alter those limits (McDonald, 1964). Dewey, who was a student of Hall's, and other educators in the early 1900s, rejected those views. Although some of Hall's views were rejected, he was instrumental in implementing the multidisciplinary approach to early education programs. But the majority of the programs at that time remained maturational in character.

In summary, teachers who were educated to have attitudes and conduct lessons in accordance with Froebellian and Deweyian philosophies implemented programs based on their beliefs. With the advent of graded classrooms, graded materials, and principals or supervisors (who also helped standardize teaching practices for the masses), few of the progressive education techniques could be employed. The supposition that learning should be likened to play, that children should be allowed to grow and develop naturally, and encounter new experiences as they were ready, were beliefs that did not fit well into educational designs beyond the kindergarten. Perhaps there were too many children, too much for them to learn, too much faith in American education, too many social pressures, and other interferring variables. As a result, schools became learning factories rather than institutions modeled after the home as Pestalozzi recommended. But, the kindergarten and preschool remained relatively untouched and teachers in those schools were free to employ the techniques that reflected maturational thinking.

RESEARCH INTO THE NATURE OF EARLY EDUCATION PROGRAMS AND TEACHER EDUCATION PRIOR TO 1964

Earlier in this chapter reference was made to Hom and Robinson's (1977) cogent observation that early childhood or preschool programs were designed and implemented with little, if any, regard for existing research in child development. Thus far in the chapter an attempt has been made to indicate the events that led to the development of preschool and kindergarten educational programs that were essentially maturational in nature. Inferences were also made as to some of the possible reasons why preschool and kindergarten teachers retained teaching techniques associated with maturational thinkers and why elementary teachers could not continue to employ those techniques. One research study (Morphett & Washburne, 1931) was cited as being interpreted to mean that children with mental ages of 6.5 or higher were able to learn to read with more ease than youngsters of lower mental functioning. As a result of the interpretations of that study, first grade teachers were delegated the responsibility for teaching readiness; kindergarten teachers were freed from that responsibility. But, research findings *were* used as a basis for the kindergarten teachers' attitudes that they were not responsible for implementing structured, cognitive-based, early childhood programs. Other similar examples of misinterpretations of research were presented by Hunt (1964).

According to Hunt (1964), six practices of preschool and kindergarten programs based on research existed. Those views were used to support the designs of early education programs. Hunt cites the following beliefs and some of the researchers responsible for them.

1. Intelligence is fixed or unalterable (Cattell, Hall, and Terman).
2. Development occurs in stages or is predetermined (Coghill, Gesell, Thompson, Watson, and Skinner).
3. The brain operates in a manner similar to a telephone switchboard in that it is fixed and static (Thorndike, Morgan, and Hull).
4. The need for learning experiences during the early years of development, especially before speech occurs, is unnecessary (Hunt's research base is unclear on this point).
5. Experiences in the early years of development that affect development during later years are emotional reactions that result from "the fate of instinctual needs and impulses" (Freud).
6. Learning is "motivated by homeostatic need, by painful stimulation, or by acquired drives based on these" (Guthrie, Mowrer, and Freud).

Hunt identified the works of many researchers as being erroneous. He also identified the researchers who provided data that could be used to repudiate the six major fallacies. However, during the period of time when each of the concepts regarding child development and learning were accepted as truths, the psychologists and educators who were conducting early childhood programs were following or adhering to the dictates of researchers of the period. However erroneous the interpretations were, the maturationalists could cite researchers who supported their recommendations.

Hunt presented substantial evidence that errors in research and subsequent interpretations led to erroneous education practices. It may be noted that some of Dewey's beliefs, such as the need for a preparatory period and waiting until children reach 8 years of age to teach them to read, may fall into the areas of erroneous interpretation and research. However, Goodlad (1966) credited Dewey with providing a logical basis for curriculum planning. According to Goodlad, Dewey's recommendations that learners begin by experiencing primary data, then progressively learning to reorganize them, and finally "perceiving order among phenomena," is the primary avenue for involving students in subject matter. Goodlad also predicted that in the future educational decisions made by teachers will be based upon scientific facts and that practices of recognizing and providing for individual differences among children will prevail.

Goodlad's research and writing in the area of nongraded schools was an attempt to destroy or diminish the harmful effects of lock-step school arrangements, learning requirements, and student evaluations that were unsound practices not based on research. Goodlad considered the teachers' practices he observed in the maturationalist based nursery and kindergarten programs to be more commensurate with the philosophical base and research findings than were those of elementary school teachers (Range, 1978). However, Goodlad et al. (1973, p. 150) reported that when considered separately, early education and schooling was found to be deficient in three major components: "(1) the lack of fit between stated philosophy or goals and the provisions of program; (2) the narrow array of program offerings; and (3) the lack of pedagogical sophistication on the parts of teachers." In another portion of their report (p. 152) the same writers indicated that one reason for children's failure in the first grade and in subsequent grades was the failure of the designers of first, second, and third grade curricula to redesign their programs to accommodate the characteristics of children who enter from early childhood programs, especially children from Head Start (Weikart & Lambie, 1968). Goodlad, Klein, and Novotney (1973) considered the kindergarten programs they studied to be superior to the nursery school and primary school programs studied and that "They intend to provide programs . . . identified with the most frequently articulated goals of nursery schools. . . [pp. 150–152]." Again, credence is added to an earlier contention that the nursery school and kindergarten teachers prior to 1964 and afterwards who subscribed to the whole-child concept were following the established guidelines more closely than other teachers.

New early childhood programs were offered in 1965, but even with newer programs and extensive empirical evidence that emerged, proponents of those newer plans still have not been sufficiently influenced to eliminate the influences of maturational thinkers.

EARLY CHILDHOOD TEACHER EDUCATION
SINCE 1960: THE TRANSFORMATION

During the 1960s monumental changes occurred in early childhood teacher education. Federal legislation in 1964 and 1965 resulted in the allocation of large amounts of money for preservice and inservice education of teachers. A part of the Economic Opportunity Act (1964) contained provisions for preschool programs for economically and educationally disadvantaged children. The programs, coined *Head Start*, were instituted in 13,400 centers throughout the nation; the impact upon local education administrative units and the schools or departments of education in higher education was tremendous. According to Hess and Croft (1972), intense efforts were exerted on research and experimental programs to insure that the educational needs of members of the target group were met. As a result of those efforts, early childhood education programs for children as well as prospective teachers were irreversibly transformed. But even with the drastic and dramatic changes that transpired, the maturationalist point of view continued to be a viable element in the designs of many programs.

The three major programs that were developed for young children may be divided into the three major psychological theory categories:

1. Behavior/Learning/Transmission Programs
2. Developmental/Maturational Psychology Programs
3. Psychodynamic/Integration/Cognition Programs

Each has specific components based on the designers' views of learning theory and child development. However, to the untrained observer and in the implementation of the programs there may appear to be overlapping or identical elements among the three. But the reasons or basis that protagonists specify for their separate views may be very different. For the purposes of this chapter, the points of view will be categorized as: (1) behaviorist, (2) maturational, and (3) cognitive.

Many programs that were developed to be pure within a specific philosophical or psychological view or research base may also be observed as relatively impure when implemented. And in many instances, teachers change contents or procedures after the program has been implemented as a result of their perceptions of discrepancies. Subsequently, quasi-eclectic programs result rather than pure programs that are wholly or completely aligned with any one theory.

In Chapter 2 of this work, Day outlines the specific procedures of several early childhood programs that are currently in use. The Bank Street College Approach, the Cognitively Oriented Curriculum Model, the

Responsive Environment Model, and the Systematic Use of Behavioral Principles, plus other models are based upon rationales, and contain objectives, that reflect their designers' psychological viewpoints. Day and Parker (1977) presented an in-depth explanation of almost all early childhood education programs that were in existence through 1976. Fromberg (1977) described perceptual models that were designed to unify the diverse ways and tools that children can use to learn. Spodek's (1973) and Spodek and Walberg's (1977) works contain many contemporary views regarding young children's intellectual, cognitive, affective, social, and linguistic behaviors and learning. Each work cited would be very useful to prospective teachers in studying the specific elements within the various early childhood education programs. Most recently, Austin (1976) surveyed the issues, aims, objectives, and methods related to early childhood education in eight countries belonging to the Organization for Economic Cooperation and Development (OECD). Austin's work is monumental for two major reasons: (1) programs which exist in other countries that may be useful in altering or designing programs in the United States are described and (2) the international concern for young children's welfare is clearly established, providing additional support for those persons in this country who view early childhood education as essential.

The writers of this chapter used the works cited above, plus several other books, to develop a list of statements related to teacher performance or knowledge that reflect the views of the *behaviorists, maturationalists,* and *cognitivists.* The works of Bigge (1971), Stiles (1974), Hilgard (1964), and Torrence and White (1969) were essential to the project undertaken. By using information in all the works cited, it was possible to categorize and verify the beliefs of theorists and implementors of early childhood education programs. The product is a result of the recommendations of Seaver and Cartwright found on page 33 of this chapter.

If prospective early childhood education specialists are to be required to design and implement programs that are characteristic of each of the viewpoints described earlier, it is essential that they be given valid information that may be used for those purposes. The following lists may provide part of that data.

Behaviorists — Stimulus-Response (S-R) Conditioning

Behaviorists believe that overt behavior is a reflection of an organism's thought processes or mental operations. Behaviorists contend that human beings respond to cues which provide the necessary stimuli that direct the person to a subsequent movement. As responses are made to cues, these responses are "accumulated," along with the cues, to form a well-organized system or chain of behaviors that reflect learning. The behaviors that occur are believed to be reinforced through various reward systems even though the rewarders may be noncognizant of their action or deed. But, when children demonstrate desirable behaviors and receive rewards which reinforce their behaviors until the behaviors become automatic without the rewards, then behaviorists would conclude that learning had occurred (Bigge, 1971).

According to authorities who compiled the Educational Products Information Exchange document (1972), some behaviorists also accept the premise that young children learn as a result of models or persons in the family or community who demonstrate specific behaviors which are mimicked by the young observers. The postulation of that belief serves to explain the ability of many young children to perform acts prior to formal instruction.

Many researchers in the fields of genetics and the behavioral sciences have provided evidence that there are physiopsychological limits that prevent some human beings from learning information or performing specific tasks (Educational Products Information Exchange, 1972). Some behaviorists maintain that children can learn almost anything if provided the appropriate educational setting. Prospective teachers enrolled in early childhood education programs would learn to design and implement behavioristically based prereading or beginning reading programs with the following features.

1. The teachers believe that the psychological and physical environment they create will be the variable that controls the degree of learning in the classroom (Bijou, 1977).
2. The teachers develop lessons in which reinforcement contingencies or rewards are provided for appropriate behavior (Bijou, 1977).
3. The teachers carefully prepare or choose learning packages that are broken into small units and specific activities developed to insure that proper cues are preplanned, with reinforcement, to elicite proper responses (Camp, 1973).
4. The teachers design each lesson to know which response to expect following each cue and to know that the response confirms that a learning or accumulation of learnings has occurred; learning must be explicit and observable (Bereiter & Engelman, 1966).
5. Students' motivation is provided by the actions of the teacher (Berieter & Engelman, 1973).
6. When students demonstrate that they did not learn, the teacher reorganizes or refashions the learning environment to create a new

situation or degresses to a previous step or stage that is preventing the present learning from occurring (Berieter & Engleman, 1973).

7. Students are not held accountable for their inability to learn; teachers are the master planners and in complete control of the students' destinies (Bushell, 1973).

8. Teachers develop activities that will allow children to practice the learnings that occur (Bushell, 1973).

9. Children should learn formal language and mathematics skills at an early age in a variety of structured situations (Spodek, 1973).

10. Teachers must view children's physical, linguistic, cultural, and ethnic characteristics as pertinent to the success they achieve in learning, but teachers must know that those variables are secondary—the teachers' role is of primary importance and diminishes all other effects (Camp, 1973).

11. In addition to academic learning, children should be provided with specific opportunities to learn appropriate work habits such as: raising hands, waiting patiently for the teacher's attention, persisting and persevering in completing a task, delaying gratification, and following established rules, regulations, and procedures (Bereiter & Engelman, 1973).

12. Teachers should provide many prereading and prearithmetic skills such as recognizing objects and words, performing divergent and convergent mental operations, as well as teaching children to evaluate and show appreciation for materials, ideas, and the thoughts and feelings of other persons (Bereiter, Engelmann, Osborn, & Reidford, 1964).

13. The teacher is a technician who is responsible for the direct teaching of specific, prescribed lessons to children (MacDonald, 1973).

14. Teachers must design or select programs in which the areas of study are separated into small, specific units and programmed into a logical, sequential order for presentation; all lessons should be highly task-oriented (MacDonald, 1973).

15. Teachers must stress children's attention to the tasks presented and their ability to master the material; however, competition among or between children must be deemphasized and, if possible, eliminated (MacDonald, 1973).

16. Training programs for children must be academic in nature and include formal language and mathematics instruction (MacDonald, 1973).

17. Teachers must provide learning environments in which a process of operant conditioning is employed to develop appropriate or desired responses or shape the behaviors of children; positive rewards will be superior to negative ones (Spodek, 1973).

18. Children must have frequent opportunities to practice the learnings to be acquired and be provided with immediate feedback as to the quality of their response; programmed-type materials are useful in this respect (Spodek, 1973; MacDonald, 1973).
19. Teachers present lessons that are preplanned and carefully designed; children's interests are not viewed as important; there is little room for spontaneous activities or discovery learning (Blank, 1973).
20. Teachers must provide lessons in which abstract thinking is stimulated early (Blank, 1973). Teachers are in complete control of the children's activities; parents and other persons may be used as aides or be taught how to reinforce school-learned behaviors at home (Bijou, 1977); however, as a result of the highly technical teaching procedures, parents and untrained adults would not *teach* (Educational Products Information Exchange, 1972).
21. Children who exhibit linguistic or academic handicaps in learning must be provided special learning programs designed for them; teachers should not disengage from the learning tasks to be mastered, but rather, redesign activities to allow children to be successful (Bereiter & Engelmann, 1966).
22. Teachers must develop systematic, continuous reinforcement procedures, especially when initial learning experiences are developed—sporadic or inconsistent reinforcement is ineffective (Spodek, 1973; Bushell, 1973).
23. Teachers must plan activities in which children demonstrate that they have developed adequate self-concepts, self-esteem, and the esteem of other persons.
24. Teachers will develop several sets of sequential learning tasks that may be learned simultaneously by children. Objects, symbols, ideas, and vocabulary terms would be manipulated by children as they learn to enumerate, categorize, systematize, perceive relationships, and synthesize the information presented directly by the teacher. Such activities would develop auditory and visual discrimination skills, imagery, vocabulary, and cognition as substructures to success in beginning reading and arithmetic.
25. Children may be taught to read through use of the synthetic method in which they learn grapheme–phoneme relationships and advance to synthesization processes (Layton, 1979).
26. As lessons are planned and conducted, teachers must be cognizant of the children's stamina and physical endurance and provide rest and relaxation periods; however, claims that behavioral teaching techniques are too exhausting for young children should be discounted (Educational Products Information Exchange, 1972).

27. All lessons should begin with simple, concrete learning experiences and advance to abstract, complex, and more difficult levels as children develop response chains (Spodek, 1973).

For educators who view the behaviorists' views as inappropriate for young children, especially 3-, 4-, and 5-year-old children, perhaps maturationalist ideas will be more acceptable.

Maturationalists — Whole-Child Concept

A large portion of the beginning of this chapter was devoted to the events that led to the predominance of the *whole-child* concept or maturational theorists' influence on preschool and kindergarten programs in the United States. Even in view of psycho-scientific research, the *whole-child* advocates, or maturationalists, maintained their beliefs and influence in matters of child growth and development. As new programs emerged in the 1960s and as the 1980s are entered, the maturational early childhood education programs still exist and prospective teachers are being educated to operate those programs in fashions not dissimilar to those of Susan Blow.

Behavioral theorists adhere to the belief that the environment is dominant and that through appropriately designed activities and teacher behaviors children can learn almost anything. Maturational theorists view children's inherited characteristics and growth patterns to be the basis upon which early childhood educational programs should be designed. The behavioral advocates accept that various forms of immaturity do exist in young children but believe that procedures may be employed to educate the children and remove the immature characteristics. Maturational protagonists contend that through natural growth processes in physical, mental, and emotional attributes, guided by genetic processes, children will achieve appropriate stages of readiness to learn. Therefore, it is believed that educators in early childhood programs should provide activities similar to those used in the home and allow children to follow their interests, felt needs, and desires as they progress through specific stages of internally controlled maturation. Advocates of the whole-child concept do not deny the importance of or influence exerted by environmental variables upon a human being's development. They merely contend that environmental variables do not produce the maturation of children (Johnson, 1961; McCandless, 1961).

Teachers in departments or schools of education and psychology or child study who emphasize this approach will probably teach prospective teachers to design and implement early childhood education programs with distinctive features. They contend that young children's development and behaviors (cognitive, affective, psychomotor, and creative) will be controlled ultimately by genetic variables, but exogenous conditions may to some degree alter specific growth patterns. Young children's development in school may be enhanced by designing and implementing programs with the following features.

1. The teachers believe that the psychological and physical features they create will provide learning areas for the children. As the children's natural unfolding or growth occurs sufficiently for them to be able to successfully manipulate the materials provided, learning will occur (Spodek, 1973).

2. The teachers will provide learning centers or areas which will contain materials especially designed and selected to be commensurate with the children's genetic growth stage or level (physical, intellectual, social, and emotional) (Spodek, 1973).

3. The teachers will schedule specific activities for the children and will present structured lessons; however, supervised free play, creative and exploratory activities, as well as physical and discovery experiences will be essential to the children's success (Spodek, 1973).

4. The teachers will provide academic and social learning environments that will allow children to learn individual and group-member responsibilities, but every child will not be expected to reach the same maturational levels at the same time (Spodek, 1973).

5. Teachers will develop activities and materials that follow the development of children rather than shape them unnaturally (Elkind, 1973).

6. Teachers will design activities in a manner that information and skills are learned by children at appropriate stages in their development; those learnings will provide substructures or prelearning for complex thinking at a later time (Spodek, 1973).

7. Teachers will provide a wealth of experiences with figural or concrete objects for the children (Spodek, 1973).

8. Teachers will establish nonthreatening, nonanxiety-producing situations for children, and even invite parents to participate, thereby creating a school environment that reflects the home environment (Spodek & Robinson, 1973).

9. Teachers will schedule adults, older children, and other resource persons into the school to serve as models for the children who are enrolled (Biber, 1977; Biber & associates, 1971).

10. The teachers will design lessons that would develop children's readiness (prereading and premathematics) skills. Attention would be given to visual efficiency skills, visual memory, attention,

auditory and visual discrimination, enumerating, counting, and so forth (Biber, 1977).

Teachers and parents should provide many learning activities that would result in children's developing the readiness or prereading/pre-mathematics skills prior to entry into first grade. However, children who do not reach the desired levels should be provided activities that would insure that their development continue. Those children's activities, leading to that development, should not be interrupted. Forms of art, music, and literature would be presented to the children.

Young children's total development is dependent upon many inter-related areas of development (social, emotional, language, physical, and intellectual). Any surface behavior, interpreted as a lack of learning, could be erroneously attributed to one area, when in reality another one or a combination of others may be the source. Therefore, to correct the prob-lem, the whole child must be treated. Attempts to force learning in one area of development without due consideration of the others may produce harmful effects (Biber, Shapiro, & Wickens, 1971).

It is apparent that the contemporary view of maturational thinkers regarding child growth and development and educational programs that should be provided for children is very similar to the Froebellian or Deweyian philosophies. In many instances there is a marked difference be-tween the beliefs of the whole-child advocates and those of the behaviorists; however, there are some beliefs regarding the role of teachers that are similar even though the philosophical or research based reasons may be different. But there is one other major group of psychologists and educators who support an eclectic curriculum design for young children.

Within the recommendations of the cognitivist theorists, aspects of the maturational and behavioral thinkers may be recognized. However, it is necessary to present the complete views of the third group to specify not only the principles they accept, but also to allow the reader to determine the beliefs that are rejected.

Cognitivists

Early childhood education prospective teachers may encounter pre-service programs in which higher education instructors subscribe to the beliefs that: (1) emotional and affective variables are important to a human being's development and (2) psychosexual personality is paramount in the development of children and adults (Educational Products Information Ex-change, 1972). However, members of the two schools of thought share similar views in their attitudes toward the overt behaviors of young children and the variables that affect a human being's development into adulthood. Those points of agreement are:

1. Environmental forces will provide the main sources for children's learning, but that learning will be controlled in part by the children's genetic characteristics as well as developmental growth patterns (Biber, 1977).
2. Familial and community members and other persons will serve as models or consultants to children who are developing language and behavior patterns based on the information they receive from those persons (Biber, 1964).

Combined into a single psychological point of view, cognitive theorists believe that from infancy human beings develop perceptions of their environment that result in conceptual or cognitive maps that serve the human being as guides for behavior. Prospective early childhood education teachers educated in the beliefs of cognitive theorists would learn to base their educational programs upon the following ideas or beliefs (Educational Products Information Exchange, 1972).

Young children's development is genetically and environmentally controlled within limits, and their behaviors (cognitive, affective, psychomotor, and creative) can be altered and stimulated in predetermined, desired directions. However, all human characteristics are interdependent and interrelated, therefore skills should not be taught in isolated lessons. But, specific learnings may be separated into components for teaching if provisions are made for children to synthesize the learning into the "whole" as it relates to other areas of growth, development, and learning. To provide educational programs for those desired behaviors, parents and teachers should work cooperatively to establish appropriate learning environments.

1. Teachers will design educational programs and physical school plants that would insure children's happiness and safety but at the same time be conducive to the children's participation in a wide range of social, physical, and psychomotor vicarious experiences (Nimicht, 1973).
2. Teachers will provide opportunities for children to exercise options in choosing learning activities, but also guide and stimulate the children in directions that insure learning will be fostered and children will be successful, and become happy, productive, and efficient (Kamii, 1973).
3. In the teaching of various skills, teachers will integrate all learning into wholes and relate each skill to other learning tasks. Also,

children's preferences for learning must be duly considered (Kamii, 1973).

4. Teachers will provide learning experiences for children—as the children become ready—that are within the developmental stages provided by Piaget: sensorimotor, preoperational, concrete–operational, and formal–operational (Kamii & Radin, 1967).

5. Teachers will know and understand that children's development of skills and abilities is uneven and that readiness for formal learning in reading and mathematics may be reached by individual children at different points in time.

6. Teachers will emphasize a wide variety of language-based, cognitively oriented activities that relate to a large number of subject matter or content area disciplines. Emphasis would be placed on discovery and inquiry techniques and interaction between the teacher and children, and children and children.

7. When providing a wide range of activities for children to learn individually and in groups, teachers should also ascertain that a careful balance of human relational as well as academic problem-solving challenges are provided (Nimnicht, 1973).

8. Teachers should provide a wide variety of activities in reading, mathematics, and handwriting preskills on a horizontal plane rather than rushing upward along a vertical pathway designed to move students to higher levels of achievement (Kamii, 1973).

9. Teachers must attend to children's learning preferences or modes, as well as their abilities to achieve success in the tasks encountered; however, children should develop self-initiative, self-discipline, self-direction abilities, and other personality characteristics (Nimnicht, 1973).

10. Teachers should provide readiness activities that will allow for the manipulation of figural materials, pictorial representations, visual-vocal and auditory-vocal interactions, as well as kinesthetic, tactile, olfactory, and gustatory learning experiences. Such experiences will insure that cognitive maps are well-established when children enter formal skill-learning experiences (Kamii, 1973).

Teachers must learn to attend to children's learning preferences, interests, genetic and cultural characteristics, and other aspects of child growth and development to develop true, eclectic, prescriptive classrooms. Genetic and environmental variables will be interactive in controlling the degree to which a child will learn; the degree to which teachers and parents can cooperate in designing learning programs for those individual characteristics will be directly related to the success the children will realize.

Summary

The presentation of the specific practices that would be employed in accordance with the principles of maturationalists, behaviorists, or cognitivists would also be used to develop educational programs for prospective or inservice teachers. The last group, cognitivists, may be viewed as believing in an eclectic or functionalist approach to the development of early childhood education programs for children. However, Hilgard (1956) was critical of the functionalism theories of the 1950s. He contended that the proponents were recommending too many uncontrollable activities and did not "satisfy the requirement for a neat system [p. 49]." In 1964, McDonald considered the functionalism advocates to have exerted their greatest influence in curriculum studies that were conducted by researchers who argued that beliefs underlying curriculum design must be generated from the measurement of effects. McDonald further stated that the researchers were not interested in developing a systematic, evenly balanced theory. Instead, they insisted that views concerning learning and educational activities that were employed must make sense and be relatively well confirmed by carefully controlled research studies. Apparently, since the 1950s the functionalist point of view has become a hybrid plant in the form of the eclectic, cognitivist view toward early childhood education.

Gordon and Jester (1973) reviewed the research literature on teaching in early childhood education between 1963 and 1970. The authors concluded that researchers had presented enough evidence to be pieced together, but called for more comprehensive studies using common instruments to make accurate determinations as to the effectiveness of preschool teaching and learning. However they viewed the efforts through the 1970s to be promising.

The struggle for the supremacy of the psychological point of view may never be completely settled. Specific early education programs that have been carefully designed, based upon reputable research (e.g., Follow Through models), and implemented have been found to be extremely successful for some children. Unfortunately three situations were identified within or as a result of the programs: (1) some children failed to learn; (2) some children met failure in future years or were not superior to students who did not receive the formal early childhood experiences; and (3) successful programs that were shown to be effective in one geographical area were considered failures when replicated in another geographic area. As the programs' efficacies were analyzed, hypotheses were posited by various professional groups as to the reasons for the failure. The second thrust, following the Head Start/Follow Through movement begun in 1964 resulted in attention to suggestions for additional considerations that would later be added as coordinate units or programs to the existing early childhood education programs. Among those coordinate programs were multicultural education, learning style, early diagnosis and screening, mainstreaming, basic skills, and mass media.

COORDINATE EARLY
CHILDHOOD EDUCATIONAL PROGRAMS

Multicultural Education

One of the first reasons cited for children's failure in learning basic skills in the primary grades was that children from diverse cultural and linguistic groups did poorly in educational settings that were designed for the mainstream of the middle-class children in the United States. In 1973 the National Council on Education Research was established. One priority of the members was to investigate, through research and development, educational programs that would be necessary for children from distinct cultural and linguistic environments to attain the skills necessary to compete successfully in school and society. That charge is still in force.

One of the first discoveries that resulted from the studies was that educators who designed programs for young children were unaware of the young children's backgrounds upon entering school. And even though the maturationalists and cognitivists stressed the importance of community and familial variables and other societal aspects in providing for young children's welfare, they too were ignorant of the specific and global differences among cultural groups. Therefore their educational programs for teachers were relatively void of references to children who were distinct, not only in looks, but in knowledge, values, attitudes, and learning preference.

One of the major misconceptions of educators that surfaced as a result of the multicultural studies was that of the intelligence of children who lived in diverse sociocultural systems. Lesser and associates (1965, 1971) discovered that children from various ethnic and cultural groups did not possess the same intellectual patterns of performance as did their middle-class counterparts when contemporary tests were employed, and also that specific ethnic and cultural groups differed from one another. In view of those findings, it is not difficult to understand why young children entering formal schooling for the first time would encounter not only value conflicts but other strange and bizarre conditions that would possibly lead to neurosis and academic failure rather than success.

Lesser (1971) and Cohen (1969) were partly responsible for encouraging faculty members in schools and colleges of early childhood education and psychology to stress the importance of teachers' being aware of the cognitive styles of linguistically and culturally distinct children. As research continued, evidence was also collected to support the belief that not only should children's cognitive styles be studied and identified but that those of the teacher also be taken into account. As a result of their studies, Ramirez and Castaneda (1974) recommended that children be assigned to teachers according to "cognitive style matches" and that teachers be educated to redirect or teach children the use of an alternate style. In that way, children who are bicultural and bilingual would also become multicognitive.

Recent research findings were interpreted to mean that the familial environment may be responsible for the variation that exists in children's cognitive styles (Cohen, 1969). Broman, Nichols, and Kennedy (1975) found that socioeconomic class and education of the parents, especially the mother's, were variables that contributed the most to the intelligence of 4-year-old children.

Young children in all cultural groups have been observed to learn a new language easily and readily. Saville (1970) recommended that to stimulate children to learn a new language, teachers use eclectic approaches. However, Saville revealed three controversies:

1. It has not been determined whether homogeneous grouping is superior to heterogeneous grouping in allowing regular and special teachers to meet the needs of denied or linguistically distinct children.
2. It has not been determined when children should be taught English as a second dialect or language, or whether reading should be taught after English is learned, as English is learned, or by using dialectic readers.
3. It has not been determined if instruction in English should be used to replace children's dialects or first language completely, thereby making it extant, which may in reality heighten the cultural differences among children.

The extensiveness of cultural plurality in the United States has served as a source for social unrest and educational, employment, and social injustices. More importantly, the cultural and linguistic differences among people have been used as a basis for assuming one person's unnatural superiority over another person. Perhaps teachers who are properly educated to administer early childhood programs can be largely responsible for eradicating sources of bias and insure that all children enter the mainstream of education and other aspects of life with the knowledge, skills, and abilities to achieve success.

Mainstreaming

Mainstreaming connotes an educational situation in which children who are mildly handicapped in various ways are returned to regular classrooms to receive instruction. The requirement that children be screened and possibly diagnosed for special placement or mainstreaming resulted from federal legislation which stipulated that all children be afforded a free and appropriate education in the least restrictive environment (regardless of financial burden to the public).

Young children, their parents, and their teachers were excluded from the dictate that mildly handicapped children be placed into nonsegregated classes. Screening and diagnosis is required at all educational levels to identify the mildly handicapped children who are viewed to have emotional disturbances, behavioral disorders, educational handicaps, learning disabilities, or brain injuries that are not severe enough to warrant total exclusion from regular classes. In addition to the screening and diagnosis that are required, teachers are required to enlist the aid of other personnel and parents to write prescriptive, immediate, and long-range remediation programs for the children. Those prescriptions are termed IEPs (individualized educational program).

Colleges and departments of teacher education and psychology are presently engaged in preservice and inservice teacher education to prepare teachers to assume roles as prescriptive teachers. The major thrusts of those programs for early childhood education teachers usually include

1. Screening and diagnostic procedures to evaluate children's characteristics from a psychodynamic and learning theory base
2. Writing comprehensive individualized educational programs for children who are found to be mildly handicapped

Layton and Range (1978) viewed screening procedures to include

1. Selecting appropriate instruments, learning to use them, and analyzing the results correctly
2. Being able to identify high risk students who require diagnosis by appropriate resource personnel
3. Designing comprehensive screening programs that would include all aspects of young children's growth and development

Layton and Range further specified that although early childhood teachers would not be taught diagnosis, they should be able to translate diagnosticians' findings into reasonable and logical predictions or projections of the educational needs of young children. Also, the teachers of young children should be able to assist in the implementation of learning programs for both mildly and severely handicapped young children. The implementation of the learning programs would be based on the individualized educational program which all early childhood education teachers would learn to develop. Through appropriate preservice and inservice educational programs, containing a balance of lecture, onsite participation, professional reading, and competency-based instruction, early childhood teachers should become adept in screening and diagnosis, prescriptive-intervention, and interpersonal relationship skills. Seemingly, teachers thus educated would be able to employ appropriate teaching techniques to insure that basic skills which are substructures to later learning may be realized by young children.

Back-to-the-Basics

As the *mainstreaming movement* swept across the nation's schools powered by the fuel of federal legislation, the *back-to-the-basics movement* also gained momentum. The citizenry of the United States, stimulated by educators' interpretations of statistical test data, began to view students as being relatively uneducated in areas of basic skills: reading, writing, composition, mathematics, and so forth. Demands were forthcoming that all teachers refrain from whatever they considered to be educationally appropriate and return to teaching basics. State legislators joined the ranks of the reformists and soon, either through state or local legislation, basic skills tests began to appear throughout the nation.

Prior to 1965, the back-to-the-basics movement as well as the early screening and identification movement would probably have had little effect on early childhood programs. But with the advent of Head Start and Follow Through, early childhood education programs were no longer protected, as they once were, from the influences of educational policies and practices.

A reanalysis of the proponents of the maturational and the behavioral viewpoints will reveal that reading, math, and handwriting skills were included in their curriculum recommendations. The eclecticist thinkers who subscribe to the cognitive viewpoint appeared to believe that children in early childhood education programs needed activities that would prepare them conceptually and sensorily, and were less concerned with the formal introduction of mathematical or reading verbal symbols. In reality, kindergarten became a downward extension of the first grade. It appears that while educational researchers were discovering the complicated reasons as to why many children were not learning, and were devising programs so that all children could move forward to the basics, stronger, more influential groups were forcing educational practitioners to return to archaic practices that were shown to be sources of childhood neurosis and poor self-esteem.

There is a growing trend for early childhood prospective teachers to be certified to teach children from birth through age 8. Their training is received mainly through colleges and departments of education and psychology. Therefore, they will be competent to teach reading and mathematics skills at higher levels than teachers who were once trained in schools or colleges of child development. The result may be a tendency for those teachers to ignore specific aspects of total child growth and development and overstress reading and mathematical skills as a result of societal and peer pressures. Present emphasis is being placed upon mainstreaming and aspects of multicultural education. The knowledge that children with diverse abilities, included in those two groups, will be integrated into educational programs with "normal or average" children who are equally diverse in maturational growth, should lead to the conclusion that not all of those children can be forced to be successful during the same period of time. However, if teachers are aware of alternative teaching procedures and can guide children as they progress through various stages of learning until they become competent, then success can be attributed to the teacher.

Competency-Based Programs

Zigler (1971) recognized that the increased emphasis placed on early childhood education could be disastrous to the lives of young children if teachers were not adequately educated. Zigler introduced the concept of educating day-care-center teachers in competency-based (performance-based) programs. In turn, the teachers were to implement competency-based programs for young children. The Child Development Associate (CDA) introduced by Zigler was established to be commensurate with other competency-based or performance-based teacher education (CBTE/PBTE) programs and included requirements that prospective teachers learn through actual experiences with children. Zigler referred to the education of day-care-center teachers as a socialization process and identified the goals of the program to be the development of performance objectives or competencies through which teachers would learn the attributes, behaviors, and functions of the early childhood teacher. Within the construction of those goals, Zigler specified that through actual involvement and interaction with young children, teachers would learn to (a) define their roles; (b) develop a teaching style; (c) develop teaching skills and techniques through which educational objectives for children may be realized; and (d) develop professional-level attitudes.

The employment of competency-based teacher education programs is strongly supported by members of the American Association of Colleges for Teacher Education (AACTE). A special committee of AACTE presently houses a wealth of information on CBTE/PBTE. One of the major reasons that CBTE/PBTE received such wide acclaim and was institutionalized was the public's demand that educational institutions be accountable for their successes or failures in teaching. The *accountablility movement* occurred prior to the *back-to-the-basics* movement. But a difference exists between the two concepts. Whereas back-to-the-basics advocates are essentially nonresearch oriented, nonprofessionally educationally trained, proponents of CBTE/PBTE are usually well-educated educators. They desire to develop systems approaches to teaching so that objectives can be specified and proficiency standards determined. In that way, students at all levels can progress successfully in the direction of predetermined goals.

Early childhood education programs could be designed to be perfor-manced based. The recommended activities by protagonists supporting the three points of view of early childhood education programs could be for teachers to (a) divide learnings into component parts; (b) write objectives with specific proficiency levels; (c) develop activities through which children would demonstrate proficiencies; and (d) provide for children to be recycled if the need arose. Theoretically the system would work for teachers and students—and has been employed in many schools throughout the country. However, humanists, Gestaltists, and phenomonologists view such educational practices with disdain. Many linguists and especially psycholinguists scoff at such practices, especially if employed during the years of childrens' formative language development. The PBTE/CBTE movement, like all other programs, has not received universal acceptance.

SUMMARY

Early childhood education has a vivid history. Since the time of Plato and Aristotle a deep concern for the educational welfare of young children has been foremost in the thoughts of respected philosophers, psychologists, and educators. An overwhelming movement during the 1800s established permanent kindergartens in the United States and also early childhood teacher education programs. However, it was not until the 1960s that early childhood education was recognized nationally as an essential component of a total and complete educational system.

Since the birth of Head Start in 1964, early childhood education has received much attention. Hess and Croft (1972) reported that experimental programs and research was extensive following 1964. Klaus and Gray (1968) stressed the importance of community and family variables on child development as well as formal educational programs. Joyce and Weil (1972) verified the utility of the educational models developed by Kamii and Kohlberg based on the concepts of Piaget. Hess and Croft (1972) stressed that structured activities alone would not meet all the educational needs of young children. And Tanner and Tanner (1975) expressed the idea that institutions of higher education could not furnish teachers all that would be needed to establish reputable early childhood programs; neither could the teachers work independently. The Tanners recommended that teacher centers be established for teacher interaction and sharing of ideas critical of CBTE. Bremer (1975) preferred PBTE since prospective teachers were required to interact with and teach on site. Rooze and Whitfield (1978) also view field-based educational programs to be a viable alternative to educate teachers.

A final analysis of all that has been presented leads to the conclusion that the attempts of all those persons who have been associated with early childhood education were to guide young children individually through educationally related tasks. Conte and Hanson (1978) wrote that the formal I.G.E. (individually guided instruction) developed cooperatively at the Wisconsin Research and Development Center for Cognitive Learning was that type of program. Although some writers have been critical of schools for 4-year-old children (Moore & Moore, 1973), other writers such as Evans (1975) contended that if equality in education is to be achieved, then preschools must be established for all young children.

Still, the question of which program is superior remains unanswered. Many authorities support an eclectic program. The position of those writers has merit as well as implications for prospective and inservice teachers of young children. If the best of all that is known about child growth, development, and learning, and also teaching techniques, can be effectively employed by a teacher, children will succeed. But, if there is only one teaching technique, one theory of child growth, development, and learning, what does the teacher do when a child fails?

CONCLUSION

This chapter was included to present a historical account of the nature of the education of teachers based on existing information related to early education and teacher training. To date, one of the strongest positional papers on the education of early childhood prospective teachers was written by Seaver and Cartwright (1977). In their treatise, they contended that early childhood educational specialists were attempting to develop eclectic programs by merely patching traditional views. As a result of their studies, Seaver and Cartwright believe that programs for prospective teachers in early childhood education should be designed so that students will learn the specific characteristics of the separate views regarding early childhood education as each is actually implemented in the field, and be taught to teach in those specific situations. The writers stressed that until "ideological pluralism" was fostered in teacher education programs, that the quasi-eclectic programs would remain.

Seaver and Cartwright viewed the positions of the behaviorists, cognitivists, and maturationalists to be conceptually consistent and capable of being categorized into component parts and taught as entities. In that way, prospective teachers could view the separateness of the three theoretical views while at the same time learning the overlapping and similar components of the ideas. Seaver and Cartwright suggested several courses for providing an appropriate pluralistic foundation program for early childhood education prospective teachers. In separate, but related courses, students would

1. Learn the nature of child growth and development
2. Learn to apply or connect learning and developmental theories to the developmental characteristics of young children
3. Develop separate programs for young children based upon the behaviorist, maturational, and cognitive theories, and also be assigned practicum experience to observe a variety of programs
4. Learn the nature of content areas (science, social studies, art, and so forth) and basic skills areas (reading and mathematics) in methods courses and in practicum situations in which the principles of the three theories would be studied as they relate to teaching
5. Observe, analyze, and evaluate existing model programs, on site, to determine the degree to which they meet the criteria established
6. Student teach in two early childhood education settings during the same period of time, and develop competence in teaching using the recommended procedures generated from the three theories

Seaver and Cartwright should be applauded for their cogent recommendations and for designing carefully controlled and measurable procedures for teacher education. Their earlier work (1976) in successfully field testing student teaching experiences adds credence to their recommendations.

Based on all that is contained in this chapter, it appears that Seaver and Cartwright's position is well-founded. However, there are additional data that should be considered when early childhood teacher education programs are designed. The ideas are not presented as a rebuttal to Seaver and Cartwright, but to support their beliefs that highly structured, partly competency-performance-based teacher education programs are very necessary if prospective teachers are to be educated appropriately.

Contemporary researchers have confirmed that many successful programs were not mobile, that they could not be transferred to other geographical areas. At least two possibilities may cause this: (1) the differences among teachers and (2) the differences among children. Earlier in this chapter, researchers in multicultural education were shown to support the belief that children, especially from culturally and linguistically distinct groups, may require not only different programs from other groups but different types of teachers. The present emphasis for early detection of handicapped children has serious implications for educators of prospective teachers. Higher education faculty members will need to teach diagnostic and screening procedures to provide teachers with techniques to identify children's weaknesses and strengths, and to provide appropriate learning activities for those children.

Many teacher and student characteristics have been identified in recent years. Children have been found to be dependent-prone or independent-prone (Livson & Mussen, 1957; Kagan, Sontag, Baker, & Nelson, 1958) and also compulsive or impulsive (Grimes & Allinsmith, 1961). Those four characteristics alone will influence the success or failure a particular child will have, in a particular program, with a particular teacher.

Teachers have been characterized as being rigid or nonrigid (Flanders, 1960); well-integrated, weakly integrated, or turbulent (Heil, Powell, & Feifer, 1960); integrative or dominative (Cogan, 1975); and abstract or concrete (Harvey, Prather, White, & Hoffmeister, 1968). Additionally, teachers have been observed to use either direct or nondirect teaching techniques (Stern, 1963). The intent here is not to define or describe these teacher and pupil characteristics, but rather to direct attention to the enormous impact of all those variables when they interact in (a) teacher education institutions (prospective teachers are students also); (b) when practicums and student teaching experiences occur; and finally (c) when beginning early childhood education teachers enter teaching. Therefore, it appears ambitious to think that programs, developed for children who will be guided by teachers, can be neatly arranged in terms of materials, sequencing, and activities so that teachers and children will fit into them. Ultimately, the goal should be (a) to decide what children should learn during early childhood years, (b) then on an individual basis decide the best ways (approaches and methods) for children to achieve those learnings (and whether they are able to learn them), and (c) educate teachers to alter their behaviors to match the child's initially, and employ correct procedures to alter the child's learning behaviors where necessary. Such a system would require teachers to make more use of learning and developmental theories, and deemphasize opinions that such ideas are abstract notions with little applicability. And too, more emphasis should be placed on the child and the teacher rather than programs and materials that are sometimes employed to defeat children's and teacher's efforts rather than enhance them.

REFERENCES

Austin, G. R. Early childhood education: An international perspective. New York: Academic Press, 1976.

Bereiter, C., & Engelmann, S. Teaching disadvantaged children in the preschool. Englewood Cliffs, N. J.: Prentice-Hall, 1966.

Bereiter, C., & Engelmann, S. Observations on the use of direct instruction with young children. In B. Spodek (Ed.), Early childhood education. Englewood Cliffs, N. J.: Prentice-Hall, 1973. Pp. 176–186.

Bereiter, C. S., Engelmann, S., Osborn, J., & Reidford, P. A. An academically oriented pre-school for culturally deprived children. In F. Hechinger (Ed.), Preschool education to-day. New York: Doubleday, 1964. Pp. 105–135.

Biber, B. Preschool education. In R. Ulich (Ed.), Education and the ideal of mankind. New York: Harcourt Brace Jovanovich, 1964.

Biber, B. Cognition in early childhood education: A historical perspective. In B. Spodek and H. J. Walberg (Eds.), Childhood education: Issues and insights. Berkeley, Calif.: McCutchan, 1977. Pp. 41–64.

Biber, B., Shapiro, E., & Wickens, D. Promoting cognitive growth: A developmental inter-action point of view. Washington, D. C.: National Association for the Education of Young Children, 1971.

Bigge, M. L. Learning theories for teachers. New York: Harper and Row, 1971.

Bijou, S. W. Behavior analysis applied to early childhood education. In B. Spodek and H. J. Walberg (Eds.), Early childhood education. Berkeley, Calif.: McCutchan, 1977. Pp. 139–156.

Blank, M. Implicit assumptions underlying preschool intervention programs. In B. Spodek (Ed.), Early childhood education. Englewood Cliffs, N.J.: Prentice-Hall, 1973. Pp. 122–142.

Bloom, A. The education of democratic man. Emile, Daedalus, Summer 1978, 135–153.

Braun, S. J., & Edwards, E. P. History and theory of early childhood education. Worthington, Ohio: Charles A. Jones, 1972.

Bremer, N. A model for field-based learning. Texas Tech Journal of Education, 1975, 2, 19–25.

Broman, S. H., Nichols, P. L., & Kennedy, W. A. Preschool IQ: Prenatal and family cor-relates. New York: John Wiley, 1975.

Bushell, D. Jr. The behavior analysis classroom. In B. Spodek (Ed.), Early childhood educa-tion. Englewood Cliffs, N.J.: Prentice-Hall, 1973. Pp. 122–142.

Camp, J. C. A skill development curriculum for 3-, 4-, and 5-year-old children. In B. Spodek (Ed.), Early childhood education. Englewood Cliffs, N.J.: Prentice-Hall, 1973. Pp. 187–198.

Cogan, M. L. Current issues in the education of teachers. In K. Ryan (Ed.), Teacher education: Seventy-fourth yearbook of the national society for the study of education. Chicago: University of Chicago Press, 1975. Pp. 204–229.

Cohen, R. A. Conceptual styles, culture conflict and nonverbal tests of intelligence. *American Anthropologist*, 1969, *71*, 828–856.

Conte, A. E., & Hanson, R. J. IGE and T & E: Paralleling two major educational programs. *AIGE Forum*, 1978, *3*, 14–17.

Cordasco, F. *A brief history of education.* Totowa, N.J.: Littlefield, Adams, and Company, 1970.

Cremin, L. A. *The transformation of the school.* New York: Vintage Books, 1964.

Curtis, S. J., & Boultwood, E. A. *A short history of educational ideas.* London: University Tutorial Press, 1961.

Day, M. C., & Parker, R. K. (Eds.). *The preschool in action: Exploring early childhood programs.* Boston: Allyn and Bacon, 1977.

Demiashkevich, M. *An introduction to the philosophy of education.* New York: American Book Company, 1935.

DeYoung, C. A. *Introduction to American public education.* New York: McGraw-Hill, 1950.

Dowley, E. M. Early childhood education. In *Encyclopedia of educational research* (4th ed.). London: Collier-MacMillan Limited, 1969. Pp. 316–327.

Educational Products Information Exchange, *Early Childhood Education, How to select and evaluate educational materials, number 42.* New York: E P I E, 1972.

Elkind, D. Preschool education: Enrichment or instruction? In B. Spodek (Ed.), *Early childhood education.* Englewood Cliffs, N.J.: Prentice-Hall, 1973. Pp. 108–121.

Evans, E. D. *Contemporary influences in early childhood education.* New York: Holt, Rinehart, and Winston, 1971.

Evans, E. D. *Contemporary influences in early childhood education* (2nd ed.). New York: Holt, Rinehart, and Winston, 1975.

Flanders, N. A. *Teacher influence, pupil attitudes, and achievement: Studies in interactional analysis.* University of Minnesota, U.S.O.E., Cooperative Research Project Number 397, 1960.

Froebel, F. *The education of man.* (W. N. Hailmann, trans.) New York: D. Appleton, 1889.

Fromberg, D. P. *Early childhood education: A perceptual models curriculum.* New York: John Wiley and Sons, 1977.

Goodlad, J. I. *School, curriculum and the individual.* Waltham, Mass.: Blaisdell, Publishing Company, 1966.

Goodlad, J. I. Klein, M. F., & Novotney, J. M. *Early schooling in the United States.* New York: McGraw-Hill, 1973.

Gordon, I. J., & Jester, R. E. Techniques of observing teaching in early childhood and outcomes of particular procedures. In R. M. W. Travers (Ed.), *Second handbook of research on teaching.* Chicago: Rand McNally, 1973. Pp. 184–217.

Grimes, J. W., & Allinsmith, W. Compulsivity, anxiety, and school achievement. *Merrill-Palmer Quarterly*, 1961, *7*, 262–303.

Harvey, O. J., Prather, M., White, B. J., & Hoffmeister, J. K. Teachers' beliefs, classroom atmosphere, and student behavior. *American Educational Research Journal*, 1968, *5*, 151–166.

Heil, L. M., Powell, M., & Feifer, I. *Characteristics of teacher behavior related to the achievement of children in several elementary grades.* Washington, D.C.: U.S.O.E., Office of Education, Cooperative Research Branch, 1960.

Hess, R. D., & Croft, D. J. *Teachers of young children* (2nd ed.). Boston: Houghton Mifflin and Company, 1972.

Hilgard, E. R. *Theories of learning.* New York: Appleton-Century-Crofts, 1956.

Hilgard, E. R. (Ed.). *Theories of learning and instruction.* Sixty-Third Yearbook of the National Society for the Study of Education, Part I, Chicago: University of Chicago Press, 1964.

Hom, H. A., Jr., & Robinson, P. A. *Psychological processes in early education.* New York: Academic Press, 1977.

Hunt, J. Mc. The psychological basis for using preschool enrichment as an antidote for cultural deprivation. *Merrill-Palmer Quarterly of Behavior and Development,* July 1964, *10.*

Hutchins, R. M. (Ed.). *Great books of the Western world: the dialog of Plato* (Vol. 7). Chicago: Encyclopedia Britannica, 1952.

Johnson, D. M. *Psychology: a problem solving approach.* New York: Harper and Brothers, 1961.

Joyce, B., & Weil, M. *Models of teaching.* Englewood Cliffs, N.J.: Prentice-Hall, 1972.

Kagan, J., Sontag, L. W., Baker, C. T., & Nelson, V. L. Personality and I.Q. change. *Journal of Abnormal and Social Psychology,* 1958, *56,* 261–266.

Kamii, C. A sketch of the Piaget-derived preschool curriculum developed by the Ypsilanti early education program. In B. Spodek (Ed.), *Early childhood education.* Englewood Cliffs, N.J.: Prentice-Hall, 1973. Pp. 209–229.

Kamii, C., & Radin, N. A framework for preschool curriculum based on some Piagetian concepts. *Journal of Creative Behavior,* 1967, *1,* 314–324.

Klaus, R. A., & Gray, S. W. The early training project for disadvantaged children: A report after five years. *Monographs of the Society for Research in Child Development,* 1968, 33, Serial Number 120.

Layton, J. R. *The psychology of learning to read.* New York: Academic, 1979.

Layton, J. R., & Phillips, M. P. Susan Elizabeth Blow. In J. F. Ohles (Ed.), *Biographical dictionary of American educators* (Vol. I). Westport, Conn.: Greenwood Press, 1978. Pp. 140–141.

Layton, J. R., & Range, D. G. Development of area workshop in screening and diagnosis. Mimeographed proposal submitted to the State Department of Elementary and Secondary Education of the State of Missouri, Springfield, Mo., 1978.

Lee, G. C. *An introduction to education in modern America.* New York: Henry Holt, 1953.

Lesser, G. Postscript: matching instruction to student characteristics. In G. Lesser (Ed.), *Psychology and educational practice.* New York: Scott-Foresman and Company, 1971.

Lesser, G. S., Fifer, G., & Clark, D. H. Mental abilities of children from different social-class and cultural groups. *Monographs of the society for research in child development.* Number 102, 1965.

Livson, N., & Mussen, P. H. The relation of control to overt aggression and dependency. *Journal of Abnormal and Social Psychology,* 1957, *55,* 66–71.

Lundgren, E. C. Susan Blow Founds the public kindergarten. In O. L. Davis, Jr. (Ed.), *Perspective on curriculum development 1776–1976.* Washington, D.C.: Association for Supervision and Curriculum Development, 1976.

McCandless, B. R. *Children and adolescents.* New York: Holt, Rinehart, and Winston, 1961.

McDonald, F. J. The influence of learning theories on education. In E. R. Hilgard (Ed.), *Theories of learning and instruction.* Sixty-Third Yearbook of the National Society for the Study of Education. Chicago: University of Chicago Press, 1964.

MacDonald, J. The open school: Curriculum concepts. In B. Spodek (Ed.), *Early Childhood Education.* Englewood Cliffs, N.J.: Prentice-Hall, 1973. Pp. 92–107.

Master, L. S. Margarethe Meyer Schurz. In J. F. Ohles (Ed.), *Biographical dictionary of American educators* (Vol. 3). Westport, Conn.: Greenwood Press, 1978. Pp. 1156–1157.

Miller, L. *Experimental variation of headstart curricula: A comparison of current approaches.* Progress report number 5, Grant number CG8199, OEO. Louisville, Kentucky: University of Louisville, January, 1970.

Moore, R. S., & Moore, D. R. The dangers of early schooling. In *Reading in education.* Guilford, Conn.: Rushkin, 1973.

Morphett, M. V., & Washburne, C. When should children begin to read. *Elementary School Journal*, March, 1931, *31*, 496–503.

Neff, J. C., & Engle, J. Francis Wayland Parker. In J. F. Ohles (Ed.), *Biographical dictionary of American educators* (Vol. 2). Westport, Conn.: Greenwood Press, 1978. Pp. 990–991.

Nimnicht, G. Overview of responsive model program. In B. Spodek (Ed.), *Early Childhood Education*. Englewood Cliffs, N.J.: Prentice-Hall, 1973. Pp. 199–208.

Osborn, D. K. *Early childhood education in historical perspective*. Athens, Ga: Education Associates, 1975.

Perkinson, H. J. *The imperfect panacea: American faith in education, 1865–1965*. New York: Random House, 1968.

Pestalozzi, J. *How Gertrude teaches her children*. London: George Allen and Unwin Limited, 1892.

Pyle, W. J. Marie Krause-Boelté. In J. F. Ohles (Ed.), *Biographical dictionary of American educators* (Vol. 2). Westport, Conn.: Greenwood Press, 1978. Pp. 765–766.

Ramirez, M., & Castaneda, A. *Cultural democracy, bicognitive development, and education*. New York: Academic Press, 1974.

Range, D. G. The influences affecting the preparation of teachers for early childhood education. Mimeographed Paper, Southwest Missouri State University, 1978.

Rooze, G. E., & Whitfield, E. Improving field-based instruction using the ULIGE model. *AIGE Forum*, 1978, *3*, 31–33.

Saville, M. R. Language and the disadvantaged. In T. D. Horn (Ed.), *Reading for the disadvantaged*. New York: Harcourt Brace Jovanovich, 1970. Pp. 115–134.

Seaver, J. W., & Cartwright, C. A. A pluralistic foundation for training early childhood professionals. *Curriculum Inquiry, 1977, 7*, 305–329.

Seaver, J. W., & Cartwright, C. A. *Early childhood student teaching*. University Park: Pennsylvania State University, 1976; also, E.R.I.C. Document Service, pp. 130–759.

Smith, N. B. *American reading instruction*. Newark, Del.: International Reading Association, 1965.

Soar, R. *Follow through model implementation*. Interim Report on Project Number OEG-0-8-522, 471-4618(100), U.S.O.E. Gainsville, Florida: University of Florida, 1970.

Spodek, B. *Early childhood education*. Englewood Cliffs, N.J.: Prentice-Hall, 1973.

Spodek, B., & Walberg, H. J. (Eds.). *Early childhood education*. Berkeley, Calif.: McCutchan, 1977.

Stern, G. C. Measuring non-cognitive variables in research teaching. In N. L. Gage (Ed.), *Handbook of research on teaching*. Chicago: Rand-McNally, 1963.

Stiles, L. J. *Theories for teaching*. New York: Dodd, Mead, and Company, 1974.

Tanner, D., & Tanner, L. *Curriculum development*. New York: Macmillan, 1975.

Torrance, P. E., & White, W. F. *Issues and advances in educational psychology*. Itasca, Ill.: F. E. Peacock, 1969.

Weikart, D. P., & Lambie, D. Z. Preschool intervention through a home teaching program. In J. Hellmuth (Ed.), *Disadvantaged child* (Vol. 2). New York: Brunner and Mazel, 1968. P. 442.

Wyckoff, D. Patty Smith Hill. In J. F. Ohles (Ed.), *Biographical dictionary of American educators* (Vol. 2). Westport, Conn.: Greenwood Press, 1978. Pp. 644–645.

Zigler, E. A new child care profession: the child development associate. *Young Children*, December 1971, *27*, 71–74.

CHAPTER 2

Contemporary Early Childhood Education Programs and Related Controversial Issues

BARBARA D. DAY

Simmons, Whitfield, and Layton (Chapter 1) imply that there exists a need for continuity in the educational experiences of young children. In addition, they contend that an ultimate goal of early childhood educators is to decide what to teach and then how best to teach it to individual children. Certainly, the emerging definition of early childhood education as involving the ages birth through 8 years would imply continuity for children.

In this chapter the attempt to implement Project Follow Through as a means of providing continuity in the educational experiences of children, with the resultant involvement of parents, is examined. In addition, research findings and opinions related to reading before the first grade, the role of play, and the influence of television on young children is presented. The controversies surrounding reading and play have major implications for educators concerned with the nature of early childhood education programs and continuity within programs. All three issues have implications pertaining to the effects of certain practices on the development of individual children.

39

ASPECTS OF EARLY CHILDHOOD EDUCATION
Theory to Research to Practice

PROJECT FOLLOW THROUGH

Project Follow Through was initiated in 1967 for the graduates of Head Start and other compensatory programs to offset the loss of gains made when the children entered the public school. Edward Zigler (1978), former director of the Health Education and Welfare Office of Child Development, in reassessing the effectiveness of Head Start pointed out two critical factors in sustaining the gains made: (1) involving parents in the education of their children and (2) maintaining continuity through similar support in the elementary grades. According to Zigler (1978), "We can never inoculate children in one year against the ravages of deprivation; there must be continuity [p. 5]."

It was to confront the ravages of deprivation that Follow Through was created. More specifically, however, the federal government expected Follow Through, as an experimental research program, to allow educators to identify clearly the most effective methods for educating low-income children in the early primary grades ("Annual Evaluation," 1977).

OVERVIEW OF FOLLOW THROUGH MODEL PROGRAMS

Follow Through was the first extensive, federally funded program administered with an emphasis on research and development; it represented a "unique attempt to unite educational theory and practice—to evaluate new approaches . . . in the public schools ["Follow Through: Promising Approaches," 1971]." The experiment is often referred to as "planned variation" which is viewed as the single most distinctive feature of Follow Through when compared to other compensatory programs.

The approaches range from a "highly structured instructional approach in which cognitive skills are stressed to a far less structured child-centered approach in which emphasis is placed not on curriculum content so much as on the development of the child's confidence and other behavioral characteristics ["Follow Through: Promising Approaches," 1971]." Two of the 22 approaches did not contain concerns for the classroom. One was designed for training parents to teach their children within the home, and the other for engaging parents in major school decision making. Generally speaking, communities have the advantage of selecting the approach (or a combination of approaches) best suited for meeting the needs of their children. A program sponsor is designated to supervise, provide training for teachers and parents, provide materials, and perform other services ("Follow Through: Promising Approaches," 1971).

Seven model programs were selected for discussion in this chapter. A framework will be superimposed upon each for distinguishing among their salient characteristics. The programs to be presented are Bank Street College Approach, Cognitively Oriented Curriculum Model, Educational Development Approach, Parent Education Model, Responsive Environment Approach, Systematic Use of Behavioral Principles Approach, and the Tucson Early Education Model. Each of the above-mentioned programs will be described in terms of the following: sponsor, rationale, objectives, curriculum and methods, and role of the teacher. The information for the seven selected models presented was extracted from the narrative in "Follow Through: Promising Approaches" (1971) and from information generally known by persons involved with early childhood education program development.

Bank Street College Approach

Sponsor:	Bank Street College, New York City.
Rationale:	Children need a predictable environment they can trust. Children need to learn the effects of their own actions. Skill learning and emotional development cannot be separated.
Objectives:	Each child should develop a positive image of himself as a learner. An interest in learning and greater independence should be developed.
Curriculum and methods:	Progression from child-oriented content to social content. Classroom themes are explored first; learning is later extended to community themes. Academic skills are learned in the context of relevant classroom life. Language (written and oral) permeates the classroom. A planned sequence of reading activities is used.
Teacher:	Teaches diagnostically. Plans individual follow-up.

Cognitively Oriented Curriculum Model

Sponsor:	David Weikart.
Rationale:	Derived from Piagetian theory focusing on classification, number, causality, time, and space. Children learn by doing, experimenting, exploring, and talking about what they are doing.
Objectives:	Provide teachers with a theoretical framework of cognitive goals, materials, and strategies. Materials used must encourage involvement, self-direction, and verbal interaction among children.

Curriculum   Materials used include AAAS, Nuffield and Cuisenaire math
and   program, Allen language experience approach, Miami
methods: reading series.
               Small group instruction.
               Students are actively engaged with materials.
               Home teaching program (visits by teachers).

Teacher: Asks more than tells.
               Creates discussion to encourage generation of ideas.
               Teacher dominance is minimized.
               Visits homes, teaches parents how to become involved in the
               education of their children.

Educational Development Center

Sponsor: EDC, Newton, Massachusetts.

Rationale: Children learn by being actively involved in a learning en-
               vironment that has concrete and sensory materials.
               Children learn through interacting with each other; this
               multi-age grouping pattern is rooted in British primary
               schools.
               Humanistic and basic education are integrated for effective
               learning.

Objectives: Establish a strategy to help schools make drastic changes.

Curriculum   Academic skills are important, but children are self-directed.
and   Open classroom environment.
methods: Groupings are flexible, based on the needs and interests of
               the children.
               Children and teacher plan together.

Teacher: Has freedom to structure program to fit needs and interests of
               children.
               Is given much assistance and support from an advisory team.

Parent Education Model

Sponsor: Ira Gordon, The University of North Carolina Chapel Hill
               (until his death in 1978) and formerly from The University of
               Florida, Gainesville.

Rationale: Child's pattern of achievement, motives for learning, and
               personality, are influenced significantly by the home.

Objectives: Provide ways to improve classroom organization and
               teaching patterns. (Train the teacher to work with the parent
               educator.)

Train parents to engage in learning tasks with the child in the home to increase intellectual, personal, and social competence.

Curriculum and methods:

The teacher determines the curriculum; it is not predesigned. The parents and teacher analyze the curriculum so that tasks appropriate for home learning can be developed.

Parent educator visits parents; teaches parent to teach child. Parent educator works in the classroom, instructing small groups, observing children, and so forth.

Construction of educational materials by parents, teachers, and parent educators.

Teacher:

Has an extended role; interactions with adults play an important part.

Responsive Environment Approach

Sponsor: Glen Nimnicht, Far West Laboratory.

Rationale: Children learn in different ways.
Children learn at different rates.
Children learn best when they are interested.
Problem solving is the essence of learning.

Objectives: The child should explore the environment and set his/her own learning pace.
Learning should be its own reward; emphasize how to learn, not acquiring specific facts.
Develop positive self-concept.

Curriculum and methods:

Individualized approach.
Child chooses activities and sets pace for learning.
Use of self-correcting toys (depth cylinders; matrix games).
Use of equipment with immediate feedback (tape recorders, language masters, typewriters).
Parent involvement—meetings, teaching assistants and volunteers, home instructors.

Teacher: Provides an environment that poses problems for children and encourages discovery of solutions.

Systematic Use of Behavorial Principles

Sponsor: Engelmann, Becker; University of Oregon.

Rationale: The Follow Through child begins kindergarten or first grade at a level lower in basic learning skill than the middle-class child.

If disadvantaged children learn at normal rates they will stay behind.

Objectives: Academic skills should be stressed.
Increase the rate of learning.
Many responses from the child are required.

Curriculum and methods: Programmed, DISTAR reading, arithmetic and language programs; Instructional Media of American art and music programs are used. Small group instruction (children aged 5 through 8), grouped according to skills achievement levels. Rapid presentation of tasks.
Questions to groups with some questions to individual children; children must stay alert and be ready to answer all questions.
One to 2 hours per day devoted to academic skills.

Teacher: A behavior modifier.
Knowledge of behavior reinforcement; use enjoyable activities to encourage desired behavior patterns.

Tucson Early Education Model

Sponsor: University of Arizona.

Rationale: Skills and abilities children will need as adults should be developed.
Children have a natural tendency to imitate.

Objectives: Develop thinking skills, language, and motivation.
Devote attention to reading, math, and social interaction.
Learning should become a satisfying experience.

Curriculum and methods: Individualization; unlike traditional education, children may move ahead.
Teacher models desirable behavior; children imitate.
Generous use of positive reinforcement.
Several skills are taught at once.
Small group instruction (three to six children).
Interest centers are used.

Teacher: Manager of the learning environment.
Basis learning activities on child's experience.

THE EFFECTIVENESS OF FOLLOW THROUGH

In 1977 the Office of Education issued the following statement concerning the model programs used in Follow Through. "Few can be said to have added a substantial positive increment to the expected educational outcomes of participating children ["Annual Evaluation Report," 1977, p. 145]." Other findings enumerated in this report were (1) the educational approaches used did not differ substantially in their ability to raise test scores; in some cases, test scores did improve but this occurred primarily when the more structured approaches were utilized, and (2) the most difficult factor in comparing one educational approach to another is the fact that each program varies according to its location.

Others have criticized the evaluative research conducted by the Office of Education vehemently. One critic accused the nationwide evaluations of having "Obscured as much as they have revealed [Riessman, 1977, p. 14]." The main reason for that remark was that in many evaluation studies of compensatory education researchers found no clear learning gains for disadvantaged children. The primary attack on this approach seems to be that "No effort was made in the studies to assess such positive outcomes as social services, medical care, and parent participation [Riessman, 1977, p. 14]." When the only evaluation measurement considered was intelligence scores, other important outcomes were being ignored.

Among the more conservative counterarguments are the following possibilities: (1) effects of certain approaches may take time to produce a visible effect; (2) when a large-scale study is undertaken, results of poorly executed programs may undermine the results of the good ones; and (3) some programs may be manageable on a small scale only (Riessman, 1977).

Tucker (1977) believed too much hope was placed on the possibility that through Follow Through, growing social unrest could be cured and that too much was expected of an undertaking of that sort. Problems cited by Tucker included:

1. Many of the models did not have clearly stated goals and objectives when they were first used; it was not until further on into the experiment that the idea of planned variation was fully understood.
2. When the first evaluation studies were concluded, staff members in programs in which intelligence scores for children were not raised feared the programs would be eliminated. It was not uncommon for local program developers to deviate from the original model. in efforts to improve intelligence test performance.
3. The experiment was too large and lasted too long.
4. Studying no more than six models for no longer than 5 years would have been sufficient; replication decisions could have been made at that time.

Even if evaluators of Follow Through models failed to conclude which approach was best for educating low socioeconomic children, the positive outcomes were many and were recognized even by critics. Those who had strong opinions that compensatory education failed admitted that mistakes were made but also that lessons were learned. "The compensatory approach cannot be partial, segregated, or temporary; it must be total and enduring [Riessman, 1977, p. 16]." In addition to the notion that gains can be sustained only when a continuous approach is used is the idea that the effective program will be the one designed to build upon children's strengths, not their weaknesses. The term compensatory education suggests a negative approach, one that may "Emphasize deficits, weaknesses, and inadequacies . . . [Riessman, 1977, p. 16]." Ambron (1977) and others associated compensatory programs with a pathology model which was operated under the assumption that too many things are wrong with low socioeconomic homes. She believes that *almost all* families need support, some more than others, in raising their children. A closer examination of Ambron's proposition will be made later in this chapter.

Perhaps the most important lesson learned from Follow Through models, regardless of instructional approach, is that, "With proper training . . . parents can assume a teaching role [Riessman, 1977, p. 16]."

PARENT PROGRAMS

There are a number of existing parent education and parent involvement strategies. Some of those strategies were conceived as Follow Through models or components of Follow Through models; others arose entirely from the growing concern with improving children's cognitive development by helping parents to fulfill their roles as teachers, socializers, and decision makers (Stevens & King, 1976).

Maccoby and Zellner (1970) denoted two meanings for parent involvement: (1) parent education which includes the concept of bringing parents into the classroom, training parents to better educate their own children, and general education; and (2) parent participation in the control of programs. Some program designers clearly superseded the established Follow Through guidelines and made parent involvement a core objective.

The history of parent involvement is traced in a number of sources. Morrison (1978) reminds us that parent involvement is not new but that it has evolved to mean something quite different within the past decade than it previously did.

Levitt and Cohen (1977) showed how compensatory education programs led to higher levels of parental involvement. The demand for giving disadvantaged children appropriate early education led educators to create programs like Head Start and Follow Through to counteract the effects of environmental deprivation and expected cumulative deficits. Evaluations highlighted the fear that only temporary results ensued. That impelled a search for the key component vital in producing lasting effects. Home-based programs such as those planned by Weikart, Karnes, and Gordon were among the first conceived. Attention was also drawn and interest further aroused by statements similar to Zigler's (1978) that, "The program that impacts the child most is the one involving parents in direct interaction with their own child [Levitt & Cohen, 1977, p. 166–167]."

Another source classified parent strategies into three distinct categories: (1) the consultation model, in which the parent is a teacher, subdivided into individual and group consultation; (2) the discussion-group format; and (3) the parents as policy- and decision-makers approach (Stevens & King, 1976). A synopsis of the goals and some of the characteristics of each strategy follows.

Consultation Model

Goal: Assist the parent in facilitating the learning process for the child. The premise is that if parents believe they have an effect on the child's learning, school success is likely to result.

A. Individual

1. Examples are programs developed by Gordon, Gray, Levenstein, and Weikart.
2. Procedure: A parent consultant or home visitor works with parent and child in the home. (In the DARCEE program, for example, the consultant is for the parent, not a tutor to the child; the home visitor's job is to model effective teaching.)
3. Emphasis is on fostering positive self-concept of both parent and child.

B. Group

1. An example is the Nimnicht Toy Lending Library Project.
2. Procedure: Help the parent to reorganize the home environment to maximize learning.
3. A move from dependence to independence is encouraged through the development of parent–peer support. This approach is most likely to preserve growth.

Discussion-Group Format

Goal: Parents will be effective in socializing their children when their understanding of growth, development, and family management is increased.

Parents as Policy- and Decision-Makers

Goal: Give parents control of the environment. It is expected that their self-concepts will improve, which will in turn foster similar attitudes of competence in their children.

Researchers studying different parent education strategies found that there is an impact upon children when home tutoring with parent participation was combined with parent-group discussions about child-rearing concerns. Significantly, more educational materials were found in the homes and parents relied less on authoritarian disciplinary measures when the strategy was employed (Radin, 1972). Other researchers suggested that "The effect of parent education programs may be a latent one in terms of children's development; parent education combined with classroom experience may be more effective in sustaining young children's skill development than classroom experience alone [Stevens & King, 1976, p. 238]." Gordon's study led him to remark, "It takes about two years of parent participation before an impact occurs [Gordon, 1978, p. 6]."

In 1968 Gordon defined parental involvement as

> involving parents in partnership arrangements stressing the needs, strengths, concerns, and special knowledge the parents have and utilizing the expertise of the professional. This requires an atmosphere of mutual trust [p. 73].

Gordon's position adds cohesion to the territory of parental involvement. At that time Gordon also distinguished between parental involvement and parent education. He called for a redefinition of parent education so that parents could be educated to function as advisors and participators in school and community decision making. Gordon also favored home visits to reach parents for whom school represents something alien. Above all else, Gordon's chief concern was to go beyond compensatory education. He was in agreement with Tucker (1977) in feeling strongly that those efforts should begin on a small scale. "Rapid expenditures on unproven models not only waste money but also increase the level of frustration of the people for whom the service was designed [Gordon, 1968, p. 74]."

Gordon, until his death in 1978, remained a leader in the parental involvement movement. He identified six roles parents are able to assume in this regard and documented each with research data. The six roles are audience, classroom volunteer, teacher of own child, paraprofessional, decision-maker, and learner.

The federal guidelines of Follow Through contained stipulations for parental involvement. Gordon, Olmsted, Rubin, and True (1978) were firm in their declaration that evaluations of those guidelines should also be made. Gordon thought that the practice of many educators was to measure the wrong things. Looking ahead, he foresaw a movement toward a different form of evaluative research accounting for case history, personal history, and anthropological factors to supplement child achievement data. Only then, he believed, could the interrelationships between instructional and other strategies, and learner characteristics and environmental conditions be fully investigated; only then could they be systematically applied and studied comprehensively.

As a result of the diversity of early childhood programs (Follow Through Models, Open Education, and "new directions of cognitively oriented nursery schools"), the trend has been toward the acceptance of pluralism in our society—that different educational approaches may be needed for different locations and populations. Whatever the model program may be, from highly restricted, teacher-oriented approaches to more child-centered ones, one theme is clear: Educators and parents are not minimizing the importance of preschool experiences and the tremendous impact of a child's home upon later school performance. Parents are being given the opportunity to engage in discussions and decision making, learn best how to help their children learn, and further their own education.

THE ISSUES OF READING, PLAY, AND TELEVISION

It would be impossible to present all of the many issues related to early childhood education in this chapter. Consequently, the writer has chosen to discuss three issues that have major implications pertaining to the effects of certain practices on the development of children. Those issues include:

1. Reading: Should We Encourage It Before the First Grade?
2. Play: Is It Important in Early Childhood?
3. Television: What Are the Influences on Young Children?

Issue Number One: Teaching Reading Before First Grade—Should It Be Encouraged?

Reading before first grade has been a controversial issue for years and is still a topic of wide debate. Arguments for or against this issue have been based in part on changing beliefs about child development. Those changes have been influenced by research literature, governmental decisions, and many other social forces. The influences provide insight into the development of this issue. Of primary importance are the questions:

1. How did the issue develop?
2. When is a child ready to read?

3. What do researchers and other persons say about reading before first grade?
4. Should reading be taught formally or informally?
5. How may present instructional practices be improved?

Each of these questions will be explored as subtopics of the major concern, "Should reading be taught before first grade?"

How Did the Issue Develop?

The roots of this issue extend back to the development of curriculum for the first American preschools and kindergartens. Early curricula were play-oriented, free, and flexible with emphasis on social, emotional, and physical development. Educators were influenced by the maturational viewpoints of Rousseau, Pestalozzi, and Froebel, who believed that education should coincide with children's physical growth and development and that their growth was a continuous process. In 1898 Dewey and Patrick also supported the maturational view. Furthermore, Dewey (Downing & Thackray, 1972) indicated that as a result of their limited physiological development, children below age 8 should have only incidental experiences with reading and writing.

Those influential men set the stage for the postponement of reading until first grade. However, the practice became a source of controversy as a result of further research and studies. For example, in 1918 Terman reported a child who learned to read at 14 months of age and later, in 1925, Terman noted that a high percentage of gifted students read before first grade (Mason & Prater, 1966). Still, there was support for the postponement of reading. Morphett and Washburne (1931) concluded that a mental age of about 6.5 was an optimum point for beginning reading instruction. Nonetheless, further questioning occurred in 1964 when Benjamin Bloom published *Stability and Change in Human Characteristics.* He stressed that the first 5 years of life are a child's period of most rapid intellectual development (Durkin, 1977). As a result of those developments emphasizing the importance of early childhood, Americans began to seek better ways to educate young children.

Because of the concern for early education, there eventually arose pressures for earlier reading. Government impetus to that idea began with Head Start, a compensatory education program using reading readiness programs with preschoolers. In the 1970s James Allen, Jr., the United States Commissioner of Education, placed additional emphasis on the importance of reading with the national Right to Read Campaign. Parents, too, have contributed to the early reading movement. They expressed concern over the play-oriented structure of kindergarten. Parents wanted assurance that schools would meet the needs of children who began reading before entering school. The trend toward earlier reading continues today as educators weigh its advantages and disadvantages.

When Is a Child Ready to Read?

As educators plan curriculums for early childhood education, they must determine the proper time to begin reading instruction. Generally, instruction should begin when a child reaches the appropriate readiness level. However, readiness has a variety of definitions. Some reading specialists express a maturational view while others express a more comprehensive view. According to Dolores Durkin (1973), the term *readiness* was first used in the 1920s in connection with the teaching of Hall and Gesell. Growth and development supposedly proceed in stages; progress from one to another is dependent upon spontaneous maturation or, put more simply, the passing of time. Later, educators such as Rupley, Sutton, Downing, and Thackray began to support a more comprehensive definition of readiness. Rupley (1977), for example, stated, "A child's readiness for beginning reading instruction is a combination of many factors, including heredity, maturation, and learnings [p. 450]." In his opinion teachers should concentrate on children's experiential backgrounds and specific learnings to prepare them *for* reading. As a result of a longitudinal study of children who read in kindergarten, Sutton (1969) reported a number of additional psychological factors that influenced readiness such as "need to compete with older siblings, willingness to try new experiences, desire to break down the written code or to test one's self in a specific situation [p. 602]." Downing and Thackray (1972) suggested that psychological, environmental, emotional, and intellectual factors are all influential in determining reading readiness.

At the present time many educators share the comprehensive view of reading readiness which takes into account the total child. They suggest that a combination of maturation and experiential background prepare a child for reading. Thus, preparation for reading is beneficial and reading readiness should be determined by considering not only age but also experience and interests.

What Have Researchers Reported about Reading Before First Grade?

Research, studies, and opinions can be used to support opposing views about early reading. Much of the literature contains important topics such as the mental and physiological capabilities of young children, the value of early reading, and the possibility of harmful effects to young readers.

Advocates of early reading cite numerous cases which give evidence that young children are capable of learning to read before first grade.

Evidence of early reading without direct instruction include Terman's 1925 study in which he indicated that 44% of gifted boys and 46% of gifted girls read before age 5. Kasdon studied college freshmen and concluded that 54% of them read before they began school (Mason & Prater, 1966). Variables correlating with early reading reported by researchers were (a) parents who read, (b) siblings or parents who answered questions for the child, (c) children who played school, and (d) children who were very curious. Other investigators presented evidence of children who read early as a result of direct instruction. Gates and Boecker reported instances in which kindergarteners read through the use of picture word cards, and Moore reported that 2- to 5-year-olds were taught to read using an electronic typewriter (Mason & Prater, 1966).

Additional support for the argument that children can read before first grade comes from Templin's research in 1957 in which he indicated that today children have larger vocabularies and greater abilities to construct sentences (Austin, 1968). That suggests that young children are better prepared for kindergarten than they have been in the past.

Gates (1937) concluded that mental age could not be the sole criterion for determining a child's readiness for reading. He contended that mental age would vary in relationship to teaching styles and skills, the types of approaches (materials) employed, and class size. The amount of preparation the teachers afforded children prior to the actual teaching of reading and provisions for meeting individual needs were also cited by Gates as a variable that could influence children's mental age status. MacGinitie (1977) added that every 4- or 5-year-old child should be able to learn some reading if instruction were suited to the child. Also, Durkin (1977) explained that the age of 4 is a time of children's high interest in written language and that teachers should capitalize on those interests. Thus, researchers have indicated that children can and do learn to read before first grade if they are in the proper environment.

Opponents of early reading contend that children generally cannot effectively learn reading at an early age as a result of mental and physiological immaturity. Morphett and Washburne (1931), for example, indicated a high correlation between mental age and reading achievement. They suggested postponement of reading until a child reached a mental age of about 6.5. Waller (1977, p. 4), a follower of Piaget, also considered cognitive development of most young children a block to learning to read. He maintained that children progress through four sequential stages of cognitive development: (a) sensorimotor, (b) preoperational, (c) concrete–operational, and (d) formal–operational. In his opinion, a majority of pre-first-grade children are in the sensorimotor period and cannot read because "The children simply do not possess the mental equipment to cope with the many complex demands of even simple reading tasks." Other opponents cite physiological problems for young readers. Both Cole and Sheldon pinpoint immature auditory and visual development as key problems. Cole observed that many children experience difficulty focusing on objects at a close range until they are older than 8 years. Furthermore, she added that a normal 6-year-old will be unable to distinguish consistently between pairs of related sounds (Moore & Moore, 1974). Sheldon's (1968) views were consistent with other writers; he stated that young children would also be handicapped if (a) auditory acuity and discrimination skills were underdeveloped, (b) speech skills were absent, (c) an adequate listening vocabulary was not developed, and (d) children were unable to use grammatical constructions correctly. Harris and Sipay (1975) also offered a wealth of evidence to support their beliefs that although young children with mental ages below 6 years could learn to read, there were many children in that mental age group who failed in their attempts. Apparently, researchers have continued to collect data that support the beliefs of Dewey, as well as his disciple Patrick, that knowledge of children's minds, physiological and nervous systems, and other systems should lead early childhood specialists to introduce reading at a later period (Downing & Thackray, 1972).

Few of the studies contained information concerning the long-term effects or the future value of early reading to a child; however, many experts have expressed opinions on this subject. Many share the belief that reading before first grade is not only helpful, but is essential to the development of the child. Bloom, for example, believed that by age 4 up to 50% of a child's intelligence is flexible, but attempts to raise their intelligence at a later time is difficult (Pines, 1974). Ferguson added emphasis to the future value of early reading by explaining his demonstration day care facility in Washington, D.C. Ferguson stated, "If the brain is not stimulated at the right time, something is lost forever. The right time is early childhood—as early as eighteen months [Dribin, 1972, p. 46]." In his opinion, any help given later is simply remedial. Other educators such as Johnson (1971) and MacGinitie (1977) argued that the earlier children begin reading, the more time they will have to assimilate the reading process.

Researchers have supported the value of early reading. For example, from Hillerich's 1965 study, in which kindergarten children were taught to read, he concluded that they had more reading skills at the end of first grade than children who started reading in first grade (Wilson, 1976). In both the 1960 Denver experiment and Durkin's 6-year study, early readers had a lead on other children in first grade, although their lead was maintained only with adjusted reading programs in later years (Durkin, 1973, 1977). Based on her studies, Durkin concluded that the lower the child's intelligence quotient, the greater seems to be the advantage of starting early. Additionally, Sutton (1969) indicated that the early readers' advantage not only continued, but actually increased as they progressed through the grades.

Opponents of pre-first-grade reading do not believe that it is of significant future value to a child. Those opinions are based on research and theories of child development. Of the few longitudinal studies on early reading, from Vernon's 1955 study, it was concluded that the advantages of early training may not be maintained in intermediate grades (Mason & Prater, 1966). Keister and Durkin also have shown that early reading advantage lasts *only* if subsequent instruction is adjusted (Leeper, 1974).

Beliefs about child development also lead to ideas that pre-first-grade reading is not of future value to a child. Elkind (1974) stated that a child must reach a certain stage of development before reading instruction can be productive. Before that time a child is unable to assimilate and generalize rules. Hock (1978) added that children who begin reading at 8 years of age will be at an advantage because they will learn more quickly than those who read at 5 years of age. Furthermore, Glass (Adelphi) asserted that the curriculum *must* suit the development of the child. He argued that of all a young child's communication skills, reading is the least mature. Therefore, if youngsters depend primarily upon reading in their early years they will not only be cheated of using their highest level of cognitive skills (at that stage of development) but they may associate reading (initially and forever) with the act of reading and not expect that it can result in learnings and joys beyond other modes of communicating (which reading cannot do in the early grades). Hock (1978) suggested that children's early education should be through listening and speaking until age 8 when language would become a dominant factor in their lives.

In summary, the future value of early reading has not been established. Proponents are encouraged by researchers who indicated initial advantages for early readers in first grade. But, that advantage, to be maintained, is accomplished only by adjusting the curriculum in later grades. Opponents argue that, generally, children are not developmentally ready to read before first grade and that a majority of them are incapable of assimilating rules and processes involved in reading. More longitudinal studies are needed before any final answers are possible.

Another important topic considered by educators and researchers is the question of harmful effects resulting from early reading. Some of the suggested harmful effects include fear of visual damage or psychological damage.

Proponents of pre-first-grade reading cite the results of the Denver study in refuting those claims. Brzeinski, Harrison, and McKee (1968, pp. 158–159) wrote, "No evidence was found that early instruction in beginning reading affected visual acuity, created problems of social adjustment, or caused a dislike for reading." Heigartner, a Texas opthamologist, agreed that there is no evidence of early eye damage, although he indicated that the eyes of young children focus better on distant objects (Moore & Moore, 1974).

Educators in favor of early reading do not believe that it leads to emotional problems such as dislike of reading, poor social adjustment, or poor self-concept due to fear of failure. LaConte (1970) surveyed kindergarten teachers and reported that the teachers' consensus was that teaching reading in kindergarten was neither psychologically damaging nor a cause of children's dislike for reading. Kelly (1963, p. 58) found that many 5-year-olds arrive at kindergarten with "built-in readiness" and that the kindergarten environment is no longer needed as a "socializing agency." Apparently, self-concept and fear of failure depends more upon the kind of environment provided for children than what is taught to them. According to Gates, reading print should not be harder for children than understanding spoken language (Lifton, 1974).

Opponents of those who support teaching young children to read firmly believe that early reading can damage a child both physiologically and psychologically. Hock (1978), stated that there are two hemispheres of the brain. The right is used to create and the left is used to process information. Hock believed that the hemispheres are balanced when children are 5 years of age. However, he contended that too much reading instruction may overdevelop the left side and cause the right (creative) hemisphere to become underdeveloped. Many educators primarily oppose teachers' practice of placing undue emphasis on formal reading instruction before first grade. The results may be damaging psychological effects. Dolch, Agnew, and Bloomster (Sheldon, 1968) suggest that confusion and failure may occur when word analysis or identification skills are presented to young children. Carpenter (1968) listed (a) fright, (b) dull techniques, (c) parent concern over grouping, and (d) discipline problems.

Having considered the question, "Is early reading harmful to a child?" it is apparent that the evidence may be interpreted as inconclusive. However, many educators are in agreement that reading need not be harmful to any child who is ready to read. Harm results from teachers and parents who coerce children to try to read when they are not developmentally ready and from the employment of inappropriate teaching approaches and methods, without due consideration of the children's learning preference.

Should Reading Be Taught Formally or Informally?

Researchers have indicated that young children may be taught to read by employing a variety of approaches and that the approach used to teach reading should be related to the program that is developed for developing children's readiness. Instructional techniques may be broadly classified as formal (i.e., basal approach) or informal (i.e., open learning approach).

Some of the earliest research indicating the effectiveness of formal and structured programs comes from the work of Moore who taught 2- to 5-year-old children to read using an electronic typewriter (Mason & Prater, 1966). Bender also viewed the use of machines and a structured environment advantageous in teaching disadvantaged 4-year-old children to read (Wilson, 1976). Kelly (1963) was another supporter of formal reading instruction. Kelly compared formal and traditional readiness programs and concluded that the formal program was more effective. In addition, Bissel and Stanchfield concluded that disadvantaged children progressed more in reading skill development in highly structured sequential programs than when assigned to other organizational plans (Smith, 1976). Thus, it appears that direct, formal reading instruction has been effective as a means of teaching pre-first-grade reading in specific circumstances. However, studies cited contained only one aspect of child development, reading ability. Educators are responsible for the total child, including social, emotional, and physical development.

Many authorities believe that informal or loosely structured reading programs are more beneficial for early readers. Many program developers are highly critical of formal methods. Piaget supported informal approaches. Hymes (1973), one of Piaget's supporters, questioned formal instruction. Hymes contended that just because children today have a wider range of experiences does not mean they are more mature or that they need less experiential learning. Sheldon (1968) also believed that Piaget's work could be interpreted to mean that children 5 years old and younger would learn best through individual attention rather than through formal instruction. Through informal programs, teachers may provide flexibility as they determine when and how each child learns to read. Thus, teachers can provide a greater degree of individualization as well as a relaxed atmosphere in which self-esteem and confidence in reading ability can be built.

Many authorities who support informal approaches consider formal approaches to be very damaging to young children. In a formal program, Hymes (1968) cited inpersonal instruction, authoritarian teacher control, and sparse evidence of child enthusiasm as very damaging. Hymes contended that formal teaching techniques may result in psychological damage to young children. He condemned practices of pressuring children to achieve before they were ready. To Hymes, children were being manipulated by adults; in turn the children would be persistent in their efforts to receive rewards of love, affection, and approval; the final outcome would be children with unhealthy personalities. Furthermore, Hymes accused educators of using formal reading methods as a means of managing overcrowded kindergarten classes rather than seeking the most beneficial programs. Another criticism, shared by Dolch and Bloomster, is that young children cannot assimilate the complex rule systems inherent in formal reading programs until they reach a mental age of about 7.0 (Sheldon, 1968). A final shortcoming indicated by Elkind (1974) is that in the formal programs, forced learning may result in negative attitudes toward reading and school in general.

In conclusion, supporters have shown that formal approaches employed to teach young children to read can be successful. But they have not disproven the criticisms posited by the advocates of informal approaches. Informal approaches have been shown to have many advantages. Through them, teachers can offer flexibility and individualization that are essential characteristics of good programs since all children do not reach readiness at the same time and do not learn in the same ways. Through informal approaches teachers can capitalize on the natural curiosity and interests of young children while, at the same, fostering healthy attitudes toward reading. Teachers can also provide for the needs of children who are reading and those who are not.

How Can Present Instructional Practices Be Improved?

Educators and parents have proposed numerous suggestions for changes in present instructional practices in reading for pre-first graders. Commentators suggest more individualization, integration of curriculum, use of spiral curriculum, concern for the total child, and parent involvement.

Durkin (1973) suggested that in individualizing instruction, teachers should consider not only children's readiness to read but also their readiness for a particular kind of instruction. Similarly, Hymes (1973) wrote that children under 6 years of age should be taught to read, but methods used must be shaped to fit the child.

Improvement of reading through integration of curriculum is the suggestion of a committee of educators in an article in *Educational Leadership.* Their recommendation was, "To provide opportunities for reading experiences as an integrated part of the broader communication processes that included listening, speaking, and reading [Corbin, Plunkett, Kyer, Myer, Day, Durkin, Nurss, Ollila, Strickland, Pharis, Engstrom, Smith, & Roderick, 1977, p. 325]." Through that approach, purposes could be established for reading that would increase motivation.

Another recommendation involves a greater use of a spiral curriculum in reading. Glass (Adelphi) believed that skill learning required of beginning readers should be built upon previously learned listening and speaking skills. Through that type of program the interrelationship of communication processes could be provided and also employed to build the young readers' confidence in themselves.

A final suggestion for improvement is in the area of parent involve- ·

ment. According to Hoskisson (1974), parents should play a significant role in pre-first-grade reading. He believed that since parents were more knowledgeable of their children's experiential backgrounds, accumulated information, and linguistic competencies, the parents were better prepared to guide children through speaking skills and into the act of reading. Closer communication and cooperation between teachers and parents can be very beneficial to a child's development. Parents can be excellent teachers if they are given adequate and appropriate direction and instruction in how to guide and direct their children.

Conclusion

Reading before first grade remains a critical issue in early childhood education. Many parents and educators continue to demand pre-first-grade reading programs. The research available has flaws. Most reporters have indicated short-term effects only. Researchers have not confirmed that pre-first-grade reading is harmful to all children, although various individuals have expressed that concern. The results do show that early reading instruction is helpful only if later programs accommodate early learning.

Studies of child development have made educators more aware of the many factors influencing reading readiness. Today most educators are in agreement that readiness is a combination of maturation and experience. Thus, readiness is not solely dependent upon age; all children do not reach readiness for reading at the same age or in the same grade.

As educators have sought the most effective means of teaching reading to pre-first graders, much of their support has been directed toward informal instruction which suits the child. An informal program tends to have more of the critical attributes which educators consider essential to a child's cognitive, social, emotional, and physical growth and development.

**Issue Number Two: Play in the Life of the Young Child —
Is It Important?**

Every child plays spontaneously and by choice. Play is an intrinsic and enjoyable activity of childhood. But does play do anything other than provide pleasure? Clepper (1974), in *Growing Up with Toys: A Guide for Parents*, stated, "Play is the work of childhood, the way a child develops his mind and his muscles, and finds out who he is and what he can do about it [p. 8]."

This issue is presented to shed light on the importance of play in early childhood. How was it regarded in the past, and more importantly, what value is placed on play in the present?

Definition of Play

A logical starting point in examining the importance of play in early childhood is first to define play. But Butler, Gotts, and Quisenberry (1978) presented a view that makes it difficult to generate an explicit definition. To them, the definition of play is fluid, and dependent upon the perceptions of the definer. The young child enters the environment of play with knowledge, skills, and attitudes; additionally children have opinions and attitudes about themselves (self-esteem, self-concept, and so forth) and also views or perceptions of other children who will enter the play environment. The activities and outcomes will vary in accordance with the interactions of those same variables. Therefore, Butler and her associates contend that play is not an isolated act or group of actions by children; that much more is involved. They also believe that persons who observe children's play may classify the activities as related to learning or growth and development processes, or completely foreign, unrelated, and unnecessary. Therefore, Butler and associates (1978) conclude, "A formal definition (of play) is difficult (to create) [p. 6]."

Frank (Hartley & Goldenson, 1963) was aware of the concerns many people expressed regarding children and the significance of play. Frank wrote that the meaning of, and needs for, play were still not clear in the minds of many persons. Frank presented the essentialistic view held by many that work (labor) and play (fun) are different. But Frank believed that "Play is the child's work [Hartley & Goldenson, 1963, pp. vi–viii]." Through play, Frank contended, children gain a view of *their world* and *their position* in it. As children explore, develop percepts, concepts, linguistic, and intellectual skills, they work and learn. Though formulating a formal definition of play is difficult, certain descriptive characteristics of play are widely accepted. Garvey's (1977) characteristics included several variables that were referred to by Frank and by Butler and Gotts; still the list is different enough to warrant inclusion. Garvey contended that play should be an enjoyable activity motivated by internal drives. Play should be a voluntary act, and no extrinsic goals should be established for it. Garvey further stipulated that children must become actively involved in play and find it a pleasurable experience.

Any reference to *play* throughout this discussion of the issues will connote the sense of activity possessing the descriptive characteristics just cited.

Some Early Views on Play

"Play is as old as recorded history [Frost & Kissinger, 1976, p. 319]." Views about why children play have been abundant in history, but until recently there was little systematic examination of the nature and values of play. The value of children's play and regard for its potential contributions to cognitive and affective development appear to have been re-established among early childhood educators during the 1970s. Over the century, many people have considered play to be sinful and a waste of time and energy. One nineteenth-century educator saw little value in play, aside from its function in expending surplus energy (Frost & Kissinger, 1976, p. 319). Some schools and parents consider the release of excess energy to be the sole purpose of play, leaving nothing to imagination and planning. As long as the child remains active, one form of play is as valuable as another.

Some early theorists perceived play to be a means of helping children to relax and replenish their energies. Other theorists assumed that play served more meaningful functions, yet they disregarded, almost entirely, the content and developmental sequences of play (Barnett, 1977). Those views of play are being replaced or expanded by contemporary thinkers who are adding to a rapidly growing body of literature that contains support for play.

Historically, some early theorists regarded play as being of limited significant value. Early Greek thinkers recognized play as a vehicle for learning. They believed that play was important; through play children could practice functions that would be essential for their safety and economic security as adults. John Locke believed that all children's activities should be sport and play, not only because it was important in sustaining and improving health and physical fitness, but also because it allowed young children to "test their limits to find out what they could and could not do [Frost & Kissinger, 1976, p. 320]." Froebel gave play an essential role in the educational process. He believed spontaneous play to be the most important avenue for children's learning. In Froebel's thoughts, play was the one free expression of what is in a child's soul. Play was the purest and most spiritual product of children.

Why and How Children Play

Young children play to develop an understanding and mastery of their environment; play is the most important aspect of a young child's life. To a child, play is serious business. It is that seriousness of purpose that gives play its educational value. Young children at play combine a seriousness of purpose with an enjoyment that is often envied by adults. "Young children bring a fervent intensity to play activities. It is as they are little researchers, working at a job they love [Marzollo & Lloyd, 1972, p. 3]."

Play permits children to learn to exhibit behaviors appropriately and to control a *variety* of human encounters they must cope with throughout life. Goldsworthy (1971) described play as the greatest psychological need of growing children. He believes that play, if provided under really good conditions, produces not only mental vigor, shown in thinking and reasoning, but also much learning as the result of rich experiences.

Children also utilize play as a means of expressing themselves creatively. Role-playing, building structures, singing, dancing, and artistic endeavors provide children with creative outlets.

Words alone are not enough for the young child. Children learn best through active play by manipulating concrete and sensory materials. Play is the way young children explore and experiment with the world around them. They form relations with that world, other human beings, and themselves. Play is the avenue through which children learn to concentrate, to exercise imaginations, to try ideas, and to practice grown-up behaviors. Through play, children discover how to come to terms with their world, to cope with the tasks of life, to master new skills, and to gain confidence in themselves as worthwhile individuals. Play provides a medium through which children can learn through trial and error; it is a way in which they learn to cope with the real world.

Play is the natural way a child learns. Nature has always been on the side of young learners. When children are born, they are bestowed with an insatiable curiosity. The more they learn, the more they want to learn. They want to talk; they want to imitate other people; they want to explore. Unless children suffer from some abnormality or are placed in a restricted environment, they seem to be unable to keep from playing. When materials are left for them to manipulate and explore, their curiosity and inquisitiveness leads them to investigate and solve problems.

The Value of Play in a Child's Life

Earlier thinkers considered play and education to be opposites, but contemporary educators, psychologists, and early childhood specialists have discovered that play is one of the most effective means for learning known. Young children are some of the best learners known. During the preschool years, children learn more and faster than at any other time in their lives. The concept of early childhood as strictly a time for fun and physical growth is obsolete and inadequate. "The early childhood years are exciting and powerful years for building the foundations of intelligence. The act of play is the extraordinary process by which it (intelligence) happens [Marzollo & Lloyd, 1972, p. 2]."

Play serves an important function in the intellectual, emotional, social, and physical development of the child. Some contemporary theorists attempt to analyze the content of growing children's play and relate it to more fundamental aspects of their total development. For example, play has been suggested to influence the child's self-development, resolution of conflicts, control of aggression, and development of motor skills (Barnett, 1977).

Cognitive Growth

Play provides for children's cognitive growth during early childhood; it is the motivating force in children's intellectual development. Piaget interpreted children's play as "a predominance of assimilation over accommodation (Barnett, 1977, p. 39]." Play is a means of "taking the outside world and manipulating it so that it fits a person's organizational scheme. As such, play serves a vital function in the child's developing intellect, and remains to some extent, always present in human behavior [Spodek, 1972, p. 204]." Piaget suggested that play, especially make-believe, may be a source of creative imagination. In playful interactions with the environment, children are thought to form unique relationships and associations among objects and ideas which are usually "unrelated in less freely assimilative thought [Barnett, 1977, p. 40]." Through manipulation, children begin to attend to similarities and differences among objects encountered. Those early, playful encounters are viewed as helping children to classify and develop simple categories and concepts as they progress to more advanced, abstract, technical modes of thinking.

Bruner (Barnett, 1977), viewed young children's interactions with their environment as a way of making possible the "playful practice of subroutines of behavior that later come together in useful problem solving." Singer suggested that "The ability to fantasize freely is a cognitive skill related to concentration, fluency, and spontaneity of thought, as well as to the ability to organize and integrate diverse stimuli [Barnett, 1977, p. 40]."

Leeper *et al.* (1974) indicated that play encouraged language development. Children's language growth is stimulated as they come in contact with other children and their need to communicate is made evident. Play thoroughly engages the attention of the child. Play provides for repetition which is one of the chief means through which children learn. Through play, children practice until a skill is mastered. The resulting success provides satisfaction and motivation. Play is the setting in which children develop their communication and relationship skills—skills that provide the foundation on which future learnings are built.

Through play children learn to follow a task to completion. They learn skills basic to reading: (*a*) the ability to concentrate and persevere; (*b*) the ability to discriminate between shapes; (*c*) the ability to gain the meaning of words; and (*d*) the ability to solve problems and make decisions. Through play, children discover who they are, the rules of their world, and the rules and expectations of their culture.

Children in their play begin to reason, to develop logical thinking abilities, to increase their vocabularies, and to discover mathematical relationships and scientific facts. Play experiences are essential if children are to use all of their innate abilities and develop the skills necessary to solve abstract problems.

Emotional Growth

Play is of great value to children's emotional satisfaction and stability. Play is an avenue for children to externalize feelings through dramatic and artistic expressions that are shared with others. The deep satisfaction of creative achievement provides a motive for self-discipline and self-control.

Play is necessary for mental health. Children engage in play wholeheartedly, without restraint, discarding self-consciousness. They reveal their true natures, thus providing subtle indicators of their emotional well-being. While observing a playing child, a person may note behaviors of joys, fears, or hopes.

Play serves as a means of coping with emotional stress. It may serve as one means through which children learn to solve problems. For example, a child may choose a toy that represents something he fears or toward which he has resentment (Leeper et al., 1974). Playing-out a problem enables the child to gain a sense of mastery and self-assertion.

Play helps children deal with their angry thoughts. With a better understanding of those thoughts, children can actualize acceptance of those thoughts, and play can become more peaceful. It is through imaginative and fantasy play that the children learn about the outer and inner worlds of their lives.

Cass (1971) described children as entering into their imaginary play environments with fresh and spontaneous actions with unique characteristics. Cass believed that those same attributes would not only be useful, but necessary, for success later in life. To Cass, imagery skills developed during childhood are substructures of problem solving, anticipating outcomes, foresight, and many other cognitive, affective, physical, and creative tasks encountered at all ages above the early years. Cass (1971, pp. 52–55) bemoaned the condition that the "freshness and spontaneity to their imaginative play" and each child's unique qualities thereof were "easily lost as they grow older." To prevent that deterioration, Cass admonished all those persons concerned with children's welfare not to preclude the provision of activities that "feed and stimulate the imaginative life"; to do so would be to "impoverish their whole education."

Children need outlets for their feelings, both positive and negative. Play provides an avenue for children to learn that feelings can be safely expressed and that hostility and aggression can be managed and controlled.

Social Growth

In the environment of play, children gradually learn the difference between *mine* and *yours*. Children learn first to discover themselves, and then to reach out to others. While at play, children provide themselves with practical experiences for learning what they are like, how their actions bring results, and how people react to them and they to people. Children usually go through a developmental sequence of play. The sequence usually includes activities in which children aged 3 through 5 years engage. The six categories of play behavior are (1) unoccupied, (2) solitary, (3) onlooker, (4) parallel, (5) associative, and (6) cooperative.

Perhaps the most important socializing value of play experiences is that children, as members of a group, begin to learn to understand each other. Their interaction helps their development of attitudes and behavior toward others. It is through play that young children learn about their culture, their personalities, and their emotions. Participation in play helps children learn to follow rules, to allow the group to rule, to receive the fulfillment of group identity, and to learn to live with others. Children's interests fuse in play, bringing them into new social contacts and new situations which they learn to handle. Cooperation can reach its highest level through play.

By playing, children learn basic patterns of living. Their imagination and love for creative dramatics enable them to assume various rules, feelings, attitudes, and emotions. Children rehearse skills that will be useful in later life. Spodek (1972) viewed play as a means for children to learn principles of economics and geographical knowledge of their communities, as well as to gain ability in measurements. Spodek viewed the environment of play, in which children assumed social roles, to be an opportune period for children to grow in many ways.

Physical Growth

Play provides for physical development. As children run, skip, jump, climb, and hop they gain in physical fitness. They gain new skills through exercising and using the coordination that exists. Climbing the jungle gym, hammering, and putting puzzles together all foster muscular control. Large objects, long play runways, large sheets of paper, and lots of room for active play are essential in early childhood learning environments. Play in a barrel may be viewed as just fun to a young child, but getting into, through, and out of the barrel provides many needed movements for the normal physical growth of the young child. Skills in small-muscle activities are also important in building eye–muscle coordination. Using crayons and scissors and manipulative materials builds many of the skills necessary for writing and reading.

The Role of the Teacher

The good teacher is the adult who perpetuates and encourages the learning situation by sharing interests and enjoyment of the children, and ensuring that suitable challenges are met rather than allowing the distress of constant failure. The good teacher presents new situations and information in an open-ended manner that involves children rather than limits them to an adult-determined framework (Matterson, 1975).

An important task for the teacher is to provide materials which the child can manipulate, adapt, accommodate, and assimilate into his own world. The skillful teacher facilitates learning through an organized environment, one deliberately designed with many opportunities for young children to explore and to discuss. Concrete and sensory materials are a vital part of the environment, as they are basic learning devices for the young child (Day, 1975). A climate of trust is established, and children are helped to see connections and encouraged to ask questions and share learnings. Adults who play with the child and assist in setting the stage for play are vital contributors in the child's development.

Playtime at school is teaching time. Teachers must arrange special activities that foster psychomotor development. They must also insure that children grow in cognitive, emotional, social, and physical development. Teachers provide encouragement and opportunities for children to cooperate, share, and help one another. Equipment and activities are modified by teachers to extend interests, contacts, concepts, and language. Teachers are also responsible for providing safe outlets for emotions.

Playtime is diagnosis time. Through play or failure in play, children reveal themselves intellectually, emotionally, socially, and physically. Teachers gain valuable insights into the child's concept development, language development, and level of motor development. During play children's behaviors provide indications of their emotional well-being. By observing a playing child, the teacher may screen for anxieties, fears, or hostilities. The immature child who has had limited play experiences needs to be taught how to play in meaningful, constructive ways. Immature children demonstrate their inabilities through exhibiting behaviors of wandering and boredom. Aggressive behavior is exhibited through destructive play and fighting. If children play happily, it is almost always an indicator that they are mentally healthy. Well-adjusted children easily transfer from and to various roles during imaginative play.

The teacher must provide materials which a child can manipulate with confidence and competence. Those materials should be structured to encourage the learning of skills through spontaneous play and structured play. Spontaneous play is that movement to activity which is self-initiated. Structured play activities are planned and presented by teachers who match them with children's developmental capacities, interests, and experiences.

Play in Some Existing Educational Programs

Upon examination of some of the Follow Through model programs, it is evident that great emphasis is placed on the value of play in the learning process. Other models, however, do not value play as a primary way for young children to learn. Developers of the Bank Street model suggested that play is very important to young children and should be used by teachers in establishing many behavioral goals. In their model, play is implemented in the following manner: "There is a central use of play, and it reflects how the child perceives relationships, reveals how he orders the world, and this is the way he learns to integrate his ideas and develop them [Maccoby & Zeliner, 1970, p. 39]." Through playing, children learn helpful communication skills while enjoying themselves. Play serves as an excellent motivator in the Bank Street School.

A goal of the Bank Street program is to support the play mode by incorporating experience, by nourishing, and by setting the stage for dramatic play activities. "The most elaborate form of symbolizing experience is seen in the self-initiated dramatic play through which children relive the most meaningful aspects of their experience [Day & Parker, 1977, p. 441]."

In play, children assimilate experience, selecting prominent components of their impressions of the real world of how things work and what people do, and recompose them into new configurations. In the course of spontaneous invention among children, they extend their understanding, solve problems inherent in adapting props and assuming roles to serve as symbolic carriers of meaning, intensify insights, and create new situations that lead to new wondering and questioning (Day & Parker, 1977).

Since dramatic play is regarded as fundamental in representational thinking and a natural way for young children to gain cognitive mastery through reliving experiences symbolically, it is given an important place in the Bank Street curriculum. Space is assigned for it in the classroom, and time is allotted in the daily sequence of activities. An abundance of materials to foster play are provided. Those materials include blocks, trains, animal and human figures, dress-up clothes, and house-keeping toys. The role of the teacher is to be attentive to the content and movement of the children's play and to offer additional materials and content that will move the play toward a more challenging or satisfying level. Teachers must be able to accept that children may refuse certain suggestions when their choice of play has resulted in inner-directed courses.

The Bank Street program developers recognized another developmental purpose of self-initiated play. It is a way to express and deal with emotions and to merge the subjective and objective without embarrassment, since a child's sense of adequacy is not yet invested in strict adherence to rules of logic (Day & Parker, 1977).

"The essential core of a preschool program in the Bank Street view is support-guided play [Evans, 1971, p. 76]." Support-guided play is based upon the principle of active exploration in a safe, nurturing, varied environment. It is based upon the assumption of growth stages in the direction of increased differentiation and hierarchical integration (Evans, 1971). During the preschool years, a child's play shifts to take on a quality of industry and self-initiated activities (Maccoby & Zeliner, 1970). Children become more involved in understanding the physical and social environment. In addition to responding to the child's self-initiated activities, the teacher also looks for ways of stimulating children to begin searching.

Bank Street designers direct teachers to organize the classroom as the children's workroom where they are free to manipulate objects and explore various media. Children make choices and carry out plans. The Bank Street environment is a safe and ordered one.

The Nimnicht model developers desired to create a responsive environment, one that is responsive to the needs of the children. The guiding principle of the Nimnicht program is that the environment should be arranged so that children are likely to make discoveries about their physical and social world because a child better remembers what he discovers for himself (Maccoby & Zeliner, 1970). Problem solving is the essence of learning and it is best learned in an atmosphere that poses problems and encourages the discovery of their solutions. The Nimnicht model classroom environment is structured so that as children freely explore it, they will make discoveries from which they will learn. Throughout the day, the children are free to choose from a variety of activities: artwork, puzzles, looking at books, listening to records, and playing with manipulative toys. In the course of the day, teachers and assistants read to children, play games with them, and respond to their spontaneous activities. Small groups may choose to play games with specific learning objectives. There are large group activities once or twice a day, but a child takes part only if he chooses to. Although the children have a free choice of activities within the environment, the teacher and assistant structure the environment by deciding which activities and materials will be available each day, according to their planning for specific learning objectives. The adults arrange the materials and respond to the children in a way that poses problems that the children will want to solve and that will guide them to learn specific skills or concepts.

As the children engage in spontaneous play activities, the teacher assistant watches for indications of frustration and the need for help. The assistant also watches for ways to help them learn new concepts.

The British Infant School model designers attempted to create a rich environment where freedom of choice, creativity, and exploration are facilitated. It is similar to the Nimnicht and Bank Street models. A playful attitude of self-expression and messing-about with a variety of learning materials is encouraged. Areas are equipped for different activities such as small-muscle games, listening, looking (and other sensory experiences), large-muscle games, and expressive play. Children can move freely from one area to another and choose their activities as well as the amount of time to spend on each.

Evans (1971) stated that the work-play dichotomy that characterized traditional infant schools was being avoided by designers of new programs. However, Evans supported the inclusion of play in nursery and infant schools. Evans considered attitudes of many persons who viewed play as a waste of time to be erroneous and unfounded. Evans's remarks were harmonious with those of other writers who supported the necessity of play. All of them supported play as vital and as the major avenue (a) through which children learn, (b) through which concepts are developed and comprehension skills are established and become sophisticated, and (c) through which powers of attention and concentration are established. According to Evans, children have the potential to transfer habits of concentration to other learning. There is also reason to believe that the other skills are just as transferrable.

In sharp contrast to the philosophies of the Bank Street, Nimnicht, and British Infant School model designers is the Engelmann–Becker philosophy. While Engelmann and Becker recognized that it is important for children to want to learn, they believed that motivation can be taught. They contended that teachers should not rely on motivation's automatic presence or delay instruction for it to develop spontaneously.

Engelmann and Becker reasoned that making a special effort to raise the self-esteem of children is not necessary. They believed that high self-esteem will be a result of competence.

The Engelmann–Becker curriculum is focused on objectives designed to teach language, reading, and mathematics at a rapid pace. The approach is a no-nonsense one with the teacher quickly correcting the children's mistakes and making heavy work demands on them (Frost & Kissinger, 1976). The program is criticized for its insensitivity to affective development and for its narrowness of content (Frost & Kissinger, 1976).

It is concluded that play is generally excluded as a mode of learning in the Engelmann–Becker Model, and that no emphasis is placed on the value of play in the learning process in an environment like the Engelmann–Becker one, where discovery, exploration, and creativity are not encouraged.

Conclusion

In conclusion, play in early childhood is invaluable in the growth and development processes. It is indeed an avenue for intellectual, emotional, social, and physical growth and development of children. Persons who observe young children at play will notice growth and learning that become apparent. To children, play is serious business; it is their work.

Play is a very serious activity of a child from birth to 8 years of age. Play helps a child accomplish many things. It facilitates growth and helps children to come to terms with their personal patterns of growth and development, helps them find their places in the culture, and gives them a sense of power. In the world of play, the child is in control. The children can select the play activity without the restrictions of the real world. Through play, children can experience adventures of their own ordering. The abnormal can be tested to determine if it works. Play provides a base for language development and allows contacts with other human beings in a comfortable setting in order to build relationships. Play helps children master the physical self, encourages interests and concentration, and teaches them about adult roles (Caplan & Caplan, 1973).

Childhood is a unique and highly important developmental stage in a human being's life; play a fundamental and powerful aspect of that stage of development. Children need to experience that part of their lives fully if childhood is to be a rich and productive experience in the present, and a foundation for advanced learnings in the future. Childhood play is not only a pastime, it is a valuable tool which will enable children to grow, develop, and learn.

Issue Number Three: Television—What Are the Influences on Young Children?

In 1965, with the first ACEI publication on *Children and TV . . . Making the Most of It*, Christensen questioned whether television was a friend or enemy of young children. Christensen concluded that for television viewing to be of value to young children, parents and teachers would have to be responsible for (a) monitoring and evaluating the content of programs, (b) determining the purposes producers had for airing certain productions, and (c) analyzing children's reactions to various programs and presentational techniques (Swenson, 1967). Those recommendations are as valid today as they were a quarter of a century ago. In fact, television probably has an even greater influence in the lives of young children today. Approximately 97% of American homes have at least one television set. Some have two or even three sets. Researchers have indicated that children devote more time to watching television than to any other single activity except sleep (Kaye, 1974). The average home television set is on more than 6 hours a day (Surgeon General, 1972). By the time children are graduated from high school, they will have spent an average of 15,000 hours watching television compared with 11,000 hours in school (Kaye, 1974).

There is no doubt that American children spend many hours in front of television sets. But what effects does television viewing have on young children? Hundreds of studies have been conducted by researchers who tried to find answers to the question. They have only begun to sort out the complex relationship that exists between children's behaviors and televiewing habits. Some researchers indicate positive effects, but many of them have found negative ones, especially in the area of television violence.

Parents and educators of young children should concern themselves with total child development. It is important that all areas of a child's life are developed to the fullest. In the presentation of the issue of televiewing the effects of television will be presented in each major area of a child's development: cognitive, affective (including the socialization process), and physical. The presentation will also contain specific data related to television advertising and methods for helping children analyze advertisements. A section on the use of television in the home contains suggestions to parents to help them teach their children how to gain the most from television programs.

Effects on Cognitive Development

Television productions can be a powerful teacher of young children. Every day that children watch television they learn something new. Silberman (1971), author of *Crisis in the Classroom*, wrote, "Students probably learn more about certain subjects from television than from (their) schools [p. 32]." What is it about television that makes it such an effective teacher? There are several variables. Television characters capture children's attention and arouse their curiosity. Messages on television get through to kids as nothing else seems to. They learn a great deal from it, and it is not all bad.

One of the interesting facts emerging from surveys is that a large number of people think television programs, any television, is educational. Parents most often mention education as television's major advantage for children (Liebert, Neale, & Davidson, 1973).

Educational Television

In the United States, educational television exists on both the national and local levels. The only country-wide educational system is a loosely federated organization of over 100 stations, the National Educational Television Network (NET).

The Children's Television Workshop is a nonprofit organization established by a group of public and private agencies (The Carnegie Corporation, Ford Foundation, U.S. Office of Education, U.S. Office of Economic Opportunity, and the National Institute of Child Health and Human Development). Its goal was to telecast a daily program that would both entertain and foster intellectual and cultural development (Ball & Bogatz, 1970). The Workshop currently produces *Sesame Street* (since 1969), which is a television program that uses an entertainment format intended to teach preschool children skills that help them think and learn. On the program, various characters and other devices are used to teach number and letter concepts, relational concepts, problem solving, and basic prereading skills. Emphasis is placed also on helping children learn about themselves and the world in which they live.

In the United States, *Sesame Street* is transmitted daily from nearly 300 television stations and is watched regularly by an estimated 9 million youngsters 3 to 5 years old. Millions of other children in more than 50 countries and territories around the world have seen the program or its foreign language counterpart since 1970.

In the fall of 1971, *The Electric Company* was aired for the first time. That program was designed specifically for teaching reading skills primarily to second graders. The skills presented include sound–symbol analysis of printed words. Children are taught the correspondences between letters and sounds to enable them to decode words. Reading for meaning, using the context of the material, and syntax are also presented (Liebert *et al.*, 1973).

Research on *Sesame Street*

Ball and Bogatz (1970) completed a thorough, independent study of *Sesame Street* following the first year it was broadcasted. The studies were conducted in five widely separated sections of the country. Altogether, 943 children participated in all phases of the study. Each child was given a pretest and a posttest, designed to measure specific learning in the following areas: body parts, letters, numbers, forms, relational terms, sorting skills, classification skills, and completing puzzles.

The total sample was divided into quartiles on the basis of the amount of viewing. Children in Quartile I rarely or never watched *Sesame Street;* those in Quartile II watched two or three times weekly; those in Quartile III watched four to five times a week; and children in Quartile IV viewed *Sesame Street* more than five times weekly.

Results of the study were interpreted to mean that the more children watched the program, the more they tended to improve their total scores. That finding was the same for the total sample, regardless of sex, ethnicity, or socioeconomic status. In addition, gains in other skills not directly presented on *Sesame Street* were revealed. For example, *Sesame Street* apparently had some effect on word recognition skills and ability to write one's own first name.

Ball and Bogatz (1970) conducted another evaluation after the second year of *Sesame Street*. The results generally replicated those of the first study. Children who viewed *Sesame Street* improved more than those who did not. As a result of the follow-up study the researchers also concluded that frequent viewers were rated high by their teachers on attitudes toward school and toward their peers.

Criticisms of *Sesame Street*

In spite of the positive reports of Ball and Bogatz, many researchers and educators expressed criticism. Some of the most frequently voiced criticisms are (a) skills are taught separately and children will not know how to combine them, (b) the curriculum is too narrow and young children are capable of learning more, (c) children's feelings, self-concepts,' and social relationships should be dealt with more thoroughly, (d) *Sesame Street* teaches facts but not their applications to real life situations, (e) no demands are made on children for physical or mental participation, (f) the program is too fast-paced and the noise level is too high, (g) too much emphasis is placed upon rote teaching of simple right answers, (h) there is excessive repetition, and (i) the program does not truly represent city life (Holt, 1971).

In *"Sesame Street" Revisited*, Cook and associates (1975, pp. 72–74) cited evidence that "casts reasonable doubt about whether *Sesame Street* was causing as large and as generalized learning gains in 1970 and 1971 as were attributed to the program."

If evaluators search intensely they can find fault with almost anything. There is much room for improvement in *Sesame Street*, and the program designers have and are continuing to make changes in its format. The program was not intended as a substitute for a good preschool program or for a good teacher. But, the program was a step in the right direction in the area of educational television for young children. The positive aspects in terms of children's needs outweigh the negative.

Televiewing in Relation to Play and Affective Development

A major criticism of televiewing in relation to learning is that children withdraw from play. All educators and child development specialists agree that play is a child's way of learning. Watching television is a passive activity, and young children need to be actively involved in learning experiences through play. According to Maccoby (1971), as long ago as 1951, approximately 1½ hours a day shifted from active play to passive televiewing. The hours may be greater today.

Some educators of young children emphasize the importance of children's cognitive development. Cognitive development is very important, but social and emotional development cannot be overlooked. Television programs can have a great influence on those aspects of children's lives.

Feelings and Emotions

Presently, there are not enough children's programs designed to focus directly on children's feelings and emotions. Many would argue that the development of those areas of children's lives are most effectively handled by parents. Unfortunately, many children in the United States are not fortunate enough to have warm, supportive parents. What does television programming have to offer those children to help them with emotional adjustment?

Mister Roger's Neighborhood is a children's television program designed to help children manage their feelings and also to talk about them. Fred Rogers developed his program during the 1960s for the Canadian Broadcasting Company. The program began in 1967 in the United States on NET and is now carried by over 200 stations. The show usually begins with Mister Rogers coming home from work and singing "Won't You Be My Neighbor." He greets the children and then begins talking directly to them about things that are important in their world (e.g., a possible crisis, such as the death of a pet). Additionally, he reassures them about certain fears they may have (e.g., a trip to the doctor). Puppets are also used to aid in the presentation of similar problems. Mister Rogers helps children feel good about themselves when he tells them, "There is only one person in the world like you, and I like you just the way you are."

At the present time, there are no other programs as outstanding as *Mister Roger's Neighborhood* for young children. There is a program, however, for older children, *Inside/Out.* That program is geared to health education, but the designers provided a feelings approach to the subject. Day-to-day problems of children from their point of view are presented.

For some children, television serves as an escape mechanism. That is most likely to occur among children who are experiencing emotional disturbances, among children having poor relationships with their parents or with their peers, and among children who are isolated or insecure. The greater the parent–child conflict, the greater the use of television, and the less the use of printed material. That is more true of children from middle-class homes than from lower-class homes (Garry, 1967).

Fantasy and Reality

For young children, seeing is believing. Everything they see on television is real to them. They cannot separate the real from the unreal until about the age of 7 or 8. Solnit (1972) stated that prior to the ages of 6 or 7 years, children could not always separate fantasy from reality, therefore they may be confused by television characters and their actions. Solnit traced the confused states of young children to their inabilities to think tasks, not reached until the sixth or seventh year. Preschoolers have no concepts of actors and acting (abstractions). They believe that television characters are real people. Katherine R. Lustman (1972, p. 8), co-director at Yale University's Child Study Center, asked a child, "Are Batman and Robin real or pretend?" The child firmly replied, "Oh, no, they are really, real."

A response of this nature seems harmless, almost humorous. But parents should carefully observe when their children begin to imitate the characters and situations viewed on television programs. There have been many instances in the past in which children have been seriously injured or killed in their attempts to imitate their favorite television characters. For example, after the television presentation of *Peter Pan*, some children jumped off roofs and out of windows as a result of believing themselves able to fly.

Whenever possible, parents should watch television programs with their children, explaining things to them and being ready to answer their questions. Young children need help in distinguishing what is real and what is make-believe.

When a young child meets fantasy in books, he is more in control of the situation. He knows he can stop, think about what he is reading, and ask questions. Also, when a child is told or read fairy stories, folk tales, and other selections, the child usually hears the stories more than one time. The repetition of stories presented that contain violent or unkind acts usually have happy endings. The childen learn that, and although the violence occurs, the child knows that the characters will be safe by the conclusion of the story. In that way, children learn to cope with varying degrees of violence. Some television program formats do not provide for build-up/release of tension behaviors. Also, when children are actively involved in dramatic play situations, they are the initiators of their own fantasies, and again, in control.

With television, children have no control over the program they watch and cannot stop the action when a need arises for them to think about what has just been seen. Children are passive recipients whose only control of the fantasy is to accept it or turn the program off. Most children will accept it.

Socializing Effects

Children get a lot of their ideas about the world and other people from television programs. Their developing sense of social values is somewhat influenced by television characters and plots. Researchers have been concerned about the effects of both violent and prosocial programs on young children. Those research studies warrant inclusion at this point.

Television as a Facilitator of Aggressive Behavior

More research has been published about the effects of television violence on behavior than any other area of television. In 1969, Senator John O. Pastore, chairman of the Sub-Committee on Communications of the Senate Commerce Committee, wrote to the Secretary of Health, Education, and Welfare requesting that the Surgeon General conduct a study of the effects of violence on television. The report, entitled *Television and Growing Up: The Impact of Televised Violence*, took 3 years and 1 million dollars to produce (Surgeon General, 1972). Many important studies were generated from that report, and many more have been conducted since.

Bandura, Ross, and Ross (1963) pioneered studies in which children's imitations of aggressive behavior were observed. In 1963, children in the Stanford University nursery school observed an adult model who attacked an inflated Bobo doll. The doll was 3 feet tall and weighted at the bottom so that it popped up immediately after being struck. The children were divided into three groups. One group witnessed the model in real life; the second group was shown a film of it; and the third group was shown a cartoon film of the same behavior. They observed the model punch the doll in the face, kick it, and strike it with a hammer. A fourth group of children (control group) observed none of the aggressive actions.

After witnessing one of the scenes, the children were placed in a frustrating situation. They were given toys with which to play. Suddenly, the toys were taken away for no apparent reason. Next, the children were taken to the test room which contained toys classified by Bandura and his associates as aggressive (Bobo doll, mallet, dart guns, and so forth) and nonaggressive (tea set, crayons, dolls, and so forth). During 20 minutes of playtime, the children's behavior was observed and recorded in terms of imitative and nonimitative aggression.

The principal finding was that the children who had witnessed the aggressive actions of the adult model were much more aggressive than the other children. The authors concluded, "The results of the present study provide strong evidence that exposure to filmed aggression heightens aggressive reactions to children [p. 9]."

In another study, Stein and Friedrich (1971) compared the effects of television programs on the behavior of preschool children in classroom play situations. The children were observed over a period of 9 weeks: 3 weeks prior to treatment; 4 weeks during treatment; and 2 weeks after treatment. Each school day, the children saw either prosocial, aggressive, or neutral programs. The prosocial programs were composed of segments of *Mister Roger's Neighborhood*, which emphasized cooperation, sharing, and self-discipline. The aggressive programs consisted of *Batman* and *Superman* cartoons, which contained episodes of verbal and physical aggression. The neutral programs were children's films, which emphasized neither aggressive nor prosocial behaviors.

The observers recorded behavior in five general categories: (1) aggression, (2) prosocial interpersonal behavior, (3) persistence, (4) self-control, and (5) regression. Each category was subdivided into more specific behaviors, such as regression which included crying, pouting, and withdrawal. Observers did not know to which treatment each child had been exposed.

A central finding was that children who were predetermined to be high in aggression exhibited greater amounts of interpersonal aggression when they observed aggressive acts. The same children were less aggressive when they observed neutral or prosocial behaviors. Also, it was reported that children who viewed prosocial television program formats exhibited higher degrees of self-control (i.e., obeying rules, tolerating delay, and perseverance to tasks, and so forth) than the preschool children who observed program formats containing aggressive acts (Stein & Friedrich, 1971). The two studies reviewed above show the immediate effects of viewing televised violence. A number of other studies have also been conducted to evaluate the long-range effects. One such study was done by Lefkowitz, Eron, Walder, and Huesmann (1975) at The New York State Department of Mental Hygiene. Their study is of particular importance because they investigated the development of aggressive behavior in children by studying the same boys and girls over a 10-year period.

The investigators had previously determined televised violence preferences of 875 third graders. Aggression was measured by peer ratings. The children rated every other child in their class on a variety of physical and verbal aggressive behaviors. Ten years later, when the subjects were 18 years old, the investigators obtained similar measures of program preferences and aggressive behaviors for 460 of the original 875 subjects. For boys, the results indicated that preferences for violent programs at age 8 were related significantly to aggressive behaviors at age 18. The relationship was not as strong for the girls in the study.

Despite these convincing studies, not everyone accepts the idea that viewing violence increases violent behavior. Lopoparo (1977) claimed that viewing violent acts on television was healthy for young children. He believes that children and adults need an outlet or release for certain pent-up aggressive thoughts and that television program formats can provide those releases. Viewing violence on television, in Lopoparo's opinion, reduces a child's aggressive actions. That point of view is termed the *catharsis hypothesis* based on the premise that viewing violence on television provides an outlet for internalized or endogenous aggression that must be released in socially accepted manners. Accumulated aggressive urges are supposedly drained or diminished in the person after watching violence. Supposedly, the result is that the person behaves less aggressively. Many researchers, however, have found the opposite to be true.

In view of the studies presented, why do television broadcasters continue to schedule violent programs for children? The answer is obvious, *it sells products.* Lately, there has been a trend from violent program formats to more family situation dramas. In 1975, members of the National Association of Broadcasters agreed to introduce the *family hour* between 7 and 9 P.M. That move has been viewed with some skepticism. Some authorities perceived it as simply a nice gesture to appease the public, but believed that violence would continue as usual. In a report by Klapper (1977), CBS was shown to be the lowest of the three networks in violence during the 1976–1977 season. However, all the networks combined showed an increase in both the number of violent incidents and the rate of violence from the 1975–1976 season to the 1976–1977 season. In 1979 the National Federation for Decency presented data to support that ABC presented more sex-related scenes and CBS broadcasted more profanity. NBC was rated lowest in profanity, sex, and sex outside of marriage. However all national companies were considered to have high degrees of all three.

Television as a Facilitator of Prosocial Behavior

Television can also have prosocial effects on children. Evidence of this was shown in the Stein and Friedrich (1971) study. In this study, children who watched a prosocial program such as *Mister Roger's Neighborhood,* displayed prosocial behaviors (task persistence, rule obedience, sharing, etc.).

In another study by Bryan and Walbek (1970), the effects of teaching sharing through television were investigated. Third and fourth graders were taken to a research trailer and allowed to play a bowling game. When they scored high, they received a gift certificate which could be exchanged for prizes or money. The children were told that they could donate their money to the March of Dimes if they wished. After playing the game for a while, each child saw a program of another child of the same sex playing the game. The model child was either generous or selfish with his winnings. After viewing the program, each child played the game again and was given the opportunity to share privately. It was revealed that children who saw a generous television model were more likely to share than those who saw a greedy model.

Television does influence the behavior of young children, as researchers have indicated. The primary reason for that phenomenon is that children learn by imitating the behavior of a model. The model does not have to be a human one. Children imitate cartoons and fantasy programs because, as was noted earlier, the characters are real to them.

Effects on Physical Development

The major criticism of television as far as children's physical development is concerned is related to inactivity. As mentioned earlier, watching television keeps children from play. Not only do children need play for their cognitive development, but also for optimum physical development. The National Child Research Center in Washington, D.C. was critical in its 1971 filing with the FCC: "Television represses children's innate tendencies because it requires passive rather than active involvement, and activity not passivity is necessary for children's full healthful development [Kaye, 1974, p. 16]." Cohen reported that teachers in nursery schools and primary schools were observing differences in children's behaviors that resulted from the amount of time they spent watching television. The quality of nursery schools children's play was reported to have changed, and primary grade children were cited as being resistent to teachers' attempts to get them to read or become involved in other school-related activities (Solnit, 1972).

Direct physical harm from the TV set can be avoided easily. There may be some radiation from some color television sets, and manufacturers advise sitting several feet from the set in order to avoid any danger.

The American Optometric Association has studied the effect of television viewing on the eyes and has prepared a pamphlet, *To View or Not to View*. The text of the booklet contains information that may be interpreted to mean that televiewing is not harmful to young children's eyes if the set is correctly installed and correct viewing habits are observed. Sitting too close to the screen (proper distance is five times the width of the picture tube width) and concentrated viewing for extended periods of time (which causes fatigue) were cited as examples of poor viewing habits.

Children's Television Advertising

The major concerns about television advertising are (*a*) the amount of advertisement and (*b*) the messages conveyed to children.

Barcus (1975) conducted two studies recently in relation to children's programming and advertising. One study dealt with the content of children's television during the weekday afternoon hours. The other study dealt with children's programming on weekends. Regarding programming during the week, Barcus found that 46% of the commercials were for food and 61% of those foods were high in sugar content.

In his "weekend" report, Barcus found that cereals and candy accounted for almost half of the products advertised, with toys, food, and other products accounting for the remainder. Findings showed that there are up to 12 minutes of commercials every hour on children's Saturday morning shows, and 16 minutes on other daytime programs.

What effect does television advertising have on young children? Parents and other concerned adults state these as the major influences: advertising deceives children; it frustrates them through false and misleading promises; it promotes the sale of dangerous toys; it fosters dietary habits which endanger health; it encourages greed and materialism; and it takes advantage of the fact that children are gullible.

Perhaps the most outspoken critic of television commercials for children has been Action for Children's Television (ACT). The organization was founded in 1971 by Mrs. Peggy Charren in Boston. ACT members believe that poor programming can be blamed on advertisers and sponsors, and that programming can be improved by putting pressure on them. Its work now focuses mainly on commercials. Their intent is to reduce their frequency and eliminate their misleading and dangerous content.

Children need help in understanding television commercials. Kaye listed eight suggestions or recommendations that parents could use in aiding their children to become able to critically evaluate television commercials. The list included (1) recognizing exaggerated claims, (2) allowing children to create their own commercials and determine the reasons for using specific terms and statements, (3) learning certain propaganda devices such as band-wagon effects, glittering generalities, and so forth, (4) making on-site visitations to stores to compare advertising claims with the product, (5) obtaining nutritional charts or books to determine the scientific food value of products advertised, (6) developing a set of standards to follow in purchasing cereals and snack foods, and (7) teaching children, through practice, that meals should be nutritionally balanced. Kaye also recommended that snack foods be nutritional and not of the cookie, cake, or other high-sugar content types. High-sugar content cereals were also considered less than desirable. One warning that Kaye issued, along with the recommendations, was that some children may become rowdy or uncontrollable when taken to a store to compare a product with an advertiser's claim. It was also suggested that young children be allowed to view only public broadcasting service programs in which no commercials were presented. The last two statements are especially important if Solnit's (1972) views toward fantasy from reality are accepted.

Parents and the Use of Television in the Home

Unfortunately, parents sometimes exercise very little control over their children's television viewing. Researchers at Columbia University discovered that as few as 5% of families control television viewing, and those families are most concerned with the amount of watching instead of content.

Parents must take into account the importance and permanence of television in our society and its attractiveness to children. They should protect them from the bad things on TV as much as possible. They should help their children understand that television can be intellectually stimulating as well as entertaining.

In controlling TV viewing, it is important that parents be positive and not repressive. The parents' attitude is the key to a child's acceptance of the controls placed on him.

Rutstein (1974) developed a set of standards that parents could adopt when setting limits for young children's televiewing habits. Rutstein viewed 1½ hours for children through age 6 and 2 hours for children aged 7 to 10 to be the maximum time allowed. Rutstein also contended that the time be fragmented rather than continuous. Also, it was stated that parental permission was to be secured prior to the children's turning on the television set.

Rutstein's recommendations were stringent. He also believed that parents should carefully evaluate every program that children watched and that worthwhile substitute activities be provided for children when they were not watching television. Violence themes, racial and ethnic prejudice or stereotype themes, unrealistic home situation themes, and commercials were all listed as aspects of television programs that parents should either avoid or evaluate carefully. Finally, Rutstein stated that children should not view television after the dinner hour, but if a worthy production was transmitted, that the family should watch it as a group. The reader is urged to secure Rutstein's *Go Watch TV!* and read his complete message.

Summary

The television portion of this chapter contains an overview of the influence of television in the lives of young children. It focuses on the critical issues involved: (a) the potential for educational television, (b) the importance of providing programs that deal with the affective realm, (c) the effects of televised violence versus prosocial television, (d) the influence advertising has on children, and (e) the responsibility of parents to set standards for their children.

Much research has been conducted in the area of television's influence on young children. Researchers continue to seek answers to questions dealing with this important aspect of the society in which we live.

One of the most up-to-date works related to preschool children and televiewing was written by Lesser (1977). Lesser's proposals that conclude his propitious offerings contain ideas that are directed to the "yet unrealized potential of instructional television [p. 237]." Lesser summarized the present state of television instruction for young children as follows:

1. Television does not allow for audience interaction with the presentor.
2. Young children must have instruction commensurate with their cognitive abilities; programs for those children must be distinctly related to preschooler thought processes; not watered-down adult presentations.
3. Additional, specific instructional television programming may be necessary for children from distinct linguistic or cultural groups.

Lesser cited the controversy of figural content manipulation by young children or just visual learning through pictures as being one issue that should be settled. Lesser further contended that educators should not confuse "education" with "entertainment" or "intrigue" when evaluating children's responses to television. However, Lesser cogently observed that, "Public policy will ultimately determine . . . the extent . . . and nature . . . (of) instructional television [p. 239]."

Lesser appeared to prefer computer assisted television instruction. Through that system, teachers would design their own programs and be able to use them in school or home via special closed-circuit cable systems. But Lesser's main contribution appeared to be his observation that present knowledge of instructional television and learning may take years to translate into practical purposes; and that, "research in the instructional uses of television shift from the popularity of presentations to the type and amount of learning among preschool viewers [p. 242]."

SUMMARY

The desire for innovative early childhood educational programs in the 1960s led to the design of many new specific programs. Those programs, as presented earlier in this chapter, may be categorized as either (a) behavioral, (b) cognitive, or (c) maturational in nature.

As a result of the reawakening to the needs of young children, preschool and childhood programs that existed largely in a vacuum prior to the 1960s were no longer operated as entities, unrelated to the total welfare and education of children, youth, and adults. Instead, the programs became an integral part of every educational system throughout the United States.

It would appear that the design and implementation of new early childhood education programs would be accompanied by competent and sophisticated research designs. In many instances, that research was conducted, and investigators presented their findings in professional journals, at conferences, in books, and by other sundry means. In 1970, Goodlad *et al.* wrote that the worthwhile aspects of innovative educational programs had not been integrated into contemporary teaching procedures. They also judged the observable changes that were instituted to have resulted in insignificant differences in the lives and minds of those who were taught. Goodlad *et al.* (1970) supposed that one of the reasons for many educators to preclude the employment of reputable, innovatative designs and practices was their resistance to change. The writers also believed that teachers and administrators tend to rely on traditional methods even though valid and reliable, newer methods of instruction have been formulated.

Other observations by Goodlad *et al.* (1970) may have implications for faculty members in departments and schools of education, psychology, or child development. The writers further supposed that many teachers organized their classes and conducted lessons in the same manner as they were taught in elementary schools. Additionally, Goodlad *et al.* contended that merely exposing prospective teachers to innovative designs without showing how to implement them would be of no value. Seemingly, until prospective teachers are educated in a manner similar to those prescribed in Chapter 1, then traditional procedures will be the rule rather than the exception. An additional component that also may need to be developed for the preservice education of prospective early childhood education teachers would be a carefully devised plan to considerably reduce or eliminate their tendencies to revert to traditional methods or the ways in which they were taught. To accomplish that, specific, intensive participation, practicum experiences, and student teaching experiences under controlled conditions would be necessary. It may be that higher education faculty members are as prone as other educators to employ traditional methods.

Whatever the nature of the educational programs designed for prospective teachers and whatever the nature of the programs they design for their students, the prospective teachers must know at least one thing. As the 1980s are entered, teachers will teach children who come from a wider variety of backgrounds than ever before; the children will have been exposed to a great diversity of playmates as well as ideas. The prospective teachers must desire to become educated to be able to provide those children with an educational program the result of which will enable children to relate well to other human beings, exhibit kindness, be more altruistic, be respectful of members of other cultures, and generations, and have world focus. In many instances, teachers who provide traditional plans for instruction cannot effect those changes in children.

REFERENCES

Ambron, F. R. A review and analysis of infant and parent education programs. In M. Day and R. Parker (Eds.), *The preschool In action.* Boston: Allyn and Bacon, 1977. Pp. 196–215.

Annual evaluation report on programs administered by the U.S. Office of Education: Fiscal year 1977. Washington, D.C.: Office of Planning, Budgeting, and Evaluation. Pp. 143–147.

Austin, M. Reading in the kindergarten. In D. Schubert & T. Torgerson (Eds.), *Readings in reading.* New York: Thomas Crowell, 1968. Pp. 494–498.

Ball, S., & Bogatz, G. A. *The first year of Sesame Street: An evaluation.* Princeton, N.J.: Educational Testing Service, 1970.

Bandura, A., Ross, D., and Ross, S. A. Imitation of film-mediated aggressive models. *Journal of Abnormal and Social Psychology*, 1963, *66*, 3–11.

Barcus, E. F. *Television in the afternoon hours.* Newtonville, Mass.: Action for Children's Television, 1975.

Barnett, M. A. Role of play and make-believe in children's cognitive development. *The Journal of Education,* November 1977, *159* (4), 38–48.

Bryan, J. H., & Walbek, N. B. Preaching and practicing generosity; children's actions and reactions. *Child Development,* 1970, *41*, 329–353.

Brzeinski, J., Harrison, M., & McKee, P. Should Johnny read in kindergarten? In V. M. Howes & H. F. Darrow (Eds.), *Reading in the elementary school.* New York: Macmillan, 1968. Pp. 157–160.

Butler, A. L., Gotts, E. E., & Quisenberry, N. L. *Play as development.* Columbus, Ohio: Charles E. Merrill, 1978.

Caplan, F., & Caplan, T. *The power of play.* Garden City, N.Y.: Anchor Press, 1973.

Carpenter, E. Readiness in being. In V. M. Howes & H. F. Darrow (Eds.), *Reading in the elementary school.* New York: Macmillan, 1968. Pp. 138–141.

Cass, J. *The significance of children's play.* London: B. T. Batsford, 1971.

Clepper, I. *Growing up with toys: A guide for parents.* Minneapolis: Augsburg, 1974.

Cook, D., et al. *"Sesame Street" revisited.* New York: Russell Sage Foundation, 1975, 24–25.

Corbin, J., Plunkett, Kier, Myer, Day, Durkin, Nurss, Ollila, Strickland, Pharis, Engstrom, Smith, & Roderick. Reading and pre-first grade—a joint statement of concerns about present practices in prereading instruction and recommends for improvement. *Educational Leadership,* February 1977, *XXXIV*, 325.

Day, B. *Open learning in early childhood.* New York: Macmillan, 1975.

Day, M. C., & Parker, R. K. *The preschool in action.* Boston: Allyn and Bacon, 1977.

Downing, J., & Thackray, D. V. *Reading readiness.* London: University of London Press, 1972.

Dribin, E. Reading with joy. *Education Digest,* March 1972, *XXXVII* (7), 45–47.

Durkin, D. Facts about pre-first grade reading. In Loyd Ollila (Ed.), *The kindergarten child and reading.* Newark, Delaware: International Reading Association, 1977.

Durkin, D. What does research say about the time to begin reading instruction? In Robert Karlin (Ed.), *Perspectives on elementary reading.* New York: Harcourt Brace Jovanovich, 1973. Pp. 135–142.

Elkind, D. Misunderstandings about how children learn. In Richard Miner (Ed.), *Readings in education 75/76.* Guilford, Conn.: Dushkin, 1974. Pp. 48–50.

Evans, E. D. *Contemporary influences in early childhood education.* New York: Holt, Rhinehart, and Winston, 1971.

Follow Through: Promising approaches to early childhood education. Washington, D.C.: U.S. Department of Health, Education and Welfare, Office of Education, U.S. Government Printing Office, CE 20165, 1971.

Frost, J. L., & Kissinger, J. B. *The young child and the educative process.* New York: Holt, Rhinehart, and Winston, 1976.

Garry, R. *Children and TV: Television's impact on the child.* Washington, D.C.: Association Childhood Education, 1967, 12.

Garvey, C. *Play.* Cambridge, Mass.: Harvard University Press, 1977.

Gates, A. The necessary mental age for beginning reading. *Elementary School Journal, XXXVIII,* 1937, 497–508.

Glass, G. Let's not read so soon (even those who can). Unpublished paper, Adelphi University.

Goldsworthy, G. E. *Why nursery school?* Buckinghamshire: Colin Smythe, 1971.

Goodlad, J. I., & Klein, F., & associates, *Behind the classroom door.* Worthingham, Ohio: Charles A. Jones Publishing Co., 1970.

Gordon, I. J., *Parent involvement in compensatory education.* University of Illinois Press, 1968. (ERIC Document Reproduction Service No. 252–00115x.)

Gordon, I. J. Parents as teachers—What can they do? Paper prepared for presentation at the International Conference on Parents and Young Children. St. Louis, June 20, 1978.

Gordon, I. J., Olmsted, P., Rubin, R., & True, J. Continuity between home and school: Aspects of parental involvement in Follow Through. Paper presented at the Fifth Biennial Meeting of the Southeastern Conference on Human Development, Atlanta, Ga., April 27–29, 1978.

Harris, A. J., & Sipay, E. R. How to increase reading ability. 5th Edition. New York: McKay, 1975.

Hartley, R. E., & Goldenson, R. M. *The complete book of children's play.* New York: Thomas Y. Crowell, 1963.

Hock, R. Dangers of early emphasis on reading. *Intellect,* March 1978, CVI, 352.

Holt, J. Big bird meets Dick and Jane. *Atlantic Monthly,* 1971, 227, 72–74.

Hoskisson, K. Should parents teach their children to read? *Education Digest,* April 1974, XXXIX, 44–47.

Hymes, J. L., Jr. *Teaching the child under six.* Columbus, Ohio: Charles E. Merrill, 1968.

Hymes, J. L., Jr. Teaching reading to the under-six age: A child development point of view. In R. Karlin (Ed.), *Perspectives on elementary reading principles and strategies.* New York: Harcourt Brace Jovanovich, Inc., 1973. Pp. 131–135.

Johnson, J. C., II. *Scholars before school.* Durham: Moore, 1971.

Kaye, E. *The family guide to children's television.* New York: Pantheon, 1974, 7.

Kelly, M. L. When are children ready to read? *Saturday Review,* 1963, XLIV, 58ff.

Klapper, J. T. *Network prime-time violence tabulations for 1976–77 season.* New York: Columbia Broadcasting System, Inc., N.Y. Office of Social Research, May 1977.

LaConte, C. Reading in the kindergarten: Fact or fantasy. *Elementary English,* March 1970, XLVII (3), 382–386.

Leeper, S., Dales, R., Skipper, D., & Witherspoon, R. *Good schools for young children.* New York: Macmillan, 1974.

Lefkowitz, M., Eron, L., Walder, L., & Huesmann, L. H. Television violence and child aggression: A follow-up study. *Television and Social Behavior*, 1975, *32*, 35–135.

Lesser, H. *Television and the preschool child.* New York: Academic Press, 1977.

Levitt, E., & Cohen, S. Parents as teacher. In Lilian G. Katz (Ed.), *Current topics in early childhood education.* Norwood, N.J.: Ablex, 1977.

Liebert, R., Neale, J. M., & Davidson, E. S. *The early window: Effects of television on children and youth.* New York: Pergamon Press, 1973.

Lifton, B. Why some preschoolers are ready to read before school. *Parents Magazine*, March 1974, *XLIX*, 35–37.

Lopoparo, J. J. Aggression on TV could be helping our children. *Intellect*, April 1977, *43*, 345–346.

Lustman, K. R. The subject of play, its importance to children, and how it is affected today by television. In P. Charren and E. Sarson (Eds.), *Who is talking to our Children?: Third national symposium on children and television.* Newtonville, Mass.: Action for Children's Television, 1972.

Maccoby, E. E. Television: Its impact on school children. *Public Opinion Quarterly*, Fall, 1971.

Maccoby, E. E., & Zellner, M. *Experiments in primary education: Aspects of project Follow Through.* New York: Harcourt Brace Jovanovich, 1970.

MacGinitie, W. H. When should we begin to teach reading? *Education Digest*, February 1977, *XLII*, 60–62.

Marzollo, J., & Lloyd, J. *Learning through play.* New York: Harper and Row, 1972.

Mason, G., & Prater, J. Early reading instruction. *Elementary English*, May 1966, *XLIV*, 483–489.

Matterson, E. M. *Play with a purpose for under-sevens.* Harmondsworth, Great Britain: Penguin Books, 1975.

Moore, R. S., & Moore, D. R. The dangers of early schooling. In Richard Miner (Ed.), *Readings in education 75/76.* Guilford, Conn.: Dushkin, 1974. Pp. 55–60.

Morphett, M., & Washburne, C. When should children begin to read? *Elementary School Journal*, 1931, *XXXI*, 496–503.

Morrison, G. S. *Parent involvement in home, school, and community.* Columbus, Ohio: Charles E. Merrill, 1978.

Pines, M. A child's mind is shaped before age 2. In Richard Miner (Ed.), *Readings in education 75/76.* Guilford, Conn.: Dushkin, 1974. Pp. 45–47.

Radin, N. *Three degrees of parent involvement in the home, school, and community.* Columbus, Ohio: Charles E. Merrill, 1972.

Reissman, F. Has compensatory education failed? *National Elementary Principal*, 1977, *56*(5), 14–18.

Rupley, W. H. Reading readiness research-implications for instructional practices. *The Reading Teacher*, January 1977, *XXX*(4), 450–452.

Rutstein, N. *Go watch TV!* New York: Sheed and Ward, 1974.

Sheldon, W. Teaching the very young to read. In V. M. Howes & H. F. Darrow (Eds.), *Reading and the elementary school child.* New York: Macmillan, 1968. Pp. 145–151.

Silberman, C. E. *Crisis in the classroom.* New York: Vintage Books, 1971.

Solnit, A. J. Fantasy and reality in children's programs. In P. Charren and E. Sarson (Eds.), *Who is talking to our children?: Third national symposium on children and television.* Newtonville, Mass.: Action for Children's Television, 1972.

Smith, M. L. *The effect of preschool experience on achievement in reading.* Department of Health, Education and Welfare, National Institute of Education, October 1976. (ERIC ED 130–256).

Spodek, B. *Teaching in the early years.* Englewood Cliffs, N.J.: Prentice-Hall, 1972.

Stein, A., & Friedrich, L. Television content and young children's behavior. In J. P. Murray, E. A. Rubenstein, & G. A. Comstock (Eds.), *Television and social behavior (Vol. II), Television and social learning.* Washington, D.C.: U.S. Government Printing Office, 1971. Pp. 202–317.

Stevens, J. H., & King, E. W. Models of parent education and involvement. In *Administering early childhood education programs.* Boston: Little, Brown and Co., 1976.

Surgeon General's Scientific Advisory Committee on Television and Social Behavior. *Television and growing up: The impact of televised violence.* Washington, D.C.: U.S. Government Printing Office, 1972.

Sutton, M. H. Children who learn to read in kindergarten: A longitudinal study. *The Reading Teacher,* April 1969, *XXII*(7), 595–602.

Swenson, P. L. Parents, their children and television. In *Children and TV: Television's impact on the child.* Washington, D.C.: Association for Childhood Education, 1967.

Tucker, E. Follow through planned variation experiment: What is the pay off? Presentation at the Annual Meeting of AERA, New York, April 5, 1977.

Waller, G. *Think first, read later! Piagetian prerequisites for reading.* Newark, Delaware: International Reading Association, 1977. (ERIC ED 146–570.)

Wilson, S. A content analysis of kindergarten reading curricula in 13 large American cities. Unpublished doctoral dissertation, The State University of New Jersey, January 1976. (ERIC ED 128–760.)

Zigler, E. F. America's Head Start program: An agenda for its second decade. *Young Children,* 1978, *33*(5), 4–11.

CHAPTER 3

Research and the Child:
The Use of Modeling,
Reinforcement/Incentives, and Punishment

HARRY L. HOM, JR.
SUSAN L. HOM

For decades, psychologists interested in human development have been studying the determinants of children's behavior. Their investigations have led them into many topics directly or indirectly related to the child's behavior in the educational classroom. Some of their research has been inaccessible to anyone but other professional psychologists, buried in the esoteric jargon and methodology of research journals. Fortunately, however, with the advent of educational psychology as a recognized area of specialization, and, more recently, with the growth of early childhood education as another specialty, often a multidisciplinary one, much of what psychologists have learned about children's behavior has been interpreted in terms of principles which may be directly applicable by the classroom teacher. In no area of research is this relevance more obvious than in psychologists' investigations of learning processes, which have yielded much information potentially valuable for the teacher of preschool or early elementary grade children.

There are substantial problems in attempting to formulate practical suggestions for professionals in one discipline based on research findings from another discipline. It is possible that some of the following suggestions might prove to be inappropriate for the classroom teacher even though they make sense from a psychological perspective. In the final analysis, it is

ASPECTS OF EARLY CHILDHOOD EDUCATION
Theory to Research to Practice

the preschool and early elementary school teachers who must decide what works best for them with their students.

It is our intent to stimulate teachers to re-examine their teaching and behavioral strategies. It is our contention that an awareness of these learning principles can help a teacher produce an effective classroom situation. For a more detailed exposition of this approach, teachers may find it useful to refer to two excellent sources on the topic (Hom & Robinson, 1977; Krumboltz & Krumboltz, 1972).

This section deals with learning principles of particular relevance to the field of early education, namely, modeling and reinforcement/punishment effects. Two ways in which young children learn and change their behavior are through their observations of others and by the consequences of their own behavior. Modeling techniques can be seen as potential forms of indirect intervention by the teacher, whereas reinforcement/punishment techniques require more direct involvement.

MODELING

Young children watch other people constantly, whether they be adults or other children. From these observations, they learn how to perform new behaviors and they develop expectations concerning the consequences of their own actions. Informally, there are a great number of incidents occurring in the social milieu of the home and the classroom to support this notion. For example, Andrew, the 2-year-old son of the authors, has acquired and demonstrates the same mannerisms in getting ready for a service return in tennis exhibited by his father. In an example of modeling influence in discipline, Brian, Andrew's 10-year-old brother, was recently reprimanded for throwing toys. The younger boy subsequently picked up his toys, started to throw them, but stopped and said "no-no-no." That children are diligent observers of others' behavior is demonstrated by the clarity and precision which characterizes their imitations. How often have we failed to recognize that we acted or spoke in a certain way until we saw a child imitate our behavior?

Perhaps the most significant factor influencing an observing child to imitate involves consequences to the model (Zimmerman, 1977). A model's actions which result in rewards are more likely to be imitated than those punished or ignored. This research indicates that teachers can be extremely effective models for their students, since they are in control of a wide range of desired resources in the classroom.

Whether or not the child will actually perform the observed behavior is dependent on many factors (Bryan, 1977; Zimmerman, 1977) inherent in both the model and the observing child. With regard to the characteristics of the model, involving physical dimensions such as age, sex, and social group and acquired characteristics such as competence or status, their effects have been reported to be modest and inconsistent (Zimmerman, 1977). That investigator concluded that a similar situation exists for observer characteristics prompting imitative behavior, including the need for social approval, dependency, race, and sex; the effects of these factors are limited.

One factor which seems to be a more important influence is age of the observer. Older children seem to be influenced more by a model than younger children are (Midlarsky & Bryan, 1967; Elliott & Vasta, 1970). Yet there is evidence to show that children as young as 4 years of age are capable of imitative behavior involving complex skills and abstract tasks (Zimmerman & Rosenthal, 1974). There are also data which suggest that younger children (3–4 years) show unsuccessful imitation of complex skills demonstrated by a competent model, but that imitative behavior greatly increases when the complex skill is broken down into smaller units of behavior. Great care must be taken by the teacher in demonstrating even the most basic skills, such as tying shoe laces. In addition, it may be effective for the teacher to use peers as models (Bandura, 1969). For example, arrange for a child to see other children hanging up their coats in an appropriate fashion. Then draw the child's attention to this behavior through praise and other acts of recognition. The teacher's effectiveness may be enhanced also through being a good model for his or her children, some of whom in turn, may serve as good models for other students.

In summary, teachers can use modeling principles to teach a wide variety of skills, ranging from social to verbal to motor skills, and to eliminate undesirable behavior such as aggression (Liebert, Neale, & Davidson, 1973). For example, modeling principles can be used to teach motor skills like ball throwing, climbing, pouring liquids, and tricycle riding.

Though the research into factors important in eliciting imitation has been less than clear-cut in some instances, the results still indicate that modeling techniques may be effective teaching strategies for the teacher who is cognizant of them. Much psychological research is directed at the behavior of groups of children, whereas the teacher is often concerned with the individual child. In those particular instances where it is noted that an individual child is receptive to observational learning, it is an effective teacher who takes advantage of this opportunity to influence that child's behavior.

POSITIVE INCENTIVES AND THEIR CONSEQUENCES

The behavior of children often results in a consequence to them from the environment. Many of these consequences, such as peer attention, are unplanned by teachers and seem to be somewhat beyond their control. However, to the extent that it is possible for teachers to manage the classroom situation and to take full advantage of naturally occurring consequences, they will be more effective in promoting desirable and eliminating undesirable behavior in their students.

Psychologists have defined the consequences of behavior in the following manner. Positive reinforcers are those events which influence appropriate behavior to recur. Punishers are those events which suppress or eliminate the recurrence of behavior. It has been our experience that teachers often believe any pleasant event is a positive reinforcer. But, when a psychologist uses the term *positive reinforcement,* it is defined by the effect it has on a particular behavior, not by an evaluation of the event as being pleasant or unpleasant. A particular event may have differential effects on children's behavior, depending on the child and the circumstances. Receiving a hug may be encouraging to some children but discouraging to others. The way teachers can be sure that any particular event is a positive reinforcer or a punisher is by its consequences on the child's behavior: It either increases or decreases the behavior in question. The important factor is the child's evaluation of the event. For example, a teacher who employs verbal praise for appropriate behaviors might be surprised to find those behaviors decreasing rather than increasing. He or she should recognize that, for many children, verbal praise is an effective positive reinforcer, but for some others (the shy, painfully self-conscious child or the child who actively dislikes the teacher), verbal praise may have an opposite effect and may actually suppress the desired behavior, in which case it is a punisher rather than a reinforcer. In some instances, children are resistant to a teacher's attention and approval. Under these conditions, material or activity rewards may be the only recourse the teacher has available. The critical aspect in the teacher's selection of positive reinforcers is the child's reactions to them, that is, their effects on his or her behavior.

With other psychologists, we have noted that teachers and parents often are offended by the term *positive reinforcer* because of its suggestion that the child is a passive organism under the control of a powerful external force, the adult teacher or parent. Many psychologists use the concept of incentives in place of positive reinforcers. Incentives connote a more active role for the child in the learning process, that is, the child "chooses" to engage in the desired behavior because of the incentive value of the positive reinforcer.

There are some who criticize the use of incentives as being the equivalent of giving a bribe. Krumboltz and Krumboltz (1972) argue in the following manner that the use of incentives is not bribery. They note that reinforcement can be used to enhance both desirable and undesirable behavior but that bribery is the illegitimate use of reinforcement to accomplish only these ends: to encourage the child to behave undesirably. As long as the teacher's goal is the development and strengthening of desirable, adaptive behavior, the use of rewards or incentives is unrelated to bribery.

Different Types of Incentive Systems

It may come as a surprise to the teacher to find that psychologists have no definitive system for classifying the various types of incentives. The most common categories mentioned in research are material, activity, social and verbal, and token incentives.

Material incentives include tangible or concrete objects such as consumables, toys, stars, or money. Activity incentives are composed of many activities which may occur in a classroom setting: free play, running errands for the teacher, a field trip, recess, and playing with a specific object or group of materials. Social and verbal incentives are those which involve attending to or praising the child and engaging in physical contact, such as giving a hug.

Teachers should be reminded that these various incentive systems are often combined in the naturalistic environment, where the child is provided with both a material or activity reward, followed by social praise. While there are research psychologists whose primary concern is establishing the differential effectiveness of these particular incentive systems, the practitioner, in order to promote the desired behavior, often employs a combination of incentives without great concern for which incentive system is most effective.

The token economy is a special class of incentives used in many research projects and classrooms. In such a system, the child receives a token when the desired behavior is performed. Tokens may be poker chips, marks on a sheet of paper, or symbols on the blackboard, anything which symbolizes reward and which can be exchanged for one of the incentive classes (called "back-up reinforcers") previously mentioned: material, activity, social, and verbal rewards. The token system has a number of distinct advantages over the other incentive systems in that it is (a) not as distracting, (b) allows the teacher to reinforce immediately, (c) provides for longer periods of good behavior before the back-up reinforcer is received, and (d) is more economical in that the back-up reinforcer need not be presented for the desired behavior as often. The authors are reminded of an incident in which the use of a token economy would have been highly appropriate. A child was reinforced with M & Ms for sitting in his seat. This procedure proved to be ineffective, since everytime the child received an M & M, he promptly consumed it, which proved to be so distracting that the eventual consequence was an increase in his out-of-seat behavior! Had the teacher given him a token each time she noticed his sitting in his seat and had she allowed him to exchange the tokens for M & Ms or another reward at a time when it would have been more appropriate to enjoy the reward, she might have more effectively increased his in-seat behavior.

Choice of Incentives

There are two general approaches used in choosing incentives. One is to offer the child activities or objects the teacher thinks will be effective incentives. Hopefully, the teacher's judgment is based on previous observations of the child's preferences and not on personal preferences. Teachers have a wealth of incentives at their disposal. They must be constantly alert to each child's classroom behavior in order to note which activities, toys, and even best friends the child enjoys the most. Some incentives present in naturalistic settings are often overlooked. For example, one of the authors is reminded of an occasion when their older son found it extremely desirable to sit at the head of the table during mealtime. This unrecognized incentive was employed very economically to encourage the boy to feed his dog, wash his hands, and be at the dinner table on time.

Another approach is to allow each child to choose the preferred incentive from a variety of available incentives. Each of these approaches has its advantages and disadvantages. The first, although it is more expedient, suffers from the fact that the teacher-selected preference may not be of equal value for all of the children and, therefore, may influence their behavior unequally. The latter approach has the advantage of taking into consideration individual differences but is limited because it requires more planning and more time by the teacher, therefore it is less convenient. However, the limitations of this latter approach might be circumvented by having the teacher periodically administer an incentive preference questionnaire to the children. The teacher could develop his or her own questionnaire or utilize assessment scales which have been developed by others. For example, Cartwright and Cartwright (1970) have devised an instrument for use with children which is directed at assessing the child's incentive preferences, varying from social and material incentives to other forms such as competition and the need for independence. This particular scale could be modified for use with prekindergarten children. In addition, the teacher could alter the instrument for use with parents, providing yet another source of information regarding individual children's incentive preferences often overlooked.

How To Use Incentives Effectively

Under most circumstances, the incentive should be presented immediately after the desired behavior occurs. The teacher must be cognizant of the importance of timing, particularly during the initial phases of establishing a new behavior. Immediate presentation of the incentive allows the child to associate clearly his or her behavior with the receipt of the incentive. However, the teacher should refrain from presenting the incentive too soon, before the child has actually begun to improve, otherwise the teacher might be reinforcing the wrong behavior. For example, think of the common situation in which a parent arrives to pick up a child from a day-care center. The child is engaging in an interesting activity and does not wish to leave. The result is a temper tantrum. In such a situation, we once observed a parent promising the child a surprise for leaving the center. The child ceased. On the way home, the parent did in fact purchase a storybook for the child. The next day, when the parent came to pick up the child another temper tantrum ensued. What had happened? The parent had inadvertently reinforced the child's misbehavior. The incentive was the promise of a surprise, which we would expect to increase the frequency of the child's behavior. But the incentive came while the child was having a tantrum, thus that was the behavior which was strengthened. The parent should have promised the incentive only after the desired behavior occurred, that is, when the child actually left the center in an acceptable fashion.

Besides timing, another factor important in the effective use of incentives is frequency. The incentive can be given on a continuous or partial schedule. A continuous schedule is one which the child receives one incentive for each desirable response, while, in a partial schedule, an incentive is presented occasionally for the desired behavior. As with timing, it is particularly important to present incentives continuously in the initial phases of establishing a new behavior.

The teacher who uses an incentive system in the classroom will have to determine the correct kind and proportion of the incentives he or she decides to use. As a general rule, the teacher should be economical in the use of incentives and try to obtain the most performance for the smallest quantity of incentives. Otherwise, the child may rapidly tire of the incentive and cease to exhibit the desired behavior. This is of utmost importance when the teacher desires the child to exhibit a particular behavior daily, such as working on spelling or arithmetic. A teacher could afford to be somewhat more generous in the use of incentives for infrequently occurring behaviors, such as readying the classroom for the annual PTA open house. It should come as no great surprise that teachers vary in their effectiveness of dispensing incentives. Although these effects are modest (Drabman & Hammer, 1977), there is some evidence to support the notion that race, sex, and socioeconomic class of the authority figure, in this case, the teacher, differentially influence the effectiveness of his or her use of incentive systems.

Although we have discussed in some detail the teacher's choice of incentives, a few more words of advice seem wise regarding the use of "love" as an incentive. If we decide to use love as an incentive, we must be prepared to withhold its delivery for inappropriate behavior, a technique which often presents some difficulties. Krumboltz and Krumboltz (1972, p. 14) have stated appropriately that "So many other possibilities for reinforcers exist that there is no need to produce emotionally insecure children by giving and withdrawing love." Many feel that noncontingent positive acceptance of a child should be the basis on which the teacher establishes a relationship with that child. Their relationship may then include the teacher's disapproval of certain of the child's behaviors, but not withdrawal of acceptance of him.

Goals of the Teacher

Ultimately, it should be the goal of the teacher that each child learn self-reinforcement for engaging in self-control. Children should learn evaluative standards for judging their own behavior and should develop methods of self-reinforcement. For this reason, teachers need to be aware of those techniques which allow for this transition from external to self-control. In applied settings, incentives are not presented immediately and the child must learn to delay his or her receipt of an incentive, that is, to wait for the reward. Presentation of immediate incentives for correct behavior is necessary in the beginning, but once a behavior is established, the child should learn that immediate incentives do not always occur. The same line of reasoning holds for gradually thinning-out the administration of incentives from a continuous to a partial schedule, where the behavior is sustained by infrequently occurring incentives, more like a "real-life situation." The transition from external to self-control is provided for optimally by the use of delayed and partial schedules of administering incentives. It encourages the child to turn to verbal and social incentives which are multifarious in these classroom settings and which are also more practical and economical for use by the teacher.

Limitations of Incentive Systems

Skills which are easily taught to some children cannot be taught to others if the skills require performance capabilities they do not have. Children vary in their rate of development, and the alert teacher is constantly aware of this factor. Children also differ in the time at which they are most likely to benefit from certain instruction. When an individual child is having difficulty mastering a particular skill, perhaps it needs to be broken down further into its prerequisite components. For example, Harris, Wolf, and Baer (1964) have provided such an example in teaching a very passive preschool boy to play on a climbing apparatus. The child was successively reinforced for engaging in the behaviors of approaching the apparatus, for touching it, for climbing a little, and eventually only for vigorous climbing behavior. It is highly recommended for the teacher to engage in a task analysis, breaking down a behavior or task into its component parts, of even the most simple skills, such as tying bows, or more complicated academic skills, such as spelling.

Using the same incentive repeatedly can be ineffective because repetition tends to reduce its value. It is necessary to use a wide variety of incentives or incentive systems so that a particular incentive will not lose its potency. Teachers have available many social incentives: approval, smiling, patting, hugging, whispering, and giving attention. They should try to vary their use of these incentives so as to avoid the problem mentioned above. Personally, we are aware of cases in which a verbal statement like "that's very good" becomes ineffective in motivating a child's behavior, apparently because the teacher uses it so often. It may, in fact, become unpleasant and aversive to the child. We have observed situations in which children actually cringe when their teacher uses a "pet" phrase to indicate approval. Making an effort to use various social and verbal reinforcers will enhance the teacher's success.

Recently, a controversy has erupted concerning the possibility that the use of external incentives might undermine a child's subsequent interest in a particular activity (Deci, 1975; Lepper, Greene, & Nisbett, 1973). It is assumed that the external incentive induces the child to engage in the activity as an "explicit" means to obtain the incentive, thus eliminating or reducing any "intrinsic" interest he or she may have had in that task. It is not completely clear why the external incentive should decrease the child's interest and, although there exists research support for this argument, the issue still is in doubt. For example, Lepper et al. (1973) reported that these detrimental effects were of a long-term nature, but Hom and Maxwell (1978) found them to be temporary. There is also evidence that these reported effects are not common to all forms of external incentives. Anderson and her associates (Anderson, Manoogiam, & Reznick, 1976) found that the use of verbal rewards enhanced the children's subsequent interest in a coloring activity. Our conclusion is that much more research is required to ferret out the factors of importance in promoting or maintaining a child's future interest in an activity. However, the research of Lepper and his associates, and that of Deci, points out that we have much to learn about the administration of incentive systems. This research forces us to consider a possible deleterious side effect of incentive systems which we have previously ignored: that by using them we may inadvertently discourage the behavior we seek to encourage. For the teacher, this means that a degree of caution is required in setting up and using incentive systems.

Incentives have been useful in promoting compliance behavior, cooperative peer interaction, teaching of pre- and academic skills, and even in enhancing creativity and racial integration. For a more complete survey of the wide range of behaviors which have been promoted through incentive means, the teacher is referred to Drabman and Hammer (1977).

PUNISHMENT (NEGATIVE INCENTIVES)

Our discussion so far has focused on the use of positive incentives. Now we turn our attention to punishment. Some psychologists refer to this process as the use of negative incentives. From this perspective, we are interested in those events which suppress or eliminate a child's misbehavior through the presentation of an unpleasant event or the withholding of a privilege or a desired object following the behavior. Again, just as in assessing the effectiveness of positive incentives, the teacher must rely upon his or her own judgment in evaluating the appropriateness of a negative incentive. An unpleasant event for one person does not necessarily function as an adequate negative incentive for another. The teacher must attend to the child's reaction to the unpleasant event—does it suppress or eliminate the behavior in question for that child? If so, then it may serve as a negative incentive or punishment for that particular child.

It is not our intent to deal with the social and moral issues concerning punishment which have been brought forth by the recent interest in child abuse. We would argue that punishment when viewed as an effective socialization tactic represents a viable behavioral technique to be used by the teacher, not a means to oppress children. We wish to concentrate on disciplinary methods which presently are used or could be used by teachers in their classes. For a more complete discussion of these techniques, teachers should refer to Parke (1977) and Walters and Grusec (1977). This section will include discussion of the different types of punishment, important factors in their effective use, choice of punishment, teachers' goals, and, finally, limitations of the various techniques.

Different Types of Punishment

It has been our experience that there exists some confusion about the definition of *punishment*. College students frequently associate the term only with corporal or physical forms. It is our contention that there are other punishment techniques which are more humane and perhaps even more effective than physical punishment, and that this narrow definition of punishment prevents many persons from employing these useful non-physical forms of punishment.

Physical punishment varies from a tap on the hand to a spanking to a severe beating. Some psychologists have argued that physical punishment is unique to lower-class parents, but Gil (1970) has concluded that its use is much more prevalent in all social classes than previously realized. One might believe that it is used primarily by parents in home settings, but that it does not occur in the classroom. However, in a 1969 survey conducted for the NEA, more than 65% of the teachers interviewed favored the use of physical punishment in elementary schools. It seems reasonable to conclude that the teachers' preference for the use of physical punishment might be reflected in their actual behavior in the classroom, although we would expect the percentage of users to be lower. Also, we might conclude that, since so many parents use it and teachers approve its use, it must be effective. This notion is difficult to dispel since there are few, if any, experiments dealing with the effective use of physical punishment with children. In one exception, Bucher and Lovas (1968) used electric shock as a therapeutic device in a treatment setting for autistic children. However, most classroom teachers probably would not generalize from techniques developed to deal with extreme maladaptive behaviors to their own teaching methods. The closest approximation to physical punishment found in experimental settings has been the use of a loud and noxious noise as a form of physical punishment. For more information about this research, the reader is referred to Parke (1977).

Verbal and social punishment are probably the most common forms used in schools and on playgrounds. These include facial gestures, criticism, reprimands, ridicule, name-calling, and the use of emotion-related tactics such as accusing the child of hurting someone's feelings.

Punishment may involve the loss of a privilege or a material object or the withholding of affection. A common example of punishment used by many teachers is the loss of a favorite toy or the taking away of a special privilege. LaVoie (1974) has found that loss of a material object is an effective means of inhibiting further misbehavior. Withholding of affection may take the form of refusing attention or ignoring the child. One technique that has been employed effectively in many settings with children is the use of a time-out. In this procedure, the child is isolated from his peers as well as from the teacher for a few moments. During this brief period, the child is restricted from interacting with other children and is not permitted to engage in any privileges or activities. This technique was originally called "time-out from reinforcement."

The teacher must use great care in employing the time-out effectively. A "good" time-out is brief, with the length dependent not on a number of minutes specified by the teacher but on the child's willingness to show more appropriate behavior. "John, you must sit here by yourself until you feel you can play with the other children without hitting them. When you feel that way, then you may come back to the group." In addition, choice of the time-out place must involve concern for the child's physical and psychological well-being. In one example of overzealous use of time-out procedures, children were forced to spend their lengthy time-outs in a coffin-like structure. Obviously to most of us but, unfortunately, not to everyone, coffins, locked closets, dark basements or attics are *not* appropriate time-out places because they may be associated with fear and possibly with physical harm. On the other hand, places which may be used effectively for time-outs include a chair in an isolated corner of the classroom, the hall outside the classroom (provided there is little traffic), an empty room adjoining the classroom, or the old-fashioned cloakroom. In choosing the time-out place, a teacher needs to determine a location which is void of social, material, and activity reinforcement.

Kazdin (1975) has reported that time-out procedures are effective in eliminating a variety of behaviors, including antisocial and aggressive behaviors. Understandably, early education teachers are often perplexed by these behaviors which occur quite predictably when, for the first time, children are exposed to large group situations. These situations require a great deal of cooperation and sharing to ensure group harmony.

It has been our observation that teachers frequently employ several different punishment techniques in combination with one another. Unfortunately, there is little systematic research available on their respective effectiveness, either singly or in combination with one another. In an exception involving first and second graders, LaVoie (1974) varied negative incentives, including withdrawal of affection, use of a loud noise, and loss of a material object. Initially, the loud noise was most effective, but by the end of training there were no significant differences among the various punishment strategies. These results suggest that the various punishment techniques available may be of equal effectiveness. It is up to the teacher to exercise judgment in choosing which will be used, and he or she should govern the choice by knowledge of the possible negative side effects of some punishments, to be discussed in a later section. There may be little need to employ a physical punishment if other alternative forms are equally potent in eliminating or suppressing the child's misbehavior.

How To Make Punishment Effective

It is difficult to discuss those factors affecting punishment's effectiveness in the same fashion as we did positive incentives. Perhaps this indicates the many complexities of punishment processes and that we have much to learn about their effects. Nonetheless, the information, however limited, which is available should be given consideration by any teacher using punishment techniques in his or her classroom.

Mild, immediate punishment has been found to be effective when accompanied by the statement of a rule or a rationale (Cheyne, 1972; Leizer & Rogers, 1974; Parke, 1969). Parke (1977) reported that punishment severity interacts with its timing. When punishment severity is mild or moderate, the immediate delivery of punishment is more effective than delayed. Under more severe conditions, the timing effect is less crucial, and both immediate and delayed punishment are of equal effectiveness. However, in these studies, delay of punishment was minimal and did not involve long periods of time, that is, hours, but, rather, minutes. Clearly, further research is necessitated to delineate the role of these factors in the punishment process.

In addition, it is evident that the social setting in which punishment occurs requires increased attention from research psychologists. O'Leary, Kaufman, Kass, and Drabman (1970) found that "soft" reprimands were more effective than loud reprimands in dealing with disruptive second-grade children. It is reasonable to assume that the effectiveness of loud reprimands as punishers was undermined by its reward value in eliciting a child's peer group's attention. This is an important finding since most investigators have focused on the behavior of an individual child without much attention to the social interactions that occur in large groups of children. Apparently, punishment effects can be "washed-out" or counterbalanced by peer attention and by teacher attention.

It should come as little surprise to the teacher that consistency of punishment is a factor in determining its effectiveness, with consistent punishment being a much more effective form (Parke & Deur, 1972). Research has been devoted to some other aspects of this particular factor which are relevant to the classroom teacher. Parke and Sawin (1975) have found that when two authority figures differed in the administration of punishment they were less effective as a pair than were two authority figures who applied punishment in the same fashion. Deur and Parke (1970) found evidence to indicate that a child initially exposed to inconsistent punishment was much more resistant to further attempts to modify his behavior through the consistent use of punishment. These studies show that a child may experience some difficulty when exposed to multiple teachers (and to parents) following different standards and employing different techniques in the administration of punishment.

In addition to the teacher's consistent use of punishment, the quality of his or her relationship with a particular child influences the effectiveness of the punishment techniques used with that child. It is generally assumed and supported by research (Parke & Walters, 1967) that punishment is more effective when the relationship between the authority figure and the child is a close and nurturant one.

In classroom settings, various punishment techniques are often accompanied by the statement of a rule or rationale, a technique which has received considerable research support. Parke (1969) found that punishment accompanied by a rationale was more effective than the use of punishment alone. Interestingly enough, the use of a rationale alone can be effective without the accompanying punishment. The statement of a clear rule often is effective in promoting compliance behavior without the corresponding use of punishment. For example, "children should stay in their seats" may be an effective way to increase in-seat behavior. Apparently, the effectiveness of different types of rationales depends to a large extent on the developmental level of the child. Parke (1974) noted that concrete rationales were more effective in 3–4.5-year-old children than abstract rationales but that both types of rationales were equally effective with older children, 4.5–6 years of age. Concrete rationales emphasized the physical consequences of playing with the prohibited toy, that "it might break," while abstract rationales focused on ownership of the toy, that "it belongs to someone else." Teachers also might be interested in the research findings for other types of rationales that involved an appeal to emotions. Children at three different age levels, 3–4, 5–6, and 7–8, were exposed either to fear rationales, "I will be angry with you," or empathy-centered rationales, "I will be sad with you." Fear rationales were more effective across all age conditions but the empathy rationale was increasingly more effective with the age of the children. Length of the rationale also influences the effectiveness of punishment, with some evidence suggesting that with young children brief explanations are more effective than lengthy ones (Hetherington, 1975).

Goals of the Teacher

The aim of every teacher should be the encouragement of self-control in the child. The child who is "in control" of his or her own behavior is happier and better able to benefit from classroom instruction. In addition, developing self-control is more economical because it minimizes the need for "teacher-intrusiveness" in the child's behavior. Grusec and Kuczynski (1975) have demonstrated that children are capable of learning evaluative standards such that, under appropriate conditions, the child administers self-punishment. Children who were exposed to punishment administered by an authority figure transgressed much more often than children who learned self-punishment techniques. In addition to self-punishment leading to internalization of good behavior, it would seem that the teacher can take advantage of another technique to develop self-control in children, the use of rationales, whether accompanied or unaccompanied by a reprimand or punishment. The use of rationales seems to produce better self-control in children (Parke, 1974). This line of reasoning is consistent with the observation that, as children grow older, they increasingly expect to be given reasons for conforming to the rules stated by their teachers.

Hoffman (1970) has provided us with some provocative research regarding the effectiveness of rationales via the inductive or power-assertive techniques used by parents. Inductive techniques emphasize rules based on consequences to others and the child's own responsibility, while power-assertive techniques involve arbitrary rules enforced by the parent. Inductive methods were found to be more effective than power-assertive ones in producing self-control in the child. Hoffman concluded that consistent exposure to inductive reasoning led to greater concern for others, greater guilt feelings when transgression occurred, increased ability to resist temptation, a stronger sense of responsibility, and a greater likelihood of "telling the truth." It would be reasonable to assume that these findings also might be germane to teachers in their attempts to direct the classroom situation.

Limitations of Punishment

There is direct research support for some limitations of punishment procedures. For other limitations mentioned, there is more indirect research support, and they are offered as suggestions or guidelines to avoid undermining the effectiveness of teacher discipline.

Although we have argued that punishment can be used in an effective fashion, there are side effects which limit its frequent use by a teacher. For one thing, continued use may make the punisher ineffective, just as continued presentation of a positive incentive may weaken it. The child may learn to adapt to both. Second, punishment often has undesirable emotional concomitants. It may lead to passivity and withdrawal (Seligman, Maier, & Solomon, 1969) or, as Krumboltz and Krumboltz (1972) have argued, result in a child who "actively" fights back, through truancy and uncooperativeness. Third, these techniques may be imitated by the child, who may then scold, criticize, ridicule, or otherwise punish other children. For example, the 2-year-old Andrew, mentioned earlier, is an astute observer of his family's interactions. When his older brother's behavior doesn't suit Andrew, he says sternly, "Brian, you go to your room now." He can be just as dictatorial with the family dog, telling him "No-no-no, don't growl at me, Bernie." In both cases, his statements are exact replications of ones he hears his parents use in similar situations. Teachers must be very conscious of the examples they are setting for the child. Gelfand, Hartman, Lamb, Smith, Mahan, and Paul (1974) found with 6- and 8-year-olds that they imitated the punishing behavior of their adult teachers.

A fourth possible side effect of punishment is that the child may actively avoid an authority figure when previously punished by that adult (Redd, Morris, & Martin, 1975). The implication here is that the teacher's future influence over the child's behavior may be greatly diminished. And finally, punishment in classroom settings is often underminded by the effects of teacher and/or peer attention. The two, attention and punishment, often seem to be inextricably linked. Madsen, Becker, Thomas, Kaser, and Plager (1968) found that verbal reprimands from a first grade teacher actually produced more rather than less out-of-seat behavior. Apparently, teacher and peer attention outweighed the suppressive effects of the verbal rebuke.

Based upon these considerations, the teacher is advised to use punishment infrequently and to utilize other behavioral strategies, such as modeling and reinforcement techniques, wherever possible. For example, in the study cited earlier by Madsen and his associates, the use of teacher praise directed at those children sitting in their seats and the teacher's ignoring out-of-seat behavior proved to be effective in rapidly diminishing the incidence of out-of-seat behavior.

In those instances where punishment is deemed necessary, teachers are advised to use only those forms of punishment which are appropriate for the classroom, namely the use of mild, nonphysical punishers. There is much reason to recommend the use of time-outs or loss of privileges rather than other physical forms of punishment such as face slapping or hair pulling. In addition, the use of punishment by teachers should always be accompanied by an appropriate rationale stated to the child. The inclusion of a rationale for the punishment has a dual purpose. It not only enhances the punishment's effectiveness but it also allows teachers to monitor their own behavior as an agent of punishment. If a teacher is unable to state clearly a rationale accompanying a particular punishment, then a mental note to re-evaluate that particular prohibition should be made. And, as stated earlier, many times the statement of a rule alone is just as effective as the use of punishment.

In summary, punishment as a disciplinary technique is most effective when it is rarely used. It should be used by the teacher only in instances when an emergency is involved or when the teacher can state that other more positive methods have failed to produce a change in the child's maladaptive behavior. This undesirable behavior may be so well established that the child is unlikely to try another alternative behavior. Then punishment should be the teacher's last recourse.

CONCLUSION

In conclusion, we have outlined several behavioral techniques—modeling and the use of reinforcement/incentives and punishment—which should be applicable by the teacher in the classroom. Use of these strategies will increase his or her effectiveness in dealing with individual and group behavior problems as they occur. With the advent of Public Law # 94–142, there will exist an even greater need for the teacher to have available a wide variety of teaching and disciplinary methods, since students will be more heterogenous than in the past. No one of these techniques is generally superior to the others. Each teacher will find some more easily utilized than others. And, in the final analysis, it is the existence of change in the child's behavior which identifies a particular strategy as an effective one or the absence of any change which signals the need to try a different approach.

REFERENCES

Anderson, R., Manoogian, S., & Reznick, J. Undermining and enhancing of intrinsic motivation in children. *Journal of Personality and Social Psychology*, 1976, *34*, 915–922.

Bandura, A. *Principles of behavior modification*. New York: Holt, Rinehart, and Winston, 1969.

Bryan, J. H. Prosocial behavior. In H. L. Hom, Jr. & P. A. Robinson (Eds.), *Psychological processes in early education*. New York: Academic Press, 1977.

Bucher, B., & Lovaas, I. Use of aversive stimulation in behavior modification. In M. R. Jones (Ed.), *Miami symposium on the prediction of behavior 1967: aversive stimulation*. Miami: University of Miami Press, 1968.

Cartwright, C. A., & Cartwright, G. P. Determining the motivational systems of individual children. *Teaching Exceptional Children, II* (Spring, 1970), 143–149.

Cheyne, A. Punishment and reasoning in the development of self-control. In R. D. Parke (Ed.), *Recent trends in social learning theory.* New York: Academic Press, 1972.

Deci, E. L. *Intrinsic motivation.* New York: Plenum Press, 1975.

Deur, J. L., & Parke, R. D. The effects of inconsistent punishment on agression in children. *Developmental Psychology,* 1970, *2,* 403–411.

Drabman, R. S., & Hammer, D. Using incentives in early childhood education. In H. L. Hom, Jr. & P. A. Robinson (Eds.), *Psychological processes in early education.* New York: Academic Press, 1977.

Elliott, R., & Vasta, R. The modeling of sharing: Effects associated with vicarious reinforcement, symbolication, age, and generalization. *Journal of Experimental Child Psychology,* 1970, *10,* 8–15.

Gelfand, D. F., Hartman, D. P., Lamb, A. K., Smith, C. L., Mahan, M. A., & Paul, S. E. The effects of adult models and described alternatives on children's choice of behavior management techniques. *Child Development,* 1974, *45,* 585–593.

Gil, D. G. *Violence against children: Physical child abuse in the United States.* Cambridge, Mass.: Harvard University Press, 1970.

Grusec, J. E., & Kuczynski, L. Teaching children to punish themselves and effects on subsequent compliance. Unpublished manuscript, University of Toronto, 1975.

Harris, F. R., Wolf, M. M., & Baer, D. M. Effects of adult social reinforcement on child behavior. *Young Children,* 1964, *20,* 8–17.

Hetherington, E. M. Children of divorce. Paper presented at the Biennial Meeting of the Society for Research in Child Development, Denver, 1975.

Hoffman, M. L. Moral development. In P. Mussen (Ed.), *Carmichael's manual of child psychology.* New York: John Wiley, 1970.

Hom, H. L., Jr., & Maxwell, F. R. Effects of extrinsic rewards on intrinsic motivation. Unpublished manuscript, Southwest Missouri State University, 1978.

Hom, H. L., Jr., & Robinson, P. A. (Eds.). *Psychological processes in early education.* New York: Academic Press, 1977.

Kazdin, A. E. *Behavior modification in applied settings.* Homewood, Ill.: The Dorsey Press, 1975.

Krumboltz, J. D., & Krumboltz, H. B. *Changing children's behavior.* Englewood Cliffs, N.J.: Prentice-Hall, Inc., 1972.

LaVoie, J. C. Types of punishment as a determinant of resistance to deviation. *Developmental Psychology,* 1974, *10,* 181–189.

Liebert, R. M., Neale, J. M., & Davidson, E. S. *The early window: Effects of television on children and youth.* New York: Pergamon Press, 1973.

Leizer, J. I., & Rogers, R. W. Effects of method of discipline, timing of punishment, and timing of test on resistance to temptation. *Child Development,* 1974, *45,* 790–793.

Lepper, M. R., Greene, D., & Nisbett, R. E. Undermining children's intrinsic interest with extrinsic reward: A test of the "overjustification" hypothesis. *Journal of Personality and Social Psychology,* 1973, *28,* 129–137.

Madsen, C. M., Becker, W. C., Thomas, D. R., Kaser, L., & Plager, E. An analysis of the reinforcing function of "sit-down" commands. In A. K. Parker (Ed.), *Readings in educational psychology.* Boston: Allyn & Bacon, 1968.

Midlarsky, E., & Bryan, J. H. Training charity in children. *Journal of Personality and Social Psychology,* 1967, *5,* 408–415.

O'Leary, K. D., Kaufman, K. F., Kass, R. E., & Drabman, R. S. The effect of loud and soft reprimands on the behavior of disruptive students. *Exceptional Children,* 1970, *37,* 145–155.

Parke, R. D. Effectiveness of punishment as an interaction of intensity, timing, agent nurturance and cognitive structuring. *Child Development*, 1969, *40*, 213–236.

Parke, R. D. Rules, roles and resistance to deviation in children: Explorations in punishment, discipline, and self-control. In A. Pick (Ed.), *Minnesota symposia on child psychology.* Minneapolis: University of Minnesota Press, 1974.

Parke, R. D. Punishment in children: Effects, side effects, and alternative strategies. In H. L. Hom, Jr. & P. A. Robinson (Eds.), *Psychological processes in early education.* Academic Press, 1977.

Parke, R. D., & Deur, J. L. Schedule of punishment and inhibition of aggression in children. *Developmental Psychology*, 1972, *7*, 266–269.

Parke, R. D., & Sawin, D. B. The effects of inter-agent inconsistent discipline on aggression in children. Unpublished manuscript, Fels Research Institute, 1975.

Parke, R. D., & Walters, R. H. Some factors in determining the efficacy of punishment for inducing response inhibition. *Monograph of the Society for Research in Child Development*, 1967, *32*, No. 109.

Redd, W. H., Morris, E. K., & Martin, J. A. Effects of positive and negative adult-child interaction on children's social preferences. *Journal of Experimental Child Psychology*, 1975, *19*, 153–164.

Seligman, M. E. P., Maier, S. F., & Solomon, R. L. Unpredictable and uncontrollable aversive events. In F. R. Brush (Ed.), *Aversive conditioning and learning.* New York: Academic Press, 1969.

Walters, G. C., & Grusec, J. E. *Punishment.* San Francisco: W. H. Freeman, 1977.

Zimmerman, B. J. Modeling. In H. L. Hom, Jr. & P. A. Robinson (Eds.), *Psychological processes in early education.* New York: Academic Press, 1977.

Zimmerman, B. J., & Rosenthal, T. L. Observational learning of rule governed behavior by children. *Psychological Bulletin*, 1974, *81*, 28–42.

CHAPTER 4

Research and the Child:
A Social Learning View of
Cognitive Development and Education

PAUL A. ROBINSON

A substantial amount of research has been accumulated since 1965 in support of a social learning conception of human behavior and development. The applicability of the theory has been demonstrated not only in explaining social behaviors, such as aggression and cooperation, but also in explaining cognitive behaviors, such as concept learning, rule acquisition, and problem solving. This chapter consists of a review of the contribution of social learning theory to an understanding of children's cognitive development. The contributions of social learning theory to the field of education will be assessed, and the social learning perspective will be contrasted with the Piagetian perspective on education.

SOCIAL LEARNING THEORY: BASIC FEATURES

Social learning theory has been characterized as a "marriage" of behavioral theory and information processing theory (Rosenthal & Zimmerman, 1978; Zimmerman, 1977). According to the social learning perspective, human behavior can best be explained in terms of the interaction of *behavioral influences*, such as reinforcement consequences and stimulus conditions, and *cognitive processes*, such as attention, memory

ASPECTS OF EARLY CHILDHOOD EDUCATION
Theory to Research to Practice

processes, verbal representation processes, and problem solving strategies. Albert Bandura (1977), perhaps the foremost proponet of social learning theory, puts it thus: "In the social learning view, people are neither driven by inner forces nor buffeted by environmental stimuli. Rather, psychological functioning is explained in terms of a continuous reciprocal interaction of personal and environmental determinants [p.11]."

Although traditional learning processes, such as reinforcement, are acknowledged as major behavioral influences, social learning theory proposes a cognitive interpretation of these basic learning processes. Reinforcement is not viewed as a means of automatically "strengthening" behavior that it follows. Rather, people observe and cognitively represent the consequences of their actions; they may develop hypotheses and expectations concerning the relationship between their actions and the probable consequences, and these hypotheses and expectations guide their behavior (Bandura, 1977, Chapter 2). Furthermore, much of the reinforcement that regulates behavior, according to social learning theory, is *self*-reinforcement. One of the major emphases of this theory concerns the importance of self-regulatory processes: Based on their experiences, people internalize goals and standards, and they come to evaluate, reward, and punish themselves in terms of how their performance measures up to their goals and standards.

Within the social learning framework, the acquisition of new information, new cognitive and social skills, and new concepts results primarily from observational learning rather than reinforcement. Most social learning research has consisted of an evaluation of how observational learning processes influence various social and cognitive behaviors. The practical contribution of social learning theory, both to education and to the field of psychotherapy, consists of the development of knowledge concerning how observational learning influences behavior and learning.

The following section reviews research concerning the application of social learning principles, principally modeling, in educational practice.

APPLICATIONS OF OBSERVATIONAL LEARNING PRINCIPLES IN COGNITIVE DEVELOPMENT AND EDUCATION

Theoretical Analysis of Observational Learning

Social learning theorists consider observational learning as the most powerful and pervasive of all learning processes. "Most human behavior is learned observationally through modeling. From observing others, one forms an idea of how new behaviors are performed, and on later occasions this coded information serves as a guide for action [Bandura, 1977, p. 22]."

This statement reflects the cognitive interpretation given to modeling within the social learning framework. Modeling is construed as a means of providing information. The observer's cognitive representation of what was observed determines what is learned and remembered, and guides the observer's future behavior. Social learning theorists strongly emphasize that observational learning is not simply a matter of children or adults copying or mimicking specific overt behaviors they have observed. Observational learning is a cognitive process which may involve abstracting complex rules by observing instances of these rules.

Observational learning has been shown to be a complex process, comprising several component processes. What children learn as a result of observing some activity, behavior, or stimulus display will be influenced by what the children attend to, what memory processes and information processing strategies they apply, and how they verbally represent what they observe. The child's knowledge and cognitive skills will determine what they are capable of understanding from observing complex and subtle social and cognitive events.

Children do not necessarily put into effect what they have learned through observation. Incentive and reinforcement conditions will determine the extent to which they reflect what they have learned. For instance, children who observe models being rewarded for some behavior generally become more likely to emulate the model's behavior, and those that observe a model punished for some act become less likely to emulate the act.

Effective use of observational learning in educational practice requires careful attention to the characteristics of the modeling display used in instruction. For many activities, such as, say, drawing or solving puzzles or problems, the cognitive skills that are essential to successful performance of the activity are not evident to the observer. People generally do not learn complex cognitive or physical skills just by observing a skilled performance of these skills, because most of the cognitive processes underlying the skills are covert. In such cases, effective use of observational learning requires structuring the modeling situation in such a way that the covert cognitive skills become overt. Examples of how this can be done will be discussed in the following section.

Social Learning Procedures Used in Teaching Complex Cognitive Skills

Research has demonstrated that observational learning processes influence virtually all major aspects of cognition, including language acquisition, problem solving and information processing strategies; moral decision making; Piagetian conceptual skills such as conservation, class inclusion, seriation, and separation of variables. A comprehensive reivew of this research is available in Rosenthal and Zimmerman (1978). The present review will focus primarily on the educational implications of observational learning.

Investigation of the use of social learning procedures in teaching children intellectual skills indicates that the most effective instructional procedures generally require a combination of techniques. Modeling, for instance, may be used in conjunction with verbal instruction and explanation, the use of physical supports and guidance, and the provision of opportunity for guided practice. In order to teach a complex cognitive skill it is generally necessary to analyze the task into the component skills that make up the complex skill, then to teach each component skill, and finally to teach the child how to integrate or combine the component skills. Emphasis must be given to making sure that any covert aspects of the cognitive skills are made overt.

Zimmerman nicely illustrates how many of these procedures can be combined effectively in teaching a complex intellectual skill to young children (Henderson, Swanson, & Zimmerman, 1975; Zimmerman 1977). Zimmerman was concerned with teaching 4-year-old children the skill of seriation, that is, arranging a set of objects in serial order along some dimension, such as size, length, or weight. In this case, the seriation task of interest was to order an array of sticks according to length, from the shortest to the longest. The task was of theoretical significance since Piagetians have suggested that children of this age and developmental level cannot be taught the intellectual skills necessary to understand and perform the task successfully. Zimmerman's approach was, first, to analyze the seriation task into the component skills that it required. Seriation was not thought of as a simple skill in itself but as a skill that involved various component processes, each of which must be learned. By observing adults and children work on the task and by conducting preliminary testing, it was hypothesized that the children needed to learn (a) a technique for recognizing when an array was properly ordered, (b) a technique for aligning the bottoms of the sticks, and (c) a systematic procedure to follow in reordering a disordered array of sticks. The children were taught a rule for recognizing when the sticks were properly ordered, as follows: A model demonstrated a technique in which the model would ask himself aloud "Do they go down like stairs?" (Zimmerman, 1977, p. 61), and would proceed to walk his finger down the sticks, saying "down" each time he went down and "up" each time he went up. The children were then taught, through modeling and verbal instruction, to align the bottom of the sticks by placing them on a stand; they were then taught, through modeling and verbal instruction, to reorder the sticks by starting with the longest sticks and successively seeking the next longest, applying the "staircase" rule as they went along. The children were given guided practice where necessary to help them acquire each component skill. Zimmerman reports that these procedures were effective in teaching the children to seriate and that a televised teaching sequence of these procedures was also successful in teaching young children to seriate.

The importance of making covert behaviors and strategies clear to the observer has been demonstrated in research with impulsive children. Impulsive children are defined as those who, given a task with several alternative choices, only one of which is correct, tend to respond quickly and make many errors. The most common measure of impulsivity is the Matching Familiar Figures test (Kagan, 1965) in which a child is shown a series of pictures, and as each picture is shown the child is required to select an identical picture from an array of several similar pictures.

Debus (1970) found only limited success in using a modeling procedure to teach impulsive third grade children to respond more slowly and more accurately on the Matching Familiar Figures test. The impulsive children were exposed to reflective models who responded slowly and made few errors. The reflective models also described aloud their choice strategy of looking at the target stimulus and then comparing it with each of the alternatives. This modeling procedure was successful in decreasing the response times of the impulsive children in an immediate post-test, but did *not* significantly decrease the number of errors. Debus (1976, described in Rosenthal & Zimmerman, 1978) hypothesized that the reason for the lack of greater success in this experiment was that the covert skills necessary to do well on the task were not made sufficiently clear to the impulsive children. In a much more successful extension of this research, Debus (1976) concentrated on making the covert strategies of the reflective models more overt. The reflective models in this experiment successively evaluated each alternative aloud, explaining in detail their reasons for rejecting incorrect alternatives and choosing correct ones, and crossing out incorrect alternatives with a marking pencil. The child was given the opportunity for practice, alternating with the model, and as the child became more proficient the support of the model was gradually withdrawn. This procedure produced substantial and long lasting decreases in the response times and error rates of the impulsive children.

One of the major goals of a social learning approach to behavior modification is to teach people to effectively regulate their own behavior. In the Debus (1976) study, the strategy of the reflective model in regulating his own behavior is made overt, such that it can be discerned and adopted by the observing child in regulating his own behavior. A number of research studies (see Meichenbaum, 1977, for a review) have demonstrated that it is possible to teach children to regulate many aspects of their own problem solving behavior through verbal self-instruction. For example, in a task that required children to learn to copy line patterns (Meichenbaum & Goodman, 1971), the children observed a model who performed the task while verbally describing the problem solving and self regulation patterns that he was following:

> OK, what is it I have to do? You want me to copy the picture with the different lines. I have to go slowly and carefully. Okay, draw the line down, good; then to the right, that's it; now down some more and to the left. Good. I'm doing fine so far. Remember, go slowly. Now back up again. No I was supposed to go down. That's OK. Just erase the line carefully. Good. Even if I make an error I can go on slowly and carefully. I have to go down now. Finished. I did it! [Meichenbaum & Goodman, 1971, p. 117; also cited in Meichenbaum, 1977, p. 32].

Following exposure to the model the child was provided with an opportunity to practice verbal self-regulation of his own behavior, with further instruction and guidance by the experimenter. As the child became more successful at regulating his own behavior, the experimenter's guidance was gradually withdrawn. The child was at first encouraged to give verbal instructions to himself aloud, but as the child became more proficient he was induced to change to covert self-instructions. Meichenbaum and Goodman applied this procedure successfully to teaching children to perform a number of cognitive tasks, including following instructions, completing items on the Primary Mental Abilities test, and solving various conceptual tasks. Children undergoing this type of training scored significantly higher than an untrained control group on an IQ test and on the Matching Familiar Figures test. Meichenbaum also reported that cognitive modeling plus self-instruction was more effective than cognitive modeling alone.

Several studies demonstrate that the effective use of modeling as an educational technique may require more supportive aids and concrete referents with younger children than with older children. Denny (1972), for example, found that a modeling procedure which was sufficient to teach 8-and 10-year-old children effective question asking strategies in a 20 questions game was not effective with 6-year-olds. In a follow-up experiment, Denney, Denney, and Ziobrowski (1973) modified their modeling procedure in an attempt to make it more effective with the younger children. In a "modeling plus elimination" treatment condition, the model, after asking a question that logically eliminated several alternatives, proceeded to conceal those items which had been eliminated by the answer to the question. This elimination procedure served to highlight through concrete actions the nature and consequences of the strategy. The modeling plus elimination procedure was found to be superior to modeling alone as an instructional technique, producing substantial improvements in the ability of the children to adopt the effective question asking procedure.

The research reviewed in this section constitutes only a sampling of the available research literature on the use of social learning techniques in cognitive instruction. The experiments do demonstrate, however, that modeling, in conjunction with other techniques, can be a powerful method of instruction for a variety of cognitive skills. At this time relatively little is known about optimal combinations of social learning procedures in teaching various topics and age groups, but, with continued research of the type reviewed above there would seem to be good reason to expect that the scientific basis of pedagogy will be substantially enhanced.

SOCIAL LEARNING AND SELF-REGULATION OF BEHAVIOR

According to the social learning perspective, children and adults are not controlled exclusively or predominantly by external reinforcement contingencies and modeling influences. Much of human behavior can only be understood in terms of self-regulation processes. Individuals set goals and standards of conduct for themselves, and they regulate and evaluate their behavior in terms of these goals and standards. If their level of achievement matches their expectations and standards, they will respond with positive self-evaluation and may reward themselves by making externally reinforcing consequences available. On the other hand, if they fail to live up to their goals and standards, they may respond with self-reproof and by withholding rewards which are under their control. According to Bandura (1977), although some behaviors are maintained by anticipated external consequences, most behaviors are under self-reinforcement control. Research (e.g., Bandura & Perloff, 1967) has shown that children very often set high standards of performance for themselves on various cognitive tasks, even when they are not required to do so, and then evaluate and regulate their behavior in terms of the goals they have set.

The goals that children do set for themselves will, of course, be acquired, maintained, and modified as a result of external influences—the approval and disapproval of parents, teachers, and peers; the standards modeled by parents, teachers, and peers; the standards that are taught through instruction; and the success or failure of the child in achieving the goals and living up to the standards he or she has set. Several factors have been identified that influence the likelihood that children will adopt given standards of performance (Bandura, 1977). Children are most likely to incorporate modeled standards when the standards are modeled consistently by adults and peers, when those who exemplify the standards are rewarded with social recognition or other positive reinforcement, when the standards are realistic in terms of the child's current ability level, and when the model's own behavior is consistent with the standards the model imposes on others.

An understanding of self-regulation processes is of obvious significance to education. Effective teaching, from the perspective of social learning theory, does not involve just controlling behavior through reward and punishment contingencies, or teaching specific behaviors through modeling. Effective education requires teaching children how to regulate their own behavior effectively and inducing them to incorporate realistic standards of achievement and performance.

CONTRAST OF SOCIAL LEARNING AND PIAGETIAN VIEWS OF COGNITION AND EDUCATION

General Differences

Piagetian theory offers a much more comprehensive description of human cognitive development than social learning theory. If one wants to know how normal 2-, 4-, or 10-year-old children think and adapt to their environment, research by Piaget and Piagetians provides much more information than social learning theory. Social learning researchers have not devoted a great deal of effort to studying the sequential regularities that occur in human cognitive development. The primary area in which social learning and Piagetian theories interface is in their accounts of the role of experience in accounting for *changes* in children's intellectual functioning. The theories differ fundamentally in this respect and in their implications for education. Piagetian theory emphasizes the importance of an active self-discovery process in education and deemphasizes the role of direct instruction. Social learning theory emphasizes the role of instructional methods such as modeling, verbal instruction and explanation, analysis of tasks into component skills, guided practice, and so on.

The Role of "Activity" and "Self-Discovery" Processes in Education

One of the most fundamental educational tenets offered by Piaget is that the development of intelligence must occur through the activity of the child.

> Knowledge is derived from action, not in the sense of simple associative
> responses, but in the much deeper sense of an assimilation of reality into the
> necessary and general coordination of action. To know an object is to act upon
> it and transform it ... intelligence consists in executing and coordinating actions,
> though in an interiorized and reflective form [Piaget, 1970, pp. 28–29].

Although Piaget acknowledges that direct instruction and "imposed labor" are a necessary part of education, he emphasizes that educational programs should "give rise to active manipulation and discovery by the child itself [1970, p. 49]." This active involvement of the child refers to both physical and mental involvement.

The basic operational structures of intelligence are not acquired primarily through instruction but must be discovered, constructed, or invented by the child himself. Furthermore, the child must reach an appropriate stage of maturational and intellectual readiness before he or she will be able to develop new structures of thought. Piaget himself has not been very specific as to precisely how teachers should design a curriculum or guide the development of the child's intelligence, although he has given some very general guidelines (1970, Chapters 3 and 4). Several others, however, have developed numerous general and specific recommendations for educational practice based upon Piagetian theory (see, for example, Elkind 1976; Lawton & Hooper, 1977).

Social learning theorists do not appear to be in disagreement with the assumption that effective education requires the active involvement of the child. Within the social learning perspective, the child is viewed as an active information processor, who does indeed actively attempt to interpret or understand (assimilate) experiences by applying the information processing skills, problem solving strategies, and knowledge bases that he or she currently posseses. Effective education through social learning techniques requires that the child be attending selectively, verbally and perceptually representing information, and formulating plans and abstract rules to guide behavior. The child is *not* viewed by social learning theory as a passive receptacle into which ready-made knowledge can be directly instilled through verbalization. The goals that Piaget holds up for education—i.e., producing individuals that are critical, creative, inventive, and discoverers—are goals that can readily be shared within the social learning perspective. The differences arise between the theories in some of the assumptions concerning how such goals can be achieved.

Social learning theorists have disagreed with Piaget's emphasis on discovery processes as the primary and necessary basis of intellectual development. Certainly a major part of the child's learning does depend on experimentation and discovery, but social learning theorists argue that for many intellectual skills, methods of education that emphasize discovery may be very inefficient by comparison with social learning techniques.

Research examining discovery methods and social learning methods of Piagetian learning have consistently shown discovery methods to be less effective (see Brainerd, 1977; Zimmerman, 1977, for elaboration). This generalization applies to studies of the acquisition of Piagetian conceptual skills such as conservation, class inclusion, and seriation, as well as to other problem solving and conceptual skills. Zimmerman (1977) points out that discovery learning procedures often produce a great deal of trial-and-error groping, with a high rate of errors, and altogether, very poor learning performance.

Social learning researchers have also criticized Piaget's theory for overemphasizing or inaccurately representing the limitations and deficiencies of children at various stages of cognitive development. Piaget's stage theory, it is argued, may prompt educators to unwisely abandon efforts to teach children concepts and cognitive skills that the child may be capable of learning and may profit from learning. Much of the controversy concerning this issue has focused on the question of whether or not children at the preoperational stage of intellectual development can be taught to perform tasks that presumably require concrete operational thought structures, for example, conservation, class inclusion, and seriation. Piagetian theory indicates that the preoperational child will be able to successfully perform such tasks only when a sufficient degree of biological maturation and intellectual readiness has evolved, with the evaluation of intellectual readiness being determined by the child's physical and logical-mathematical experience in interacting with the environment. A very large research literature exists in this area, embodying a number of complicated methodological and theoretical issues. However, one aspect of this training literature is now quite clear: Contrary to Piagetian views, children who meet Piaget's criteria for the preoperational stage can be taught in a relatively brief time to successfully carry out various types of conservation, classification, and relational reasoning tasks—tasks that presumably require concrete operational thinking capabilities. Furthermore, the skills that the children learn in these training studies can often be generalized to new material, retained over long periods of time, and can be verbally explained as well as physically performed by the child. Successful methods of instruction have included modeling, verbal instruction, explanation and feedback, and other techniques (see Brainerd, 1977, for review).

Based on research such as that reviewed above, social learning theorists challenge the validity and educational value of Piaget's characterization of intelligence in terms of mental structures and question the desirability of self-discovery approaches in many aspects of education.

ACKNOWLEDGMENTS

I wish to thank GloDeen Jennings and Laura Martin for their very capable assistance in preparing this manuscript.

REFERENCES

Bandura, A. *Social learning theory*. Englewood Cliffs, N.J.: Prentice-Hall, 1977.

Bandura, A., & Perloff, B. Relative efficacy of self monitored and externally imposed reinforcement systems. *Journal of Personality and Social Psychology*, 1967, 7, 111–116.

Brainerd, C. J. Learning research and Piagetian theory. In L. Siegel & C. J. Brainerd (Eds.), *Alternatives to Piaget: Critical essays on the theory*. New York: Academic Press, 1977.

Debus, R. L. Effects of brief observation of model behavior on conceptual tempo of impulsive children. *Developmental Psychology*, 1970, 2, 22–32.

Debus, R. Observation learning of reflective strategies by impulsive children. Presented at the Congres International de Psychologie Paris, France, 1976.

Denny, D. R. Modeling effects upon conceptual style and cognitive tempo. *Child Development*, 1972, 43, 105–119.

Denney, D. R., Denney, N. W., & Ziobrowski, M. J. Alternatives in the information processing strategies of young children following observation of adult models. *Developmental Psychology*, 1973, 8, 202–208.

Elkind, D. *Child development and education: A Piagetian perspective*. New York, Oxford, 1976.

Henderson, R. W., Swanson, R., & Zimmerman, B. J. Training seriation responses in young children through televised modeling of hierarchically sequenced rule components. *American Educational Research Journal*, 1975, 12, 479–489.

Kagan, J. Individual differences in the resolution of response uncertainty. *Journal of Personality and Social Psychology*, 1965, 2, 154–160.

Lawton, J. T., & Hooper, F. H. Piagetian theory and early childhood education. In L. Siegel & C. J. Brainerd (Eds.), *Alternatives to Piaget: Critical essays on the theory*. New York: Academic Press, 1977.

Meichenbaum, D. *Cognitive behavior modification: An integrative approach*. New York: Plenum, 1977.

Meichenbaum, D., & Goodman, J. Training impulsive children to talk to themselves: A means of developing self control. *Journal of Abnormal Psychology*, 1971, 77, 115–126.

Piaget, J. *Science of education and the psychology of the child*. New York: Orion Press, 1970.

Rosenthal, T. L., & Zimmerman, B. J. *Social learning and cognition*. New York: Academic Press, 1978.

Zimmerman, B. J. Modeling. In H. Hom & P. Robinson (Eds.), *Psychological processes in early education*. New York: Academic Press, 1977.

CHAPTER **5**

Research and the Child:
The Family

PAUL A. ROBINSON

The family environment is perhaps the single most influential environmental determinant of child behavior. Children's social, cognitive,
and emotional behaviors have been shown to be strongly influenced by
parental child-rearing practices, the behavior modeled by parents and
siblings, and by many other aspects of the family environment. In this
chapter, research on parent–child and other family relationships is reviewed and related to early education. Such research is relevant to the field
of education in a number of ways. It is well established that many of the
children who pose special problems in the school—for example, aggressive
children and intellectually disadvantaged children—oftentimes reflect the
inadequacies of their home environments. An understanding of the child's
problems thus requires some understanding of the relationship between his
or her home environment and behavior. Furthermore, effective modification
of the child's behavior frequently requires intervention in the family situation. It is unreasonable to assume that schools and teachers should be exclusively responsible for dealing with the problem behaviors and intellectual deficits of students at school. Attempts to re-educate or retrain the
parents may also be necessary before long-lasting improvements can be
brought about. These ideas are, of course, not at all new. Many programs
in compensatory education for preschool children have been construed as

119

ASPECTS OF EARLY CHILDHOOD EDUCATION
Theory to Research to Practice

an attempt to compensate for the child's disadvantaged home environment, and many recent intervention projects have begun to emphasize the importance of parent education and involvement in the program if the improvement in the child's abilities is to be long lasting (Bronfenbrenner, 1974).

The main issues and questions to be examined within this chapter are these: What have we learned about the effect of the family environment— parental child-rearing practices in particular—on child behavior? What types of family environments are associated with the development of desirable, competent behavior in children? What types of family environments are associated with the development of undesirable behaviors and cognitive deficits in children? And, perhaps most importantly, What can be done about the problems that exist within families? Can parents of inadequately socialized and intellectually disadvantaged children be trained to effectively modify these behaviors?

CHILD-REARING PRACTICES ASSOCIATED WITH THE DEVELOPMENT OF DESIRABLE BEHAVIORS AND INTELLECTUAL COMPETENCE IN CHILDREN

Information about effective parenting and the characteristics of highly competent children may be of considerable value to those interested in eliminating problem behaviors and promoting positive behaviors in children. Parents who are having difficulty with their children may benefit greatly from learning some of the child-rearing practices used by more successful parents. Teachers of young children might also look to effective parents for ideas and examples of effective means of promoting competence in young children. Generally, an understanding of what is "wrong" in the environment of a child who is posing a problem at home or in school may best be understood in terms of what is *lacking* in his or her home environment. In this section we will focus on what has been learned about "healthy" children and effective child-rearing practices.

The Competent Child

Most people could probably agree at a very general level on what constitutes desirable behaviors in children. Well adjusted children would be described as energetic, cheerful, able to relate well to peers and adults, self-confident, responsible, and so on. These, however, are rather vague, global descriptions, and may not be of great use to someone concerned with making specific decisions concerning educational goals that may or may not be appropriate for children at different age levels. For a 5-year-old child, for example, what social and cognitive skills are really important for the child to possess? What is it reasonable to expect of the child at this age and what skills may be trivial or out of reach? Relatively little research has been directed at questions of this type, but the results of one study are particularly instructive and interesting. White and Watts (1973) conducted a study focusing on the question: What are healthy and well developed 3- to 6-year-old children really like? Out of a sample of 450 children, White and his colleagues selected 25 children between the ages of 3 and 6 who were judged to be very well adjusted and competent based on testing and extensive observations. Careful study of these highly competent children showed the following qualities to be particularly important to their functioning at their developmental level:

A. Social Abilities
    1. Ability to get and maintain the attention of adults in socially acceptable ways.
    2. Ability to use adults as resources.
    3. Ability to express both affection and hostility to adults.
    4. Ability to lead and follow peers.
    5. Ability to compete with peers.
    6. Ability to express both affection and hostility with peers.

B. Cognitive and Language Abilities
    1. Linguistic competence.
    2. Ability to sense dissonance or note discrepancies.
    3. Ability to anticipate consequences.
    4. Ability to deal with abstractions.
    5. Ability to take the perspective of another.
    6. Attentional abilities.
    7. Ability to plan and carry out multistep activities.

In their report of this research, White and Watts elaborate in some detail upon these and other abilities essential to the competent 6-year-old.

An important value of research such as this to the parent or educator is that it provides an empirical basis for helping make decisions as to what behaviors and skills ought to be taught or otherwise encouraged in children at various age levels. At the preschool or kindergarten level, for example, it may be beneficial to develop lesson plans systematically teaching the children ways of getting and maintaining adult attention and using adults as resources; some children may develop these skills spontaneously and easily, but others may be hampered by their deficiencies in this area throughout their development. The common sense or intuition of parents and educators may often leave a great deal to be desired as a basis for deciding what a young child should be learning at a given age. Some parents impose unreasonable demands on children, thereby frustrating them and perhaps producing a resentful attitude toward the educational process; others fail to promote behaviors in children that are critical to optimal development. The author has found that many parents who are evaluating the suitability of a particular preschool for their child will often tend to focus on a very narrow range of "educational" aspects of the preschool. Will their 4-year-old learn to count to 10 and say her ABC's? Are there many educational toys? Will she learn to write her name? While these concerns may not be trivial, the point emphasized here is that parents will generally fail to consider whether the preschool promotes some of the more basic social and cognitive skills for young children, such as those listed by White. Concommitantly, the parents may overemphasize the significance of the child learning by rote a few educational memory feats which are of little educational significance for the child's stage of development.

White's research is only a start in this area, but as further research accumulates it should be helpful in formulating appropriate educational and behavioral goals for different age levels.

METHODOLOGICAL PROBLEMS IN THE STUDY OF PARENT–CHILD RELATIONSHIPS

Acquiring accurate, replicable information about the family and parent–child relationships has been a very difficult task for researchers in child development. Family relationships are complex and change continuously throughout a child's development. If interviewed about their behavior, parents will not always be accurate or comprehensive; they may forget, confuse one child with another, bias their answers in the direction of what seems more socially desirable, or otherwise give distorted data. If the family's behavior is observed by behavioral scientists at the family's home or within a laboratory setting, the behavior of the individuals being observed may change because they are aware of being observed. Behavioral scientists, however, have not been deterred by these obstacles, and have accumulated an enormous body of research on the family in the past 30 years. Much of this research may be classified as utterly worthless because of sloppy, unreliable methodology, but there remain many studies which have been rigorous and careful in their methodology and have begun to yield some consistent, replicable findings. In this review, preference will be given to findings which (a) have been based on observation of the family, as well as interviews or questionnaire information and (b) have been reported in more than one study. There have been several recent reviews and evaluations of the parent–child literature which have been helpful in preparing this summary (Clarke-Stewart, 1978; Conger, 1978; Hetherington & Parke, 1975; Martin, 1975; White & Watts, 1973).

The Need to Examine Multiple Aspects of Parenting

One theme which emerges from the research literature on the family is that it is generally not possible to predict much about a child's behavior from examining just one aspect of parental behavior. The parent–child relationship is likely to show a predictable correlation only when multiple aspects—patterns or clusters—of parental behavior are considered. To illustrate this point, consider the global quality that may be referred to as parental love (warmth, acceptance, positive involvement). Certaintly this is an essential aspect of effective parenting, but, just knowing that a parent is in some general sense "loving" may not tell you much if anything about what the children will be like. If parents are loving, but also highly permissive and indulgent, the children may well develop a "spoiled brat" syndrome (Hetherington & Parke, 1975). On the other hand, if the loving parents are highly rigid and restrictive, the child is more likely to become compliant, obedient, conscientious, and perhaps somewhat overinhibited, dependent, and conforming (Becker, 1964). Only when factors in addition to love are taken into consideration—disciplinary practices, for example—does the parent–child relationship become reasonably predictable. As a matter of fact, parental warmth and parental discipline practices appear to be two of the most influential aspects of parental behavior, and when considered together can predict much about the child's behavior. Many other aspects of parental behavior of course can and do exert powerful influences over the child's behavior.

Effective Parenting as a Function of the Child's Age

The parental qualities that are effective with an infant or preschool child obviously may not be at all effective or appropriate with an older child or adolescent. It is no doubt quite common for a parent who does an excellent job with an infant or preschool child to be unsuccessful with the same child as an adolescent. Thus, for many aspects of parental behavior it may be silly to make a generalization about what constitutes effective parenting without specifying the age range of the child.

The importance of considering the age of the child when evaluating parental child rearing techniques is nicely illustrated in a series of studies of punishment and discipline techniques (see Parke, 1977, for a detailed review of these studies). A number of studies suggest that the effectiveness of discipline of children is enhanced when the discipline is accompanied by a rationale or explanation. For instance, in one study (Parke, 1969) it was found that first-grade children were less likely to play with a prohibited toy when they were given a rationale as to why they should not play with it (e.g., it might break) than when they were simply told not to play with it. In a study of adolescent–parent relationships, Elder (1971) found that more frequent use of explanations by parents was associated with higher confidence and independence in the adolescents and less parent–adolescent conflict. Thus explanations appear to generally increase the effectiveness of parental discipline. However, subsequent research has demonstrated that the type of rationale which is effective with children changes with age. Generally, younger children (ages 4–6, for example) seem to profit most from simple, concrete explanations (Hetherington, 1975; Parke, 1977). An abstract or complex rationale may have little effect on these children, since they will not have the cognitive sophistication necessary to understand many abstract rationales (e.g., do unto others as you would have them do unto you). For older children, on the other hand, research has indicated that they can and do begin to be influenced by more abstract rationales as well as by the more simple, concrete rationales. To be effective, then, the rationale that accompanies discipline must be adapted to the child's level of understanding.

OVERVIEW OF FINDINGS ON PARENTAL CORRELATES OF COMPETENCE IN CHILDREN

During the first 6 to 8 months of life it appears that most differences between parents in child care practices do not make a great deal of difference in their long-term impact on the child's development. So long as the parents provide good nutrition and health care and a reasonably varied, stimulating, responsive environment, the infant appears to undergo a predictable maturational path (White & Watts, 1973; Clarke-Stewart, 1977).

From about 10 months of age to 3 years, the child's social and cognitive development has been found to show a strong relationship to parental child rearing practices. Children appear to develop higher degrees of competence when their parents demonstrate these qualities: They allow the child considerable freedom to explore and interact with his environment. That is, they design the household in such a way that the child within reasonable limits has the freedom to walk about, climb, touch, and otherwise manipulate the "things" in the household without the need for his parents to frequently reprimand and control him for expressing his curiosity. In a word, the parents do a good job of "baby proofing" the house. The parents do, of course, set necessary limits to ensure the safety of the child and protect the household from unreasonable abuse. In addition, parents of the more competent young children have been found to generally provide the child with a *variety* of interesting materials (not necessarily toys) to explore, climb on, manipulate, and observe. Durring the first 2 years of life the development of the child's sensorimotor intelligence depends to a great extent upon his interacting with and observing a varied, interesting environment; to provide the child with a barren, boring, "untouchable" environment apparently hampers the development of this intelligence and the child's innate curiosity (White & Watts, 1973).

The significant caretakers in the highly competent child's environment are likely to demonstrate a quality that is generally referred to as "responsiveness." These responsive parents are noted for their sensitivity in reacting to the child's interests and behavior—showing interest in what the child does, helping, sharing, and supporting. This "responsiveness" does not generally involve the parent sitting down for long periods of time and systematically teaching the child in any formal or structured sense. Rather, it involves an availability of the parent throughout the child's day, such that when the child encounters some problem or interesting event or experience, the parent is available (usually) to comment, help, share, or respond with an interesting related idea or elaboration (White & Watts, 1973). As Clarke-Stewart summarizes the relationship, mothers of "good" infants demonstrate a pattern of behavior consisting of "looking at, talking to, smiling at, playing with, offering toys to the child—appropriately, affectionately, noninstructively, and responsively [1977, p. 25]." The parents' linguistic and conceptual activities toward the child are generally adapted to the child's interests and abilities in a nondirective, accepting manner (Nelson, 1973). Parents of the capable child in this developmental period are generally warm and loving and provide firm controls, rules, and limits.

Usually the child's mother is his most significant caretaker in terms of the frequency and intensity of interactions with the child. However, recent observations (Parke 1976) indicate that fathers appear to be as competent, affectionate, and sensitive as mothers when they do interact with their infants.

In studies of preschool children (ages 3–6), Baumrind (1967, 1971) has found that parents of the very well adjusted preschool child (energetic, confident, self-controlled, affiliative, realistic, independent) are likely to exercise what she has termed an *authoritative* (*not* autocratic or authoritarian) approach to discipline. These authoritative parents exercise firm control over the child and impose relatively high maturity demands. The children are expected and required to demonstrate appropriate responsibility and self-discipline for their developmental level—for example, to help with chores, to exercise appropriate self-care, and to show consideration for other people. But, within these limits and demands, the parents are generally warm and open in their communication with the child. They explain and discuss their rules and decisions, and may occasionally modify a decision based on the child's statements, arguments, or feelings. They encourage the child to express his or her feelings and are generally open and accepting in their comments. They encourage the child to exercise independence within the limits they have set. These authoritative parents generally do not tolerate whining and nagging. According to Baumrind (1971), they are quite consistent, demonstrating "a remarkable ability to hold a position once they took a stand." This approach to discipline has been found to be effective not only with preschool and elementary school children, but also with adolescents (Elder, 1971)—although parents allow adolescents substantially greater autonomy than they do younger children, in keeping with the greater maturity and cognitive sophistication of the adolescent. This type of approach to discipline is variously referred to as "authoritative" "moderate," "age appropriate," or democratic," although it is not entirely democratic since the parents will overrule the child's decisions if the parents are convinced they are correct.

At all developmental stages, the parents' role as *models* will exert a strong influence over the child's behavior. Generally, parents of competent children with a strong stable sense of identity are apt to model effective personal and social behavior and appropriate sex role behavior (Conger, 1978).

Academic Achievement and Parental Behavior

More specialized information about parent–child relationships can be acquired by examining parental correlates of more specific aspects of child behavior. For example, what family patterns are associated with children who have high academic achievement levels, or high standards of moral conduct, or high popularity with peers? The present section will focus only on the first quality: academic achievement behavior. Not surprisingly, parents of students that are high achievers are more likely than parents of lower achievers (of comparable ability) to *value, expect,* and *reward* academic accomplishment and to themselves *model* appropriate intellectual work habits (see Clarke-Stewart, 1977, for a detailed review). It may well be accurate to make such a generalization about *any* aspect of child behavior, that is, if the parents expect, value, reward, and model that behavior, their children are likely to manifest that behavior. What parents model and reward are without doubt two of the most powerful, pervasive influences on their children's personality development. As one looks more closely at academic achievement behavior, however, the relationship between performance and parental behavior can be seen to be somewhat more complex. Two different patterns of achievement behavior may be distinguished: Achievement within the framework of the traditional directive school setting may be differentiated from achievement in academic settings that call for more self-initiated, innovative, creative work. Achievement in the traditional classroom setting appears more strongly related to an authoritarian approach in which the parents *demand* superior school performance, as well as rewarding it and modeling it. The more self-initiated achievement pattern of school achievement, on the other hand, appears to be negatively related to an authoritarian parenting style and more positively correlated with a supportive, independence-encouraging approach to child rearing (Clarke-Stewart, 1977).

Other Determinants of Competence in Children

The correlations between parental behavior and child behavior which have been summarized here are far from perfect. There are many, many exceptions to every relationship mentioned. Many parents who are very capable and loving have children who become aggressive, or withdrawn or do poorly in school. Many competent children have parents who are not especially loving, authoritative, or good models. Within the same family, it is not unusual to have children who differ greatly in temperament, personality, academic accomplishment, and other traits—even though the parents apply basically the same child rearing practices with all the children.

What accounts for this lack of consistency in parent–child relationships and child behavior? Much of the inconsistency is due to the fact that there are many determinants of child behavior in addition to the parents—for example, the influence of peers, siblings, grandparents and other relatives; the influence of teachers and the educational system; the influence of TV, movies, radio; the influence of genetic factors on intelligence, temperament, physical appearance, rate of growth, and many other aspects of personality. All of these powerful influences on a child's behavior may counteract or otherwise modify the influence of the parents.

Consider, for example, some of the "extraparental" factors that may be associated with the child's general competence. Genetic factors account for much of the individual variation between children in traits such as intelligence, temperament, rate of physical development, and physical appearance, and *all* of these traits are significantly related to a child's personality development. Highly intelligent children are not only likely to do better in school than less intelligent children, but are also more likely to establish effective social relationships (Terman, 1954; Hallworth, Davis, & Gamston, 1965). Early maturing adolescent males tend to be rated as more poised and popular than late maturing males (Jones & Bayley, 1950). The physically attractive child is more likely to elicit positive reactions from other children and adults than the unattractive child—Dion (1974), for instance, found that college students who observed a film of a child engaging in misconduct were more likely to recommend harsh punishment when the child was unattractive than when the child was attractive. In a study of children's temperament, it has been found that some children very early in life display an "easy" temperament, characterized by an unusually positive mood and quick adaptation to new situations and demands (Thomas, Chess, & Birch, 1968). This study found no evidence that the child's temperament was caused by parental child-rearing practices.

Although a child's parents may lack important child-rearing skills and qualities, these deficiencies may be overcome to some extent by the positive influences of siblings, grandparents and other relatives, peers, teachers, neighbors, scout leaders, and other influential persons in the child's environment.

It should also be noted that the parent's influence on the child is not a one-way process. Part of the correlation that exists between parental behavior and child behavior will in some circumstances be as much due to the child's influence on the parent as vice versa. Parents may be more likely to respond positively to children that are attractive and cuddly, gregarious, and positive in mood. Thomas *et al.* (1968) found, for instance, that mothers of children with an "easy" temperament tended to feel confident, relaxed, and proud of their role as parents. Thomas *et al.* concluded that these qualities appeared to be a reaction to the child's temperament and not a cause of it.

Thus, the influence of parents must be put into perspective. Because of the multiple determinants of child behavior, there is no simple correspondence between parent behavior and child behavior, even though parental influence may be the single most important environmental influence for most children.

CHILD-REARING PRACTICES ASSOCIATED WITH PROBLEM BEHAVIORS AND INTELLECTUAL DEFICITS

Many of the problems that frequently pose difficulties for the educational system are related to child rearing practices. Two such problems and their parental correlates will be examined in this section: the intellectual deficits found among disadvantaged children and the problem of excessive aggressiveness in children. Also examined will be the characteristics of parents who abuse their children. Abusive parents are responsible for a variety of problems experienced by a large number of children. In view of the prevalence of abuse, it is likely that most teachers will become involved with a number of children who suffer from the effects of abuse and neglect.

Intellectual Deficits among Disadvantaged Children

The deficient intellectual and academic performance of disadvantaged children has been the focus of numerous research studies and many social action programs since 1960. Children from socially disadvantaged homes, on the average, score lower on IQ tests and demonstrate lower academic performance than children from middle-class homes. They are also more likely to drop out of school, to become unemployed, and to become dependent upon welfare payments for subsistence. There is considerable controversy as to the relative importance of genetic, sociological, and familial factors in accounting for the intellectual deficits of disadvantaged children. There is firm evidence, however, that at least *part* of the deficit found in many disadvantaged children is caused by inadequate child rearing practices.

Hess and Shipman (1965), for example, in a study examining child-rearing practices among mothers in middle-class and lower-class families found less optimal child-rearing practices among the lower-class families. The mothers in lower-class families were more likely than the middle-class mothers to exercise a "status oriented" method of discipline—that is, to control behavior on the basis of authority or power without explaining the reason for rules, decisions, and limits, and without discussing the consequences of the child's behavior on others. The mothers in the disadvantaged families were also more likely to engage in an "impulsive" teaching style in which they failed to organize, explain, and effectively help their child learn a new skill or task. In their verbal interactions with their children, the language of the mothers in the disadvantaged families tended to be simpler, less elaborated, and less discriminating than the language of the mothers in middle-class families.

In a study comparing the child-rearing practices of mothers with different educational levels, Streissguth and Bee (1972) found more effective child-rearing practices among mothers with college level education than among mothers with a high school or less education. In situations in which the mothers were teaching their children new skills, the better educated mothers were four times more likely than the less educated mothers to use positive reinforcement (encouragement, praise, reward, support) in their teaching and were less likely to use criticism and disapproval as teaching techniques.

Another handicap that is more likely to impair the intellectual development of the disadvantaged child than that of the advantaged child involves parental absence. Lower-class families, especially black families, are more likely than middle-class families to be one-parent families, with the father the absent parent. Prolonged father absence during the developmental years is associated with both cognitive deficits—especially in quantitative thinking skills—and deficits in self-control among children (Hetherington & Parke, 1975).

The research cited above provides only a sampling from a large body of research documenting the adverse environmental influences on the disadvantaged child. Research such as this provides a convincing empirical rationale for the proposition that improvement of the home environment will often be a necessary step toward overcoming the deficits of the disadvantaged child. A later section will consider the question of whether or how a deficient home environment may be modified.

Aggressive Behavior in Children

Cognitive deficits in children are not the only child behavior problems of concern to educators. Many children are aggressive and defiant, both in and out of school. They may defy instructions, destroy property, hit, curse, throw tantrums, and otherwise make the lives of their parents, teachers, and others quite miserable. A majority of teachers who quit teaching are reported to do so because of difficulties in discipline in the classroom (Madsen & Madsen, 1974). About one-third of all children referred to mental health clinics in the United States are referred for "conduct disorders" involving aggressive, noncompliant behavior (Patterson, Reid, Jones, & Conger, 1975). Research suggests that children who manifest aggressive, antisocial patterns of behavior are highly likely to persist in this behavior throughout childhood and adolescence and into adulthood unless some type of treatment or family intervention is instituted (Robins, 1966). Aggressive behavior in children is in fact one of the strongest predictors of behavior problems later in development.

There is substantial evidence that parental child-rearing practices are one of the major determinants of aggressiveness in children (although genetic factors, sociological conditions, and situational determinants are also implicated). Parents of aggressive children, compared to parents of nonaggressive children, have been found to be more likely to demonstrate one or more of the following traits: to encourage and reward aggressive behavior in their children; to model punitive, aggressive behavior; to rely excessively on punitive and coercive means of discipline; to fail to make effective attempts to control or discipline aggressive behavior; to fail to use positive reinforcement effectively to promote prosocial behavior (Bandura, 1973; Bandura & Walters, 1959; Patterson *et al.*, 1975; Sears, Maccoby, & Levin, 1957). Antisocial and aggressive behavior in children is also known to be related to parental rejection or indifference (Conger, 1978). It should be noted that there is more than one pattern of parental behavior that may promote aggressiveness in children—for example, either an absence of any firm discipline or an excess of discipline in the form of frequent physical punishments are known to be associated with aggressiveness in children.

If parental influences are a major determinant of children's aggressiveness, then one would expect that training parents to exercise more effective child-rearing techniques would decrease their children's aggressiveness; as will be discussed in a later section, parent training programs have achieved significant success in decreasing aggressive behavior.

Parents Who Abuse Their Children

Recent estimates indicate that as many as 500,000 children in the United States may be victim's of parental abuse or neglect each year (Light, 1973). In view of the prevalence of the problem, it is likely that most educators will come in contact with many of these children. The children are likely to pose problems in school because of a variety of childhood behavioral problems that are associated with abuse. Observations of young abused children in a preschool, for example, showed the children to be generally listless and apathetic. They generally failed to interact with other children, except for occasional episodes of unpredictable aggression among the boys (Galdston, 1971, cited in Parke & Collmer, 1975). Unfortunately, the child who is abused and neglected can often develop unattractive personality traits that may elicit negative reactions from many of the individuals that the child comes in contact with. Bakan (1971) noted that whereas "the well taken care of child attracts positive responses, the child who is abused and neglected becomes ugly in appearance and invites further abuse and neglect [p. 109, cited in Parke and Collmer, 1975, p. 35]." A number of traits in abused children may constitute problems for the teacher. The children's listlessness, apathy, aggressiveness, and sometimes frantic craving for attention are traits which may evoke further rejection. This is indeed a vicious cycle in which the child's development can be hampered because of the neglect in the home. It is noteworthy that the problem of child abuse is significantly correlated with the problem of aggressiveness in children. In one study of a group of aggressive children, it was reported that approximately 25% of the parents were classified as being physically abusive (Achenbach, 1977). Furthermore, there are several studies indicating that abused children often become child abusers themselves, thereby recycling the problem from one generation to the next.

There is evidence that parental deficiencies in child-rearing skills and information about children are among the most significant determinants of abuse. Parents who abuse their children are often very ineffective disciplinarians—quite apart from their physical abuse per se. They frequently fail to establish clear rules and expectations for their children, and fail to enforce rules and decisions in a clear, consistent manner (Young, 1964). Because of the ineffectiveness of their approach to discipline, these parents may find that the mild or moderate types of punishments which most parents find sufficient will not work for them, so they escalate the severity of the punishment until it reaches an abusive level. Abusive parents have also been frequently found to have very unrealistic expectations as to how children ought to behave at a given developmental level. These unrealistic expectations lead them to impose unrealistic demands on their children and to become frustrated and abusive when their discipline efforts are unsuccessful.

Since the source of the behavioral and intellectual problems of the abused child are often in the home, it would appear necessary to modify the home environment—specifically, to modify the parental behaviors—if one is to deal successfully with the child's problem. As noted in a later section, there is some evidence that family counseling and parent training programs can be moderately successful in such cases.

Other Determinants of Negative Behaviors in Children

As is the case with desirable behaviors in children, the relationship between parental behavior and negative behaviors in children is significant but far from perfect. Many children from disadvantaged homes do very well in school, even if their parents' child-rearing practices leave much to be desired. Conversely, children from advantaged homes with very competent parents will sometimes do terribly in school. In the case of aggressive children, one cannot assume that the aggressive child is sure to have inadequate or abusive parents. Many parents of aggressive children are very competent, capable, and loving. Many factors in addition to parental child-rearing practices must be considered if the child's aggressiveness or intellectual deficits are to be fully understood--e.g., genetic factors, the influence of peers, siblings, other adults, the schools, and so on.

An understanding of the parent–child relationship also requires consideration of the child's influence on the parents. Part of the relationship between parental behavior and negative traits in the child will be accounted for by the child's influence on the parents. Children who have a difficult temperament or are hyperactive or autistic or mentally deficient or physically unattractive appear to be more likely to elicit negative responses from parents than children without these disadvantages (see Bell, 1968; Dion, 1974; Thomas et al., 1968; for examples of this relationship).

PARENT TRAINING PROGRAMS

Since parental child-rearing practices appear to be a primary cause of many of the problems of disadvantaged and aggressive children, training or educating the parents in more effective child rearing practices may be a necessary method of treating the problems. Programs which have attempted to train, educate, or otherwise modify the child-rearing practices of parents with problem children will be reviewed in this section. The review will examine training programs for (a) parents of aggressive children and (b) parents in disadvantaged families. The review will be restricted to training programs which have been carefully evaluated through systematic research. Unfortunately, there are many parent training and education programs—even some that are in widespread use—that have not been evaluated to determine whether or not they are effective. These programs may be helping parents and their children or they may be having a detrimental effect—without the necessary evaluative research, such programs can be considered only as untested hypotheses. Perhaps the most widely used and influential parent educational program in the United States—Gordon's (1975) Parent Effectiveness Training system—fits into this category. Despite the fact that large numbers of parents around the country enroll in this program, and large numbers of teachers are taught to use a variation of this program intended for teachers, there is little rigorous research so far to indicate whether or not it is effective.

Parent Training Programs for Parents of
Aggressive Children

The most elaborated and carefully researched program in parent training has been developed by Patterson and his associates to deal with families with aggressive children (Patterson et al., 1975). For more than 10 years, Patterson has been developing, testing, and revising methods of training parents to decrease their children's aggressiveness and increase their cooperative and prosocial behaviors. Patterson's program is instructive not only because of its well-documented success, but also because it provides a great deal of information about the types of problems and obstacles that are likely to be encountered in developing and implementing an effective parent education program.

The program involves teaching parents how to apply effective behavior management procedures to modify their children's behavior. Parents are taught how to use positive reinforcement, punishment, contracts, negotiation techniques, and other procedures with their children. The parents first complete a book written by Patterson which describes such techniques of parenting and they must pass a test on this book before proceeding to the next phase of the program. Then for several weeks the parents meet in small groups with a therapist who trains them in the use of discipline and communication methods. Training includes modeling of techniques, role playing, homework assignments, verbal instructions, and discussion and analysis of problems encountered by the parents in implementing the procedures. In some cases in which parents are having difficulty applying the procedures, the therapist will visit the home and provide further consultation and training. Following the termination of the training program, the therapist continues to provide consultation services by telephone to the parents for several months. At all phases, the effectiveness of the program is evaluated by trained observers who periodically visit the family's home and record the child's behavior and the parents' behavior; parental records of the child's behavior are also obtained.

The results show that in about two-thirds of the cases in which the parents complete the program there is a significant reduction in the child's aggressive behaviors, and this improvement is maintained for 1 year after the termination of the training phase of the program. This result is particularly significant because of research indicating that aggression in children is highly likely to persist unless treatment is instituted.

Patterson's research and other related research on parenting programs with disturbed children have yielded a number of findings concerning the problems of developing and operating an effective parent training program.

1. Having parents read a book or listen to lectures about effective parenting, *in itself*, appears to have little lasting impact on parental behavior in most cases. Patterson found that most parents, after reading his book on parenting, were not able to successfully apply these procedures to alter their children's aggressiveness. Several weeks of parent training, in addition to reading the book, were necessary to produce significant change in the parents and children. For instance, Patterson found that in teaching parents how to use social reinforcement (e.g., praise) effectively with children, it was not sufficient just to tell them what to do. Effective instruc-

tion required demonstrating social reinforcement procedures and giving the parents supervised practice in applying this technique.

The ineffectiveness of books, lectures, and other didactic materials as methods of parent training has been noted also in programs for parents in disadvantaged families (Bronfennbrenner, 1974) and parents of disturbed children (Gelfand & Hartman, 1977).

2. Problems of parent attendance, motivation, and cooperation are likely to be encountered. In one study with parents of children referred for stealing, Patterson found that for only 5 of the 27 families referred did the parents keep their appointments. In dealing with this problem, Patterson found that it was necessary to incorporate incentives and prods in order to increase parental cooperation—e.g., making daily phone calls to the parents or threatening to refer the children back to juvenile authorities if the parents did not cooperate. Problems of parents failing to keep appointments or carry out assignments were frequent in Patterson's studies and have also been a problem in many other parent training programs (e.g., Karnes, 1969).

3. Programs which work well with one type of problem behavior may not work very well with other types of problems. For instance, in a study of the effectiveness of parent counseling as a method of dealing with behavior disorders in children, it was found that a program which worked very well with parents in low-income families was not at all effective with parents in upper-income families (Love & Kaswan, 1974). Patterson's program was much less successful with children referred for stealing than with children referred for aggressiveness (but no stealing), since the parents of the children who stole were generally less cooperative. However, Patterson was eventually able to modify and adapt his program so as to be more successful with the families in which children stole.

4. For a parent training program to be effective, it is often necessary for the therapist or teacher to improvise in adapting the program to individual cases. Patterson found that it was not possible to develop a completely standardized packaged parent training program that would in itself work effectively with the majority of families. In addition to presenting the standardized program, the therapists often found it necessary to develop innovative procedures to deal with individual problems that arose. Patterson and associates (Patterson et al., 1975) have emphasized the need for therapists in parent training to have a very thorough understanding of behavior management principles in order to be able to flexibly and innovatively apply these procedures in unique situations.

5. Despite all attempts at success, programs will not be effective with many individuals. In about one-third of the families participating in Patterson's program, there was no significant or lasting improvement in the

children. In some cases it was clear that the parents failed to apply correctly the procedures. In other cases, the source of the failure was not clear. Programs which claim to almost always be effective are likely to be those that have not been carefully evaluated.

6. The fact that parents *believe* that a program is effective does not mean that it *is* effective. Parents have been found to sometimes describe a program as being very effective and worthwhile, even though the program was not having any significant impact on their ability to deal effectively with their child. For example, Walter and Gilmore (1973) compared the effectiveness of Patterson's social learning program with a program in which parents met for several weeks in "leaderless discussion groups." The parents in both Patterson's program and the leaderless discussion group program reported that they felt very confident that the programs were worthwhile and effective in helping them to deal with their children's aggressiveness. The observations of the children in these two groups by trained observers, however, indicated that only the children of parents in Patterson's program showed any significant improvement in behavior during the program. The children of the parents in the leaderless discussion groups actually showed a slight increase in their aggressiveness during the time the parents were in the program. Studies such as this emphasize the need for evaluations of parenting programs to be based on information in addition to the parent's feelings about the program. Preferably, direct observation of the children's behavior should be carried out.

7. Parents often fail to generalize the techniques they learn to new problems or situations different from those that they are specifically taught to deal with.

These observations underscore the fact that a great deal of organization and skill are required to develop and implement an effective program, and that even an effective program will be limited in its successes. It obviously is not easy to change parental behavior.

A number of other programs for parents of disordered or aggressive children have been developed in recent years, and many of these programs have achieved significant degrees of success. The reader is referred to an excellent review by Gelfand and Hartmann (1977) for a review of these studies.

Parent Intervention with Disadvantaged Families

Since 1964 there have been several early childhood intervention programs which have attempted to educate or train parents of disadvantaged children in methods of promoting cognitive development. Evaluation of these programs indicates that parent education not only can be an effective strategy, but may be a *necessary* step if any lasting improvement in the child's functioning is to be attained. In a review of early intervention programs, Bronfenbrenner concluded:

> The evidence indicates . . . that the involvement of the child's family as an active participant is critical to the success of any intervention program. Without such family involvement, any effects of intervention, at least in the cognitive sphere, appear to erode fairly rapidly once the program ends. In contrast, the involvement of the parents as partners in the enterprise provides an ongoing system which can reinforce the effects of the program while it is in operation and help to sustain them after the program ends [p. 55].

There are several reviews available of these programs (Bronfenbrenner, 1974; Dudzinski & Peters, 1977; Honig, 1975; Horowitz & Paden, 1973; Peters, 1977). This review will focus on what appear to be the essential components of the more effective parent intervention programs—the methods used, the content of the programs, the amount of time, effort, and expense involved, and the problems confronted.

Karnes (1969, 1970) has developed a successful parent intervention program which has been used with mothers of 1-2-year-old and 4-year-old children in disadvantaged families. The program with 1-2-year-olds involved 7 months of training when the children were 1 year of age and 8 months of training when the children were 2 years of age. The disadvantaged mothers, who volunteered for the program, were paid $1.50 per hour to come to weekly 2-hour meetings. The meetings consisted of demonstrations of educational toys for the mothers' use with their children and discussions of child rearing. The demonstrations and discussions emphasized the importance of several aspects of parent–child interaction: mutual mother–child respect; taking a positive approach to teaching and interacting with the child; breaking complex tasks into steps; avoiding scolding, begging, or bribing. In addition to the weekly group meetings, the teachers made monthly home visits in which they pursued similar educational goals with the mothers. Throughout the program, the emphasis was on the mothers assuming responsibility for promoting the child's cognitive development. At the end of the 2-year program, the children of the parents who had been in the program showed a 16-point IQ advantage over a comparable group of children whose parents had not been involved; also, the treatment children showed a 28-point IQ advantage over their siblings. A similar program had beneficial effects on the cognitive development of 4-year-old disadvantaged children.

Although Karnes has generally found the parents in these programs to be cooperative and conscientious, he has in some programs experienced problems in obtaining parent cooperation, even though his parents are volunteers, are paid for attendence, and are given transportation to meetings. In a program in which 4-year-old children were enrolled in a compensatory preschool program *and* the mothers were involved in a parent intervention program, Karnes (1969) reported that only 50% of the mothers were in attendance at the weekly meetings and one-fourth of the mothers essentially dropped out of the program. In analyzing the difficulties experienced in the parent intervention component of the program, Karnes suggested that the teachers in this study may have unwittingly relegated the mothers to a secondary role in the program. Bronfenbrenner (1974) has suggested that the more successful parent intervention programs have emphasized the need for the mother to be treated as a colleague and as the primary agent responsible for the child's intellectual development.

Levenstein developed a succesful parent intervention program which also emphasized the importance of the parent assuming primary responsibility for the child's cognitive development (Levenstein, 1970, Levenstein, Kochman, & Roth, 1973; Levenstein & Levenstein, 1971). This program is particularly significant because the beneficial effects of the program have been observed to persist for 3–4 years after its termination. Levenstein's program involves home visits by teachers who demonstrate to disadvantaged mothers methods of verbal interaction which will promote children's cognitive growth. The teachers, referred to as "toy demonstrators," show the mothers appropriate verbal interaction behaviors in teaching their children to use toys designed to promote intellectual development. In demonstrating to the mother how to use the toys, the demonstrator models several verbal behaviors: providing information, discussing her own toy manipulations, verbally describing the social interaction, encouraging reflective thinking by the child, encouraging independence and curiosity, engaging interest in books, and giving positive reinforcement. The teachers treat the mothers as colleagues in the enterprise and take a secondary role to the mothers as soon as possible.

Children aged 2–3 who participated in weekly sessions over a 7-month period showed a 15-point IQ advantage over control children whose mothers were not involved in the program; furthermore, they maintained this relative advantage 3–4 years after termination of the program. Levenstein (1970) has commented upon "the continued cooperation and enthusiam" of almost all the mothers in keeping appointments, and carrying out toy demonstrations and other responsibilities.

Studies comparing the effects of preschool programs with and without supplementary parent intervention programs have generally (with some exceptions) found that parent involvement increases the effectiveness of the program (Bronfenbrenner, 1974).

"Washout" Effects in Early
Intervention Programs

Despite the reported successes of programs such as those described above, there remain serious doubts as to the long-term effectiveness of parent and preschool intervention programs with disadvantaged children. Almost all early intervention programs show a "washout" effect, such that after termination of the program, the beneficial effects gradually fade out. This same effect is also observed in most treatment programs for behaviorally disordered children (Gelfand & Hartmann, 1977). Although the positive effects of Levenstein's preschool program lasted 3–4 years beyond the termination of the program, the children were still only 5–6 years of age at that time. This is significant because most of the washout effects observed in early intervention programs have occurred between kindergarten and third grade. The Follow Through programs were designed to try to overcome this deterioration effect by providing continuing intervention through the third grade. However, a recent review of 17 different types of Follow Through programs, including several which involved parent intervention as well as special school programs, has yielded discouraging results (Moore, 1978). On most of the measures of cognitive development, disadvantaged children in the Follow Through programs did not do any better than disadvantaged children not in the Follow Through programs. Furthermore, the model that produced the most positive effect was a model that stressed "individual and classroom drill on basic skills" (Anderson, 1977, cited in Moore, 1978, p. 53). In this preliminary report of the Follow Through program, there is as yet no specific assessment of the effects of parent involvement, so these conclusions do not show that parent intervention is ineffective. However, results such as this do underscore the fact that there are many unresolved questions concerning the long-term impact that intervention programs have on children's cognitive development.

CONCLUDING COMMENTS

There are a number of ways in which information concerning both competent and less than competent children and the child rearing practices of their parents may be useful to educators and parents. Knowledge of the parenting practices of highly competent children may suggest procedures which both teachers and parents would find useful in disciplining and teaching young children. For example, the "authoritative" model of discipline which Baumrind (1967, 1971) found among parents of highly competent children may be effective for both parents and teachers. The responsive pattern of parenting observed in the homes of very competent children may also provide a useful model for many aspects of teacher–child relationship. Information concerning the characteristics of highly capable children may help parents and educators in selecting appropriate educational goals for children at various age levels. For those concerned with counseling families of children experiencing behavioral problems or cognitive deficits, knowledge of effective parenting should not only help in understanding the source of some problems of this type but should also provide direction in developing an effective treatment program.

Very competent parents may well constitute an underutilized resource in early education. Numerous research studies have shown that one of the most efficient ways to learn is through the observation of competent models. Seeking out successful parents and using them as models and teacher aides in training other parents or in helping to educate children may well be an effective educational strategy. The succesful parent may also be an excellent candidate for employment as a teacher in early intervention programs or day care programs. Bereiter and Engelmann (1966), for instance, in developing their effective preschool program for disadvantaged children, reported that the most capable and easily trainable teachers for their program were parents who had demonstrated skill in raising their own children.

Many parent training and education programs have been developed to deal with the problems of families with children who show behavioral excesses or cognitive deficits. Unfortunately, some of the parenting programs in widespread use are relatively untested and unevaluated—no one has a very good idea of whether they are helpful, harmless, or harmful. Of the parenting programs which have been evaluated, some have clearly been very effective. However, these effective programs have generally been complex, time consuming, and costly, and have required a high degree of organization and expertise. There is little evidence that simply providing information to parents in the form of books, lectures, or brief workshops will in itself lead to a significant change in parental behavior. It appears at least as difficult to change parental behavior as it is to change child behavior. Nonetheless, a number of programs have been effective, and if we are to be successful in modifying many problems and deficits in children it would appear to be necessary to expend the time and effort necessary to develop and implement such programs.

REFERENCES

Achenbach, T. M. Behavior disorders in children. In H. Hom & P. Robinson (Eds), *Psychological processes in early education.* New York: Academic Press, 1977.

Anderson, R. B. The effectiveness of Follow Through; what have we learned? Paper presented at the meeting of the American Educational Research Association, New York, April, 1977. Cited in Moore (1978).

Bakan, D. *Slaughter of the innocents*. San Francisco: Jossey Bass, 1971.

Bandura, A. *Aggression: A social learning analysis*. Englewood Cliffs, N.J.: Prentice-Hall, 1973.

Bandura, A., & Walters, R. H. *Adolescent aggression*. New York: Ronald Press, 1959.

Baumrind, D. Child care practices anteceding three patterns of preschool behavior. *Genetic Psychology Monographs*, 1967, 75, 43–83.

Baumrind, D. Current patterns of parental authority. *Developmental Psychology Monographs*, 1971, 4 (1).

Becker, W. C. Consequences of different kinds of parental discipline. In. M. L. Hoffman & L. W. Hoffman (Eds.), *Review of child development research* (Vol. 1). New York: Russell Sacc Foundation, 1964.

Bell, R. Q. A reinterpretation of the direction of effects in studies of socialization *Psychological Review*, 1968, 75, 81–95.

Bereiter, C., & Engelmann, S. *Teaching the culturally disadvantaged child in the preschool*. Englewood Cliffs, N.J.: Prentice-Hall, 1966.

Brofenbrenner, V. *Is early education effective?* Washington, D.C.: DHEW Publication No. OHD 74–75, 1974.

Clarke-Steward, A. *Child care in the family: A review of research and some propositions for policy*. New York: Academic Press, 1977.

Conger, J. J. *Adolescence and youth: Psychological development in a changing world*. New York: Harper & Row, 1978.

Dion, K. K. Children's physical attractiveness and sex as determinants of adult punitiveness. *Developmental Psychology*, 1974, 10, 772–778.

Dudzinski, D., & Peters, D. L. Home-based programs: A growing alternative. *Child Care Quarterly*, 1977, 6, 61–71.

Elder, G. J., Jr. *Adolescent socialization and personality development*. Chicago: Rand McNally, 1971.

Gelfand, D. M., & Hartman, D. P. The prevention of childhood behavior disorders. In B. B. Cahoy & A. E. Kazdin (Eds.), *Advances in clinical child psychology* (Vol. 1). New York: Plenum Press, 1977.

Gordon, T. *P.E.T. Parent effectiveness training*. New York: Plume, 1975.

Hallworth, H. J., Davis, H., & Gampton, C. Some adolescent perceptions of adolescent personality. *Journal of Social and Clinical Psychology*, 1965, 4, 81–91.

Hess, R. D., & Shipman, V. C. Early experience and the socialization of cognitive modes in children. *Child Development*, 1965, 36, 869–888.

Hetherington, E. M. Children of divorce. Paper presented at the biannual meeting of the Society for Research in Child Development, 1975. Cited in Parke (1977).

Hetherington, E. M., & Parke, R. D. *Child psychology: A contemporary viewpoint*. New York McGraw-Hill, 1975.

Honig, A. S. *Parent involvement in early childhood education*. Washington, D.C.: National Association for the Education of Young Children, 1975.

Horowitz, F. D., & Paden, L. Y. The effectiveness of environmental interaction programs. In B. M. Caldwell & N. H. Ricciuti (Eds.), *Review of child development research* (Vol. 3). Chicago: University of Chicago Press, 1973.

Karnes, M. B. *Research and development program on preschool disadvantaged children: Final report*. Washington, D.C.: U.S. Office of Education, 1969.

Karnes, M. B., Teska, J. A., Hodgins, S. A., & Badger, I. D. Educational intervention at home by mothers of disadvantaged infants. *Child Development*, 1970, 41, 925–935.

Jones, M. C., & Bayley, N. Physical maturing among boys as related to behavior. *Journal of Educational Psychology*, 1950, *41*, 129–148.

Levenstein, P. Cognitive growth in preschoolers through verbal interaction of mothers. *American Journal of Orthopsychiatry*, 1970, *40*, 426–432.

Levenstein, P., & Levenstein, S. Fostering Learning potential in preschoolers. *Social Casework*, 1971, *52*, 74–78.

Levenstein, P., Kochman, A., & Roth, H. A. From laboratory to real world: Service delivery of the mother-child home program. *American Journal of Ortho-psychiatry*, 1973, *43*, 72–78.

Light, R. Abuse and neglected children in America: A study of alternative policies. *Harvard Educational Review*, 1973, *43*, 556–598.

Love, L. R., & Kaswan, J. W. *Troubled children: Their families, schools, and treatments.* New York: Wiley, 1974.

Martin, B. Parent-child relations. In F. D. Horowitz (Ed.), *Review of child development research* (Vol. 4). Chicago: University of Chicago Press, 1975. Pp. 463–540.

Madsen, C. H., Jr., & Madsen, C. I. *Teaching discipline: A positive approach to educational development.* Boston: Allyn & Bacon, 1974.

Moore, S. G. The Abt report of Follow Through: Critique and comment. *Young Children*, 1978, *33*, 52–56.

Nelson, K. Structure and strategy in learning to talk. *Monographs of the Society for Research in Child Development*, 1973, *38* (149).

Parke, R. D. Effectiveness of punishment as an interaction of intensity, timing, agent, and cognitive structuring. *Child Development*, 1969, *40*, 213–236.

Parke, R. D. Punishment in children: Effects, side effects, and alternative strategies. In H. Hom & P. Robinson (Eds.), *Psychological processes in early education.* New York: Academic Press, 1977.

Parke, R. D., & Collmer, C. W. *Child Abuse: An interdisciplinary analysis.* Chicago: University of Chicago Press, 1975.

Patterson, G. R., Reid, J. B., Jones, R. R., & Conger, R. E. *A social learning approach to family intervention* (Vol 1). *Families with aggressive children.* Eugene, Oregon: Castelia, 1975.

Peters, D. L. *Early childhood education: An overview and evaluation.* In H. Hom & P. Robinson (Eds.), *Psychological processes in early education.* New York: Academic Press, 1977.

Robins, L. N. *Deviant children grow up: A sociological and psychiatric study of sociopathic personality.* Baltimore: Williams & Wilkins, 1966.

Sears, R. R., Maccoby, E. E., & Levin, H. *Patterns of child rearing.* Evanston, Ill.: Row Peterson, 1957.

Streissguth, D. P., & Bee, H. L. Mother-child interaction and cognitive development in children. In W. W. Hartup (Ed.), *The young child: reviews of research.* Washington, D.C.: National Association for the Education of Young Children, 1972.

Terman, L. M. The discover and encouragement of exceptional latent. *American Psychologist*, 1954, *9*, 221–230.

Thomas, A., Chess, S., & Birch, H. G. *Temperament and behavior disorders in children.* New York: New York University Press, 1968.

Walter, H. I., & Gilmore, S. K. Placebo versus social learning effects in parental training procedures designed to alter the behaviors of aggressive boys. *Behavior Therapy*, 1973, *4*, 361–377.

White, B. L., & Watts, J. C. *Experience and environment: Major influences on the development of the young child* (Vol. 1). Englewood Cliffs, N.J.: Prentice-Hall, 1973.

Young, L. *Wednesday's children: A study of child neglect and abuse.* New York: McGraw-Hill, 1964.

CHAPTER 6

Research and the Teacher: Teacher Effectiveness in Early Childhood Education

SYLVESTER KOHUT, JR.

GUIDELINES FOR RESEARCH METHODOLOGY AND INVESTIGATION

What are the distinguishing characteristics of a competent teacher? What personality traits are most appropriate for identifying effective teachers for preschool and primary grade pupils? What teacher behaviors are most important in creating a classroom climate which maximizes learning opportunities for pupils enrolled in early childhood programs? What basically is effective teaching? While educational researchers and early childhood practitioners grapple with these questions and often provide speculative responses to these provocative and crucial queries, in fact, there is a definite lag in the development of empirical data for evaluating teacher influence and effectiveness in classroom and learning environments.

Teacher effectiveness is an ambiguous concept, for although most educators have an idea of the "model" teacher, this image is often based on "expert opinion" or a *Reader's Digest* approach to the survey of research literature rather than relying on legitimate descriptive, casual-comparative, correlational, or experimental research findings. The issue is compounded among early childhood enthusiasts for unlike intermediate, junior, middle, or senior high school pupils, the preschool or primary

ASPECTS OF EARLY CHILDHOOD EDUCATION
Theory to Research to Practice

grade pupil often lacks the maturity or understanding to participate in sophisticated studies requiring the completion of complex written or orally administered questionnaires or the respondent-type written research instruments which in some manner attempt to measure teacher effectiveness or teacher characteristics and behavior associated with successful teaching and learning in early childhood programs.

Furthermore, there are marked differences of opinion among educators in basic and higher education concerning the major factors which reflect or relate effective classroom teaching. Beller (1969), in an analysis of the teaching process, distinguishes between teaching style and the technique of teaching. Technique of teaching relates to methods and strategies used by a teacher to accomplish learning goals and tasks. Teaching style refers to the personality traits and characteristics, attitudes, and feelings which interplay with the specific teaching methods and strategies implemented by the teacher. For illustration, a teacher in an early childhood classroom may instruct large or small groups of children or may concentrate working on a one-to-one basis. But at the same time, regardless of the teaching technique, the teacher's style of teaching might be relaxed or tense, cold or warm, sensitive or insensitive. In reviewing research related to effective teaching it is difficult to separate teacher method from teaching style. As more and more variables are accounted for or controlled by the aspiring researcher during the research process, consequently, many more qualifying statements must be incorporated in any final series of recommendations. The results of such research efforts are interesting but very difficult to generalize beyond the immediate sample or population participating in the study.

Ryans (1960), in his Teacher Characteristics Study (TCS) concluded that a person's concept of a good teacher seems to depend on (a) his or her acculturation, that is, his or her past experience and the attitudes he or she has come to accept, (b) the aspects of teaching which may be foremost in the consideration at a given time, and (c) characteristics of pupils taught. According to Ryans (1960), trying to describe effective teachers involves the social or cultural group in which the teacher operates, the grade level and discipline taught, and the intellectual and personal characteristics of the pupils taught by the teacher.

Insufficient data or conflicting research findings should not negate the importance of reviewing all available research regarding teacher effectiveness and influence in early childhood education programming. It is of paramount importance that educators understand the role of the teacher in the early childhood classroom and the numerous implications for the preservice and in-service training for early childhood administrators, teachers and paraprofessionals. Sandefur (1970 p.3), comments that evaluating teacher effectiveness has been the most difficult of all problems confronting the educational community. Very little has been done in this unexplored field. Varying opinions among authorities as to what really constitutes effective or competent teaching has hampered the development of instruments designed to uniformly assess the behaviors of teachers and the resulting outcomes and consequences.

Peck and Tucker (1971, 1973) identified six major themes regarding research related to teacher education during the period 1955–1971.

1. A systems approach to teacher education, often called instructional design, substantially improves its effectiveness. A great deal of research is clustered around three central themes—training teachers in interaction analysis, microteaching, and behavior modification.

2. Teacher educators should attempt to serve as role models for teacher candidates and in-service teachers. When teachers are treated in the same manner they are supposed to treat their pupils, they are more likely to adopt the desired style of teacher behavior.

3. Direct involvement such as clinical and field based experiences, sensitivity training laboratories and classroom simulations are more likely to produce the desired teaching behaviors in teacher candidates than remote or abstract experiences such as lectures on instructional strategies and methodology.

4. Using a variety of techniques, it is possible to induce a more self-initiated self-directed, effective pattern of learning, not only in teachers but, through them, in their pupils.

5. Traditional ways of training teachers have some intended effects but they also have some quite undesired effects.

6. The use of pupil-gain measures as the ultimate criterion of the effectiveness of any given process of teacher education is common [pp. 7–8].[1]

In proposing a model for evaluating teacher education graduates, Sandefur (1970) states that there is a growing conviction that evaluation of teacher effectiveness, in the final analysis, must rest upon the criterion of "pupil's gain," that is, evidence that the learner has achieved in some measure the intended objectives established by the teacher. As desirable as pupil-gain measures may be, they are according to Sandefur (1970) extremely elusive. In discussing pupil-gain measures, Herbert (1971) has written:

While we should do more and better research on which teacher behaviors result in changes in pupil behaviors, it is not expedient to evaluate teacher preparation programs by such changes in the schools where the teachers find employment.

---

[1] Reprinted by permission from Peck, Robert F. and Tucker, James A., "Research on Teacher Education," in Robert M. W. Travers, ed., *Second Handbook of Research on Teaching* (Chicago: Rand McNally College Publishing Company, 1973).

Combinations of variables—the school and home environment of the pupils and the decisions of the teachers's peers and administrators—may result in him being in a position where, regardless of training received or criteria used, he either cannot fail or cannot succeed. It would thus be more reasonable to evaluate a teacher preparation program by the ways pupils learn in the classroom of graduates than to evaluate a program of medical training by the health of the population its graduates serve. Therefore, though it is theoretically attractive to relate pupil behavior to accreditation, this seems unlikely to be feasible in the foreseeable future [pp. 4–5].

Another way of gathering data on the particular behaviors of teachers is to ask those who are in a position to know such as teaching colleagues, pupils, administrators, and supervisors. Keeping in mind the difficulty of administering special instruments to preschool and primary grade pupils, rating scales have been widely used in research on teaching and teacher effectiveness in the classroom. Remmers (1963) has written the following concerning rating scales:

Note that the measuring device is not the paper form but rather the individual rater. Hence a rating scale differs in important respects from other paper and pencil devices. In addition to any limitations by the characteristics of the human rater—his inevitably selective perception, memory, and forgetting, his lack of sensitivity, his inaccuracies of observation and, in the case of self-ratings, the well-established tendency to put his best foot forward, to perceive himself in a more favorable perspective than others do [p. 329].[2]

Remmers (1963), reporting on research conducted since 1927 on pupil ratings of teachers, provides the following conclusions:

1. Grades of students have little relationship to their ratings of the instructors who assigned the grades.

2. After 10 years, alumni ratings correlate highly (.92) with on-campus student ratings for college instructors.

3. Evidence indicates that students discriminate reliably among different aspects of the teacher's personality and the actual course.

4. Little relationship exists between the student's rating of the teacher and the difficulty of the course as perceived by the student.

5. The sex of the student bears little relationship to the actual rating.

6. Popularity of the teacher in extraclass activities is not appreciably related to student ratings of the teacher.

7. Teachers with less that 5 years experience tend to be rated lower than teachers with more than 8 years experience.

8. The sex of the teacher is generally unrelated to the pupil ratings [pp. 367–368].

[2] This and the following quote are reprinted by permission from Remmers, H. H., "Rating Methods in Research on Teaching," in N. C. Gage, ed., *Handbook of Research on Teaching* (Chicago: Rand McNally College Publishing Company, 1963).

The validity of using pupil ratings to assess teacher behaviors is well established in the research literature. Veldman (1970) conducted research with a rating system called the Pupil Observation Survey Report (POSR). On the 38–item POSR he found through a factor analysis five major dimensions of "space" within which pupils implicitly located their teachers. The five factors were (1) friendly and cheerful, (2) knowledgeable and poised, (3) lively and interesting, (4) firm control (discipline), and (5) nondirective (democratic procedure).

Ryans's (1960) classical Teacher Characteristics Study (TCS) identified three distinct patterns:

> Pattern X—Warm, kindly understanding, friendly versus aloof, egocentric, restricted teacher behavior.
>
> Pattern Y—Responsible, businesslike, systematic versus evading, unplanned slipshod teacher behavior.
>
> Pattern Z—Stimulating, imaginative, surgent versus dull, routine, unimaginative teacher behavior [pp. 86–92].[3]

Veldam (1970) made an effort to determine the extent to which pupil evaluations were related to supervisor evaluations of 609 student teachers. He found a definite relationship between factors 1, 2, and 3 which lends credence not only to Ryans's (1960) three distinct patterns but also to the thesis that supervisors as well as pupils can consistently identify these important teaching behaviors. Ratings from students seem a promising source of data on teaching behavior, but there is evidence that agreement between supervisors and pupils, and even intrasupervisory ratings of teachers have drawbacks. Herbert (1971) reviewing research on supervision/administrative ratings of teachers, concluded that the technique was subject to a number of limitations: (a) procedures and criteria for evaluating teachers vary considerably; (b) evidence on which ratings are based is very meager; (c) the personality of the principal seems to have a substantial effect on ratings of a teacher's ability and social competence; and (d) school district and college supervisors do not seem to agree on their ratings of teachers. Despite the lack of research evidence that peer and supervisory evaluations have validity in assessing teaching behaviors, empirically a case can be presented for systematizing a peer–supervisor rating scale which can be quantified. The fact that little evidence is available which supports such ratings is no doubt largely due to the lack of a commonly acceptable scale which consistently generates data on teaching effectiveness.

According to Sandefur (1970), the use of standardized measures to assess certain personality characteristics which seem desirable in teachers has some precedents. Hundreds of research studies have dealt with personality and teaching effectiveness. The greatest number of these have used basically three personality measures, The Minnesota Teacher Attitude Inventory (MTAI), the California F Scale, and the Minnesota Multiphasic Personality Inventory (MMPI). Getzel and Jackson (1963) comment on the failure of this type of research to produce definitive results:

> Despite the critical importance of the problem and a half-century of prodigious research effort, very little is known for certain about the nature and measurement of teacher personality, or about the relation between teacher personality and teacher effectiveness. The regrettable fact is that many of the studies so far have not produced significant results [p. 574].

The California F Scale is a most useful instrument for teacher personality and teacher effectiveness research. Sheldon, Coale, and Copple (1959), McGee (1955), Hough and Amidon (1965), and others have reported significant relationships between the degree of authoritarianism exhibited and certain teaching behaviors.

Remmers and Gage (1955) submit that in the school environment, attitude scales and inventories can be used to measure pupil attitudes toward school subjects, teacher performance, instructional practices, and special programs. Numerous rating scales for specifically evaluating the performance of the teacher by the pupil have been developed. Nottingham (1970) concludes that in curriculum and instructional research, the investigator is confronted invariably with the problem of assessing the attitude of pupils toward their particular school subject. While many useful instruments exist, he supports the employment of the Semantic Differential as the most effective. The Semantic Differential consists of a number of bipolar adjectives such as "good" and "bad," "strong" and "weak," and "active" and "passive" against which the pupil is asked to judge a particular concept or phrase.

Neale, Gill, and Tismer's (1970) study examined attitudes toward school subjects in a group of sixth graders. Using the Semantic Differential and the scores on corresponding subtests of the SRA achievement series, the researchers found significant positive correlations for male subjects on social studies, arithmetic, and reading, while female subjects showed a significant positive correlation in reading only. They concluded that a pupil's attitude toward a specific school subject is more related to school achievement in that particular subject that the pupil's general attitude toward school.

Dalton's (1962) research related to materials on teacher effectiveness and pupil ratings as a method of measurement indicates that early skepticism has given way to widespread confidence in the ability of pupils to make reliable and valid judgments of teacher performance. Dalton states that educators should accept the inevitability of evaluation, and ensure that is is handled openly and carefully, and capitalize on its findings for the improvement of instruction.

Rosenshine (1971) reported the results of available studies in which teacher behavior was studied in relation to pupil achievement. He did not report educational outcomes other than those associated with pupil achievement. In reviewing Rosenshine's comprehensive report, Flanders (1973) remarks that results from widely different samples of pupils should not be combined into the same group for interpretation; at least one can think preschool, primary, intermediate, and high school as possible boundaries between universes to be sampled. Flanders (1973) suggests that a reviewer of research on teacher effectiveness should decide whether the association being cited or described was or was not a primary topic of the research and communicate this information to his reader. Conducting research related to teacher effectiveness presents many problems involving correlation, a new knowledge of representative samples, problems of replication and research design. Even after the legitimate research effort has been completed, there are many problems involving the interpretation of the data.

With a general understanding of the special problems and research methodology associated with a review of research concerning teacher effectiveness and influence in the classroom, the information included herein is organized into two major sections. Part I includes research studies which emphasize process-product variables of research. Part II reflects investigations which focus on presage-to-process variables research and when applicable link the findings to presage-to-product variables research.

PART I: PROCESS–PRODUCT RESEARCH

In reviewing research related to process–product studies, process refers to the behaviors of teachers in a classroom environment and the resulting product in terms of pupil attitude or achievement which is observable and/or measurable. The underlying assumption of this classification of research reporting is that there is a cause-and-effect relationship between a specific teacher behavior and a specific pupil outcome related to attitude and/or achievement. For example, if a teacher behaves a certain way or exhibits a certain kind of classroom behavior, and as a result of this particular teacher behavior, there is a significant increase in pupil achievement as measured by a standardized test, then it might be possible to generalize and say that the teacher behavior, or process, was responsible for the product, the significant increase in achievement test scores.

The relationship between teacher behavior and pupils' classroom behavior is of paramount importance. Teachers typically structure and control such things as room arrangements, grouping patterns, and material organization, and in instructional situations the teacher's behavior is the most prominent of the interactional factors affecting pupil behavior. In reviewing relevant research, Miller (1975) suggests that various categories of pupil behavior have been shown to be linked directly and indirectly to teacher behavior. Fagot (1973) determined that pupil task behavior is a function of teacher praise, criticism, and direction while Katz, Peters, and Stein (1968) studied pupil task behavior, attention to teacher, cooperation with other pupils, and disruptive behavior as a function of teacher feedback control and nurturance. The program or treatment being implemented is a major factor in the behavior of teachers. Studies by Klein (1973) and Soar and Soar (1972) help substantiate that greater homogeneity of teacher behavior can result from training teachers in model programs. Aspects of teacher behavior such as whether they work with small groups or individuals, how often they elicit performance from pupils and what kind, and how reinforcing they are, have been shown to be largely a function of the program style being implemented according to Miller (1975). Even in early childhood programs which specify behaviors almost word for word, considerable variation in teacher behavior continues to occur as pointed out by Banta (1966) and Siegel and Rosenshine (1973). What accounts for this situation? According to Prescott, Jones, and Kritchevsky (1967) teachers may be affected by ecological factors beyond their control like the physical conditions of the room and the size of the center or complex, or teacher variation may be due to the individual "personality" characteristics of the teacher. This is a critical consideration, for as Mischel (1973) discusses, personality traits have been shown to be quite sensitive to situational variation.

Medley's Review of Teacher Competence-Effectiveness

Medley (1977) in his comprehensive review of process–product research related to teacher competence and teacher effectiveness reviewed 289 studies which purported to respond to the question, "How does the behavior of effective teachers differ from that of ineffective teachers?" The studies examined empirically obtained relationships between how a teacher behaves and how much the pupils learn from him. This kind of research is

commonly called process–product research. Medley (1977) used the following four criteria in determining studies worthy of further investigation:

> 1. The study from which a relationship came had to be designed so that the rela-
> tionship was generalizable to some population of teachers larger than the sample
> studied.
> 2. The relationship had to be reliable enough to be practically significant.
> 3. The measure of teacher effectiveness had to be based on long-term pupil gains
> in achievement areas recognized as important goals of education.
> 4. The process measure had to specify the behaviors exhibited in such a way
> that they could be reproduced as desired [p.5].

After application of the four strict criteria, Medley (1977) reduced the
number of studies meeting all four criteria to 14 basic process–product
studies. In almost all cases the achievement dimension in terms of pupil
gain scores related to improvement in reading and/or arithmetic. He
organized the findings into three major categories: The Competent Teacher
of Low Socio-Economic Status (SES) Pupils, Teacher Competence and
Pupil SES in the Primary Grades, and Competent Teacher Behavior in the
Elementary Grades.

The Competent Teacher of Low SES Pupils

In this category the differences between the behavior of teachers of low
SES pupils whose classes show high mean gains on achievement tests of
arithmetic, reading, or both, and the behaviors of teachers of low SES
pupils whose classes show low mean gains in arithmetic and/or reading are
compared.

Time Utilization. According to Soar (1973), the effective teacher of low
SES pupils in the third grade or below differs from the ineffective teacher in
devoting much more class time to task related or "academic" activities.
Harris, Morrison, Serwer, and Gold (1968) and Stallings and Kaskowitz
(1974) reported more reading related activities in classes of more effective
teachers. The amount of arithmetic activity and involvement according to
Harris *et al.* (1968) was found to be higher in classes taught by effective
teachers, and the frequency of teaching operational skills was reported
greater for the effective teachers by McDonald and Elias (1976).

Stallings and Kaskowitz (1974) found that the number of teacher questions asked and/or pupil responses made was higher in the effective
teachers' classrooms. However, Brophy and Evertson (1974) reported that
the proportion of opportunities a pupil had to respond per unit of time in
arithmetic lessons was lower in effective teachers' classrooms. Data indicate that even though the total amount of task related activities is higher
in the more effective teachers' classrooms, the distribution of such activities

between teacher questions and other task related activities may also be very important. Harris *et al.* (1968) and Coker, Lorentz, and Coker (1976), in separate studies, confirmed that the more effective teachers spend less class time discussing matters unrelated to lesson content and objectives.

Organization of Lessons. Effective and ineffective teachers of low SES pupils also differ in how they usually organize their classrooms. The less effective teachers usually spend more time working with pupils in small groups and less time working with the entire class or a large group of pupils. In separate studies, Stallings and Kaskowitz (1974) and McDonald and Elias (1976) concluded that effective teachers of low SES pupils spend much more time working in large groups than working with small groups. The amount of time pupils spend working independently in small groups as reported by Soar (1973) and Stallings and Kaskowitz (1974) is consistently lower in classes where achievement gain scores are high. The situation is similar in terms of seatwork as substantiated in investigations by McDonald and Elias (1976), Coker *et al.* (1976), Soar (1973), and Stallings and Kaskowitz (1974). Most teacher candidates enrolled in early childhood education programs are inundated with information which emphasizes the need for one-to-one contact with both low and high SES pupils. In terms of pupil achievement as measured by gain scores in reading and arithmetic, research would challenge this undue emphasis on one-to-one or small group instruction for low SES pupils.

There is evidence that the amount of time pupils spend in small groups without a teacher or adult present is related to their attitudes toward school. It appears that teachers who permit the least amount of individual and small group work have the greatest gains in achievement and get varied results in terms of attitudes toward school. When the individual or group is described as working independently, attitudes toward school are high according to Stallings and Kaskowitz (1974).

Qualitative Factors Related to Instruction. What kinds of questions and what ways of responding to pupils distinguish the more effective teacher of low SES pupils from the less effective teacher? There is evidence from Soar and Soar (1972), Soar (1973), Coker *et al.* (1976), and Stallings and Kaskowitz (1976) that effective teachers of low SES pupils ask more questions classifiable in the lower levels of Bloom's Taxonomy than ineffective teachers. There are also some data that effective teachers ask fewer high-level questions according to Soar and Soar (1972) and Soar (1973).

The patterns of teacher reactions to pupil responses are varied and often complex, although there are findings from Perham (1973) and Brophy and Evertson (1974) which indicate that the effective teacher of low SES pupils is less likely to be observed amplifying, discussing, or using pupil answers than the ineffective teacher. Since high-level questions requiring analysis, synthesis and evaluation, or judgment are usually associated with amplification and discussion or pupil responses, the findings are consistent for effective teacher preference for using low-level questions with low SES pupils.

According to Coker, et al. (1976) and Stallings and Kaskowitz (1976), the number of pupil-initiated questions and comments also tends to be lower in classes taught by effective teachers compared to those classes taught by ineffective or less effective teachers. Effective teachers seem to treat pupil initiated questions and comments differently than ineffective teachers. Effective teachers are less likely to listen and provide feedback to pupils or to solicit questions from the pupils in comparison to the ineffective teachers. Competent teachers of low SES pupils keep interaction at a low level of complexity. The effective teacher does not encourage pupils to engage in higher order questioning and commentary. There is an ever present strict adherence to narrow questions asked by the effective teacher of low SES pupils. If the sole criterion is the gain scores for low SES pupils in arithmetic and reading, the effective teacher tends not to encourage such pupils to express their ideas openly or to engage in lengthy discussions and conversations.

Environmental Factors. There is usually less deviant behavior or disruptive behavior in classes taught by effective teachers than in classes taught by ineffective teachers according to Bemis and Luft (1970), McDonald and Elias (1976) and Brophy and Evertson (1974). In analyzing teacher rebukes, Coker et al. (1976) and Harris and Serwer (1966) concluded that such behavior was less frequent in classrooms of more effective teachers. Studies by Brophy and Evertson (1974) and Harris and Serwer (1966) suppport the conclusion that effective teachers devote less time to managing their classrooms than ineffective teachers. Effective teachers also differ from less effective teachers in terms of the quality of the control they demonstrate in the classrooms for the effective teachers use less criticism and use more varied repertory of techniques in maintaining control and order according to Coker, et al. (1976). In three studies, Stallings and Kaskowitz (1974), Harris and Serwer (1966), and Brophy and Evertson (1974) found that effective teachers use more praise and positive reinforcement and motivation. Permissive behavior like giving pupils freedom to govern their own activities was consistently found to be more common in the classroom of the less effective teachers according to Soar (1973) and Brophy and Evertson (1974). There is evidence from the Coker et al. (1976) study that pupil attitudes are more favorable toward school in the more orderly classroom maintained by the effective teachers. Therefore, it is possible to maintain an orderly classroom and still help stimulate a positive attitude in pupils toward the formal schooling process.

Small Group and One-to-One Encounters. It may appear perplexing from previously cited studies to agree that an effective teacher would spend less time working in small groups and supervising independent study with low SES pupils when compared to the less effective teacher. Effective teachers' pupils do spend some time working in small groups and independent seatwork. It is the quality of the contact time during the small group or independent study activity that distinguishes the effective teacher from the ineffective teacher. Effective teachers tend to spend much more time checking on the progress of their pupils during periods of independent study or activity. Effective teachers actually spend more time in one-to-one encounters with their pupils than the less effective teachers. Investigations by McDonald and Elias (1976) and Brophy and Evertson (1974) support this "quality of time" interpretation and amount of one-to-one contact approach to assessing teacher interaction with low SES pupils.

When effective teachers talk to their pupils there is a marked tendency for the teachers to pay closer attention to their pupils according to Brophy and Evertson (1974). These studies indicate that when the effective teacher's pupils work independently, the teacher actively supervises them and gives careful attention to those pupils seeking or needing special help. The ineffective teacher who assigns seatwork tends to leave the pupils with little or no direct support and any pupil who needs special assistance must often take the initiative in getting the teacher's attention. In a manner, the ineffective teacher tends to give "busywork" rather than supervised seatwork. This is why the quality of the contact time is more important than the length or quantity of contact time when assessing the impact of seatwork or small group activities in the early childhood classroom.

Teacher Competence and Pupil SES in the Primary Grades

If the teacher's patterns of classroom behavior are effective with low SES pupils in the primary grades, are the same or similar patterns of teacher behavior just as effective in classes with high SES pupils? The research data directed to this question are sketchy. From his extensive review of available legitimate research, Medley (1977) concludes that in terms of process–product research findings what is successful or effective with low SES pupils is often less effective in classrooms with high SES pupils (p. 15).

Verbal Bahaviors. Based on the findings of Bemis and Luft (1970), effective teachers in high SES classes are most likely to use one of the following two questioning patterns: (1) to identify the pupil who is to answer a question before asking it, or (2) to ask a question and then call on a pupil who indicates a desire to answer the question. Some effective teachers in low SES classes are most likely to use a third approach, and this is to ask a question first, and then choose a respondent who probably has not indicated a desire to answer the question. In a high SES class taught by an effective teacher, the pupil is more likely to answer incorrectly than a pupil in a low SES class taught by an effective teacher. After the pupil has answered, the effective teacher in the high SES class is more likely to discuss the pupil's response than the teacher in the low SES class, unless the pupil's answer is incorrect. If the pupil's answer is incorrect, the effective teacher in the high SES class is more likely either to criticize the pupil's response or to answer the question personally than the effective teacher in the low SES classroom. In the case of a pupil failing to answer a question, the effective teacher in the high SES class is less likely to give the pupil another chance to react, by repeating or rephrasing the original question or posing a new question, compared to the effective teacher in the low SES classroom. What happens if the pupil merely indicated that he does not know the answer? The effective teacher in the high SES pupil class is more likely to call on another pupil than the effective teacher in the low SES pupil class (pp. 18–19).

In attempting to summarize the Bemis and Luft (1970) study, Medley identifies two distinct strategies regarding questioning patterns:

Strategy I. The questions tend to be difficult and to require the pupil to think, and the teacher tends either to indicate who is to answer the question before asking it, or to let a volunteer respond. If the answer is incorrect, the teacher is likely to be critical of it or give the answer. The pupil who fails to answer or does not know the answer is not likely to get a second chance; the teacher will give someone else a chance to answer it. The teacher who uses Strategy I successfully seems to be challenging pupils to respond near their highest level of capability. Strategy I seems to be appropriate in classes made up of high SES pupils but inappropriate in classes made up of low SES pupils.

Strategy II. The questions appear to be simple since they elicit responses that are usually correct and seldom merit further discussion. The teacher is likely to raise a question first and then to indicate who is to answer it, possible as a way of holding pupils' attention. The teacher seems to choose a respondent likely to get the answer right, since wrong answers are relatively infrequent. Criticism of a pupil's answer is rare, even when it is incorrect; and if a pupil fails to answer or does not know the answer, the teacher is more likely to help out than to turn to another pupil. The teacher who uses Strategy II appears more concerned with giving pupils a chance to experience success than to challenge them with difficult questions. Strategy II is used by effective teachers in classes made up of mainly low SES pupils and by ineffective teachers in classes of high SES pupils [p.20].

Competent Teacher Behavior in the
Upper Elementary Grades

This is another dimension of teacher effectiveness research which provides only inconclusive information. According to Soar (1966) and Spaulding (1965), teachers in the elementary grades talk more, while

McDonald and Elias (1976) conclude that effective teachers in the upper elementary grades keep pupils on task more. Good and Grouws (1975) submit that in the upper elementary grades teachers manage with less effort and fuss and that they are more selective in using rebukes and criticism with pupils.

Observational Techniques for Assessing Teacher and Student Classroom Behaviors

A review of process-product research would be incomplete without a special focus on research findings related to interaction analysis and systematic classroom observation instruments for analyzing teacher and pupil classroom behaviors.

Research instruments developed by Shaw (1977), Amidon and Hunter (1966), Flanders (1960), Cogan (1958), Hough (1966), Medley and Mitzel (1958), Taba (1964), Ribble and Shultz (1970), and others are representative of efforts to measure classroom behavior by systematic observation and analysis. Particular segments of the teacher's verbal behavior are isolated and categorized by these various instruments. Many of these sophisticated techniques have developed out of attempts to asssess "class climate" which may be defined as "generalized attitudes toward the teacher and the class that pupils share in common in spite of individual differences."

Anderson's (1939) 7–year study was primarily concerned with social behavior in the elementary classroom. He concluded that the teacher's behavior was a prime factor in determining the "class climate." Anderson introduced the concept of "dominative" and "integrative" behaviors of teachers and pupils. In the following passage, Anderson explains the basic distinction between "dominative" and "integrative" behaviors:

> What is dominative behavior? And what behavior is socially integrative? The terms . . . are merely convenient labels for two techniques of behaving that have been experimentally demonstrated to be psychologically different. In the initial investigations it was assumed, for example, that there is a psychological difference between snatching a toy out of a companion's hands so as to play with it oneself and asking the companion if one may borrow the toy for a while. It was assumed that there is a psychological difference between a command and a request [p. 73].[4]

Anderson showed that there was a relationship between the "dominative" behavior of teachers and the "dominative" behavior of students and similarly, there was a relationship between the "inte-

[4] © The society for Research in Child Development, Inc., and reprinted by permission.

grative" behavior of teachers and the "integrative" behavior of students. Furthermore, the teacher's "dominative" or "integrative" behavior influenced the behavior of students even when the teacher was out of the classroom.

A category system devised by Anderson was composed of 20 items which were divided into two major divisions of "dominative" and "integrative" behavior with two categories, teacher lecture and questions, considered neutral items. Using the category system, Anderson computed the Integrative–Dominative Index, a ratio between the total number of "dominative" and "integrative" contacts. Lewin, Lippitt, and White's (1939) study supports the findings of Anderson and emphasizes the importance of the relationship between social climate and leadership roles in the educational environment.

Among the outstanding contributors to systematic analysis of classroom behavior research is Flanders (1965). He developed hypotheses about teacher influence "that are consistent with generalizations about classroom climate but which also account for flexibility of teacher influence [p. 21]." Flanders's (1965) hypotheses are as follows:

1. Indirect teacher influence increases learning when a student's perception of the goal is confused and ambiguous.

2. Direct teacher influence increases learning when a student's perception of the goal is clear and acceptable.

3. Direct teacher influence decreases learning when a student's perception of the goal is ambiguous.

His data supported the following conclusions:

An indirect approach stimulates verbal participation by students and discloses to the teacher students' perceptions of the situation. Such an approach not only provides the teacher with more information about students' understanding of a particular problem, but also often encourages students to develop more responsibility for diagnosing their difficulties and for suggesting a plan of action.

A direct approach increases student compliance to teacher opinion and direction. It conditions students to seek the teacher's help and to check with the teacher more often to be sure they are on the right track.

The most direct teachers give twice as many directions as the most indirect, and express eight times as much criticism. These figures are consistent with what has been said about dependence. Lack of clarifying and using student ideas places the teacher in a position of giving more directions; in short, he must work harder to keep his students working successfully. When dependence is higher, progress by students depends much more on continuous teacher supervision [p. 117].

Anderson's 20 categories were reduced to 7 categories by Withall (1951), and the Integrative–Dominative Index was renamed the Climate Index. The seven categories lie on a continuum from "learner-centeredness" to "teacher-centeredness," consisting of "learning-supportive" statements, "acceptant and clarifying" statements, "problem-structuring" statements, "reproving" statements, and "teacher-self supporting" statements. Withall showed that the "class climate" of the same group of children changed as the group moved to different classrooms with different teachers.

A study by Mitzel and Rabinowitz (1953) established the reliability of the Whithall instrument in actual classroom settings. After observing four different teachers on eight separate occasions and making independent tallies for each visit, they found that differences between observers in categorization were nonsignificant. Medley and Mitzel (1958) later analyzed these data and determined that reliability could be increased significantly by increasing the number of visits and the number of observers.

The Social-Substantive Schedule, a language for the assessment of congruence between operationally stated objectives and instructional implementation, developed by Ribble and Shultz (1970) is a most appropriate instrument for early childhood classroom research. The following two assumptions prompted the research of Ribble and Shultz:

1. Teachers should be able to describe in operational terms the behavioral changes in pupils they expect to occur as a result of their instruction.

2. Teachers should choose instructional behaviors that maximize the opportunity for behavioral changes in pupils congruent with their stated objectives [p. 65.1–1].

From the writings of Bloom, Gagné, and Mager, the researchers obtained insights about the construction and classification of instructional objectives. The four classes of instructional objectives developed by Broudy, Smith, and Burnett were modified and made applicable for the Ribble–Shultz instrument (p. 65.1–2).

The following are the explicit definitions of the four types of objectives:

1. *Associative objectives*—when a teacher seeks to promote learner self-expression and hypothesis-formation in a setting where verification of learner assertions is not required and is even discouraged.

2. *Replicative objectives*—when a teacher wants learners to know or comprehend a given fact, principle, or theory. The learners are expected to demonstrate their ability to replicate information given by the teacher.

3. *Interpretive objectives*—when a teacher seeks to promote the ability of learners to extrapolate beyond a given set of relationships toward a more sophisticated conceptualization. In this situation, the teacher guides the learner toward predetermined insights.

4. *Applicative objectives*—when a teacher seeks to promote the ability of learners to synthesize or evaluate information. Given several plausible alternatives, the learner is expected to demonstrate his ability to take a position and provide a warrant for his assertions. At the highest level, the learner is even expected to establish alternative solutions to problematic situations he creates [pp. 65.1-2–65.1-3].

Ribble and Shultz (1970) identify the following modes of instruction most appropriate for the four types of instructional objectives:

Congruence of Objectives and Modes of Instruction [p. 65.1-4]

Instructional objectives	Modes of instruction
1. Associative	1. Open exploration
2. Replicative	2.1 Exposition
	2.2 Drill
3. Interpretive	3. Guided discovery
4. Applicative	4. Inquiry

In addition to the indentification of behavior patterns by means of the Social-Substantive Schedule, Ribble and Shultz define the modes of instruction in terms of the amount of learner participation in the instructional process.

Modes of Instruction and Learner Participation Rates [p. 65.1-4]

Exposition____Drill____Guided discovery ⟨ Open exploration____ / Inquiry____

Increase in the learner participation rate ____

In explaining the relationship of climate index and congruence assessment, Ribble and Shultz (1970) state the following:

Since the Social-Substantive Schedule was built on the model provided by John Withall's Social-Emotional Climate Index, the sequence of categories follows the general format of his index. We have used letters to identify our categories. The numbers and descriptions used as headings in sections one through seven correspond to the seven categories of the Climate Index. Consequently, the data collected by coding with the Schedule categories can be used to compute the Social-Emotional Climate Index as well as the assessment of congruence between stated objectives and classroom behavior [p. 65.1-4–65.1-5].

The educational community is now in the midst of a "Back-to-Basics" or "Forward-to-Basics" movement, depending on the educator's preference. During a reactionary period there is often a tendency to discard proven or readily accepted practices in the interest of rediscovery. This purging effect means that in many cases sound practices are no longer adhered to in the name of progress. This is often the situation in certain areas of educational research which are no longer considered fashionable for one reason or another. Continued research in early childhood classrooms related to a better understanding of the verbal classroom behaviors of teachers and pupils with the resulting impact on the learning environment must be expanded. "Back-to-Basics" must not be interpreted to mean "Back to Lecture–Recitation" days, for this attitude is totally incongruent with research findings. A strict lecture mode of instruction with the corresponding "dominative" behaviors by the teacher must not be tolerated in the preschool and primary grade classrooms.

There is another side to the question of establishing an effective communication network in the classroom and that is the impact of nonverbal behaviors in facilitating or inhibiting communication between teacher and pupil and the resulting outcomes. This is an area where little significant research has been done. Zamora (1974), in comparing nonverbal communication patterns between teachers and teacher assistants in bilingual early childhood programs, concluded that the regular teacher demonstrated the use of more combined positive nonverbal behaviors than the teacher assistant. Furthermore, the teacher assistant actually demonstrated significantly more negative nonverbal behaviors in everyday classroom interaction with the pupils. There are serious implications for preservice and in-service training based on her study, but there is a great deal more research needed in the area of the "silent" communication observable in any classroom. Galloway (1976) and Amidon (1971) have crusaded for years for the expansion of research efforts which focus on the impact of nonverbal behaviors in the learning environment. It is often what the teacher does not say that matters more than what he or she actually says. An early childhood teacher may very well be the most loving, talented, and concerned educator in the world, but what really counts is how the pupils, parents, aides, and professional colleagues perceive that teacher.

The personality characteristics, traits, and special training procedures associated with effective early childhood teachers are addressed in Part II.

PART II: PRESAGE-TO-PROCESS VARIABLES RESEARCH

Mitzel (1960) identifies presage-to-process variables research as an important classification in reviewing research related to teacher effectiveness. This category of research compares certain aspects of the teaching process with certain characteristics or traits teachers possess or exhibit before the formal classroom teaching or learning process begins. Linked closely to presage-to-process research is presage-to-product variables research. In presage-to-product variables research, presage still refers to certain aspects of teacher characteristics, personality, or traits which teachers possess prior to assuming a formal classroom teaching role compared to product variables which are specific pupil outcomes in terms of attitude and/or achievement which can be observed or measured in a classroom setting. When appropriate, presage-to-product variables research findings are included herein. The influence of meaningful experiences like preservice and in-service training or interaction with other teachers or parents are also reviewed from the standpoint of teacher effectiveness and pupil performance.

Models for Assessing Program and Teacher Competence

As Jones (1973) discovered, there is considerable disagreement among early childhood practitioners on such varied issues as appropriate curricula, certification requirements, and pupil evaluation procedures. In an investigation of the relationship of teacher personality variables to effectiveness of teacher role implementation in selected model categories of early education, Verzaro (1975) concluded that there were no consistent trends between predicted or generally accepted and observed personality traits among early childhood teachers. Although research findings are conflicting and often inconclusive, the amount of literature grows. Akers (1977) developed a model physical education curriculum for the first grade pupils based on concepts of early childhood education. His program exemplifies the efforts of other disciplinarians to generate curricula which incorporate an early childhood educational philosophy.

There is virtually no discipline or subject field of specialization which has not actively participated in efforts to influence and/or help determine teaching competencies or curricular priorities for early childhood teacher training programs. Another field which may seem afar from preschool and primary grade traditional subjects or activities is industrial arts education. Industrial arts educators have been extremely prolific in identifying teaching competencies and experiences related to the preparation of early childhood educators. In separate studies, Thrower (1974) and Haramis (1977) have carefully provided guidelines and policies which relate to the preparation and evaluation of early childhood teachers and the ability of teachers to provide industrial arts experiences for pupils.

Instrumentation continues to offer early childhood researchers a challenge. Falek (1974) developed an instrument and procedure for delineating attributes and providing for a comprehensive early childhood development center. The validity and reliability of using the Special Education/Early Childhood Achievement Test (SEECAT) as an instrument to measure pupil program content for master's degree candidates in early childhood teacher preparatory programs in the respective dual disciplines was established by Tsantis (1974). Beaty (1975) focused on the initial assessment of preschool teacher competencies for training purposes using another instrument called the Checklist of Classroom Competencies (CCC). She determined that the CCC was a valid and reliable instrument in prescribing appropriate learning modules or lessons for each preschool teacher trainee in the study.

Ryans's (1960) Teacher Characteristics Study (TCS)

In his TCS Ryans cited major trends observed in terms of teacher attitudes, educational viewpoints, verbal understanding, and emotional adjustment:

1. The attitudes of elementary teachers toward pupils, toward administrators, and also toward fellow teachers and nonadministrative personnel in the schools were markedly more favorable than were similar attitudes of secondary teachers.

2. The attitudes of teachers who were judged by their principals to be superior in teaching performance were significantly and distinctly more favorable toward pupils, and also toward administrators, than the attitudes of teachers who were judged by their principals to be unsatisfactory or poor.

3. Neither amount of teaching experience nor age appeared to be very highly associated with teacher attitudes, although there was a slight tendency for the attitudes of secondary teachers of greater experience to be slightly more favorable toward administrators and somewhat less favorable toward pupils than other experience groups.

4. More favorable attitudes toward pupils were expressed by women teachers in the secondary school, but among the elementary teachers there was a tendency for men to possess more favorable pupil attitudes than did women.

5. Teachers whose observed classroom behavior was judged to be more characteristically warm and understanding and more stimulating, possessed more favorable attitudes toward pupils and also more favorable attitudes toward administrators.

6. Actual pupil behavior in the classroom (based upon observers' assessments) did not appear to be related to the attitudes held by teachers.

7. The educational viewpoints expressed by secondary teachers were of a more traditional or learning-centered nature, while those of elementary teachers leaned more in the direction of permissiveness; within the secondary school, science and mathematics teachers appeared more traditional in their viewpoints and English and social studies teachers more permissive in theirs.

8. Teachers judged to be more warm and understanding in their classroom behavior, and to a somewhat lesser extent, those judged to be more stimulating, expressed more permissive educational viewpoints. Teachers judged to be more businesslike and systematic showed a slight tendency toward more traditional viewpoints.

9. The verbal understanding scores obtained by secondary teachers were significantly higher than those of elementary teachers, English and foreign language teachers excelling other subject-matter groups within the secondary school.

10. Men teachers at both the elementary and secondary levels appeared to be markedly more emotionally stable than women teachers.

11. There was a tendency for elementary teachers who were judged to be warm and understanding in classroom behavior, and also those judged to be stimulating in their classes, to manifest superior emotional adjustment.

12. There seemed to be no observable relationship between scores on the validity-of-response scale and the classification of teachers by amount of teaching experience, age, sex, grade or subject taught, or observed classroom behavior [pp. 385–386].

The TCS includes the following profile of distinguished elementary teachers based on many comprehensive surveys and studies:

> *Personal Qualities Which Appear To Distinguish Elementary*
> *Teachers Selected To Be "High" And "Low" With Respect To*
> *Overall Classroom Behavior: Characteristics of "Low"*
> *Group Teachers* [p. 360]

A. "Low" group members more frequently (than "high"):
1. Are from older age groups.
2. Are restricted and critical in appraisals of the behavior and motives of other persons.
3. Are unmarried.
4. Indicate preferences for activities which do NOT involve close contacts with people.

B. "Low " group (compared with "High" group):
1. Is less favorable in expressed opinions of pupils.
2. Is less high with regard to verbal intelligence.
3. Is less satisfactory with regard to emotional adjustment.

> *Personal Qualities Which Appear To Distinguish Elementary*
> *Teachers Selected To Be "High" and "Low" with Respect To*
> *Overall Classroom Behavior: Characteristics of "High"*
> *Group Teachers* [p. 361]

A. "High" group members more frequently (than "low"):
1. Manifest extreme generosity in appraisals of the behavior and motives of other persons; express friendly feelings for others.
2. Indicate strong interest in reading and in literary matters.
3. Indicate interest in music, painting, and the arts in general.

4. Report participation in high school and college social groups.
5. Manifest prominent social service ideals.
6. Indicate preferences for activities which involve contacts with people.
7. Indicate interest in science and scientific matters.
8. Report a liking for outdoor activities.
9. Are young, or middle-aged.
10. Are married.
11. Report that parental homes provided above-average cultural advantages.

B. "High" group (compared with "low" group):

1. Indicates greater enjoyment of pupil relationships (i.e., more favorable pupil opinions).
2. Indicates greater preference for nondirective classroom procedures.
3. Is superior in verbal intelligence.
4. Is more satisfactory with regard to emotional adjustment.

Teacher Tasks and Competencies

Traditionally, the person working with children in an early childhood program and learning environment has been referred to as a teacher. Acknowledging that the home and community have a tremendous impact upon the young child, and that the provision of short, isolated educational programs is not the most effective means to contribute to the child's full development, Kendall, Mallet, Sherwood, Zapisocky, and Nanji (1976) surveyed parents, teachers, and administrators involved in early childhood programs to determine the most important *tasks* and *competencies* of the early childhood teacher.

Tasks

1. The creation of a convenient, safe, comfortable and attractive space for the children, whether the program is in a classroom, a playground or in a home.
2. The organization of materials in that space to allow for easy access and storage. It is important that play materials—especially for sensory-motor and expressive activities be available and that the play environment encourage their utilization. Large, small, and private spaces should be available for appropriate activities.
3. The provision of a physical and interpersonal environment, ordered but flexible, in which experimentation and explorations are encouraged, without undue social or psychological risk. The environment should be carefully organized to permit the children's expectations of objects and events to be confirmed or revised. At the same time, there are a minimum of social restrictions on exploratory and motor activity. Furthermore, the teacher, as a part of the child's "interpersonal environment", accepts the ambiguity interest in exploration rather than relying on a "right or wrong" paradigm, or conventional standards.
4. Knowledgeable and accepting of the children and their families. They

understand the children's life styles, ways of thinking, feelings, their efforts and their problems. They are able, through positive interaction with the children to provide a climate of warmth, enthusiasm and trust.

5. Encouraging rapport among the children—with themselves, with each other and with other members of the community. The teachers foster the involvement of the children in the program in making group and individual decisions. They value achievement and recognize the accomplishment of individual and group efforts.

6. Responding physically, verbally, and emotionally with sufficient consistency and clarity to provide cues as to appropriate and valued behaviors and to reinforce such behaviors when they occur. Characteristically, their responses are to individual children, rather than to a group of children.

7. The provision of a wide range of direct (rather than vicarious) sequenced experiences—physical, sensory, expressive, intellectual and social, which are compatible with the experiences the child has at home.

8. The provision of a wide range of experiences which effectively initiate and/or expand the child's interest and mastery in cognitive, social, and affective learning. The activities are developmentally appropriate, sequenced in a meaningful and motivating way. The child's mastery and satisfaction, as opposed to frustration and defeat, in his interactions with the physical environment, with his peers and adults is planned for and encouraged. In most of his learning experiences, the child receives factual and specific feedback from the teacher, which he is able to acknowledge as information rather than as praise or criticism.

9. The observation and recording of the children's behavior as a basis for program planning so that the child's interest and capabilities are challenged but not overloaded. By such means, teachers can also detect any possible difficulties among the children.

10. The provision for language development, building, listening, and expressive skills which enable the child to organize and reorganize his conceptual knowledge and to communicate with peers and adults. The teachers organize the spatial arrangements so that situations are conducive to communications; they are responsive, flexible, and provocative in providing tasks and activities; they serve as models of language usage.

11. Provision for exceptional children in the classroom concerned with growth rather than compensating for deficiencies—the teachers use á diagnostic approach and resource material and personnel in working with handicapped children.

12. The provision for liaison between the program and the children's homes and the community. The teachers provide programs that are readily accessible to, motivating for, and in keeping with the values, interests and resources of the family and community. They work in a cooperative relationship with parents and other professionals, contributing and accepting ideas and directions. The teachers are viewed sources of support to parents, providing and accepting information, feedback, and alternatives. They utilize resources in the community as part of the child's learning, to ensure the child's total health and well-being, and to meet special needs of children.

13. The teacher's willingness and capability to serve as members of a network of educational and social services for young children. The most appropriate model for early childhood teachers may not be as coordinators of these services, but rather as knowledgeable resource persons themselves, in liaison with other areas of early childhood services—e.g., infant–toddler programs, guidance and services for handicapped children, and the elementary schools.

Competence: Knowledge, Attitudes, and Skills

I. Design and Implementation of the Program

Ability to relate the use of time, space, and activities to the developmental levels, learning abilities, and individual characteristics of the children.

1. Ability to involve parents, professionals, and others in the planning and implementation of the program.

   Teachers need to be able to analyze the structural elements of the system (organizational, social and physical) which affect the relationships between the teacher, the program, the families, and the community.

   Teachers need to be able to analyze situations with a view of action, that is, to understand what forces are at work and to be able to recognize and communicate alternatives for remediation or enhancement.

2. Ability to facilitate language development.

   Teachers must be able to "diagnose" the child's present level of usage, and be able to detect any possible difficulties. Teachers must profice the opportunity and structure for the acquisition of verbal skills.

   In order to promote self-expression and experimentation with symbols, children should be able to use a variety of forms of creative expression.

3. Ability to promote problem-solving behaviors among the children.

   Teachers should encourage the children's manipulation of these physical objects and set problems which can be solved through such manipulations.

4. Ability to facilitate sensory motor development.

   Children need the opportunity and encouragement to explore different sense modalities.

5. Ability to increase the child's self-knowledge, self-esteem, and self-confidence.

   The program should be designed so that a minimum of adult assistance is required in activities or in the use of materials.

   Avoiding a work–play dichotomy in programming appears to be facilitative in involving children in meaningful activity.

   Among the children in the program, it is important that teachers encourage understanding and respect for the child's own, and others' backgrounds and ethnic origin.

6. Awareness of the individual characteristics and special temporary and long-terms needs of children.

   Teachers must be skilled in observational techniques, have a sound understanding of normal development and learning and be able to recognize indications of physical and emotional distress among the children.

An awareness and accommodation of individual differences is especially important among teachers who work with handicapped children in their programs.

7. Ability to foster social development among the children.

Teacher should reinforce the child or the group for achievement or positive social behavior.

Teachers should seek opportunities to reinforce the children's positive responses to each other as an effective means to assist them in their social development.

8. Ability to facilitate physical health and development.

The teacher should be able to provide a physical environment that meets health and safety needs and, if necessary, make special provisions for the handicapped children in the program.

9. Ability to observe individual behavior, record, and plan.

It is important that the teacher be skilled in observing children objectively, be able to describe their individual characteristics and be knowledgeable about indications of problems. If the problem is to be meaningful for the children, the information collected through such observations should be used in the daily planning of activities.

II. Personal Competence

Ability to serve as an effective model of behavior for children and other adults.

1. Knowledge of self.

Early childhood teachers should be aware of their own values and prejudices. Teachers should also have a realistic view of their own needs and abilities.

2. Express to the children curiosity and exploratory behavior.

Asking questions is important. By their own nonthreatening and provocativeness in questions teachers should provide a model of inquiry for the children.

3. Sense of humor and perspective.

By a natural and unaffected manner teachers can show their personal delight in the company of the children and other adults.

4. Ability to accept people without prejudice.

Teachers need to respect the abilities and endeavors of the children, parents, and colleagues.

5. Commitment to human growth.

Teachers in the program should be aware of the strengths and concerns of others working in the program, encouraging and helping the assistants to take responsibility for different aspects of the program.

Teachers should be sensitive to the individual needs and behavior of children especially within the context of large group activities.

6. Ability to be flexible.

Teachers should be able to follow a worthwhile digression and make way for the spontaneous interest and needs of the children.

Teachers should be able to assess the children's level of involvement in an activity.

7. Ability to be emotionally responsive.

Teachers should be ready to deal with anothers' social immaturities, feelings of inadequacy, anger, and joy.

III. Interpersonal

Ability to facilitate the child's mastery and satisfaction in interactions with the physical environment, peers, and adults: to stimulate the child's exploration and explanatory of reality rather than imposing one's own which may have no meaning for the child; to view success and failure as information rather than as reward or punishment.

1. Ability to support the child's goals in a particular activity rather than curricular or teacher's standards.

Children solicit and undoubtedly need feedback from adults and it should be positive, specific and informative.

Achievement should be regarded in terms of the child's progress rather than conventional normative standards of the group.

2. Ability to recognize and use the individual characteristics of each child.

Teachers should be able to stimulate the child's expression of ideas and feelings in a natural and unaffected way. Teachers should acknowledge the children's feelings and accept but not necessarily agree with, the children's ideas.

3. Ability to provide for the children a socially and psychologically safe environment.

Teachers should foster cooperation and mutual respect rather than competition among children.

Another aspect of teachers' behavior which fosters a supportive environment is their personal interaction with individual or small groups of children.

4. Ability to provide the structure and encouragement necessary for the children to explore, learn about, and master their environment.

Teachers should be able to demonstrate procedures and give directions which are simple, positive and task oriented.

Teachers should be able to structure problem solving situations for the children rather than presenting them with information, or leaving their queries unanswered.

5. Ability to respond to the content, motivation and significance of behavior.

Teachers should be able to use a positive approach in guiding behavior rather than shaming sarcasm, threats, or physical punishment. Effective teachers use positive reinforcement to encourage desirable behaviors.

6. Ability to Communicate Effectively.

In their work with children, parents, and colleagues, teachers must be able to communicate well.

Teachers should be able to analyze how others react to them through the verbal and nonverbal messages which others express to them. [pp. 14–35].[5]

---

[5] Reprinted by permission of the Alberta Department of Education.

Summary

The research efforts of Kendall *et al.* (1976) and their assessment of appropriate tasks and competencies for early childhood educators included herein provide major implications for educators attempting to develop valid measuring instruments to assess specific teaching competencies and alternative ways of demonstrating competencies.

Special Considerations in Selecting Teachers

Who make the best early childhood teachers? How should early childhood teachers be evaluated? Taylor, Chow, Hubner, and Stripp (1976) shed some light on these concerns in regard to determining certain competencies for early childhood teachers. In their study, paper and pencil tests and classroom work samples were used to evaluate the effectiveness of three learning units for teachers in early childhood programs. Half the sample had B.A. degrees or above, and half had only high school diplomas or even less schooling. Both subsamples were assessed on the same four categories: quality of classroom arrangement; personalization of a literature experience; awareness of sense perception uses of materials; and diversity of teaching strategies which develop pupils' sense perception. In general, validity coeffecients increased from pre- to posttests for the high school educated teachers, but actually decreased for the college educated teachers. The validity coefficients were higher than the average correlations between different competencies assessed by different methods. The mean correlations between different competencies assessed by the same method suggested that at pretest, the paper and pencil test might be a more appropriate method for the college trained teachers, and the work sample method might be more appropriate for the high school educated teachers. It seems fairer to evaluate noncollege trained early childhood teachers in more practical ways than to administer paper and pencil tests which tend to usually favor the test-wise or experienced college trained early childhood teacher.

Do you really need a college degree in early childhood education to be an effective preschool teacher? While comparing the relationship between teacher academic preparation and preschool pupil achievement, Johnson and Johnson (1975) concluded that preschool pupils, including ethnic minority pupils, perform equally as well under teachers with 4 or more years of college when compared to teachers with considerably less than 4 years of formal college training. This does not necessarily imply that a college degree in early childhood education is not a valuable prerequisite for preschool teaching, but rather raises questions concerning what kind of undergraduate program is most beneficial and what kind of in-service training should be programmed for preschool teachers.

Another crucial question in early childhood education centers on the campaign for the recruitment of more men in early childhood classrooms on the assumption that a strong male figure will circumvent the "feminized' environment of pupils. Studies by Greenburg (1977), Kendall (1972), and Williams (1970) support this viewpoint. But as a counterpoint, Robinson (1977) argues that a major deficiency with previous research on sex-typed contingencies is that the studies reported employed students who were only part-time teachers as subjects in the descriptive studies. Consequently, it is possible to argue that because these students had not actually adopted the role of caregiver or early childhood teacher as an occupation, they were not representative of those men employed in the field on a full-time basis. Robinson (1977), in his study of sex-typed attitudes, sex-typed contingency behaviors, and personality traits of male caregivers concluded that findings did not confirm the flood of impressionistic reports in the educational literature which claim that males should be employed to counterbalance the "feminized" environment of the early childhood classroom.

An even more important ramification of the sex-typed contingency behavior question is what influence is best for the pupil, a male or female role model? Wolinsky (1974) investigated whether male teachers differed from female teachers in their behaviors in early childhood programs. Among her findings, she concluded that pupils generally liked their teachers and saw the teachers as liking them. From the evidence, there was a tendency for boys to affiliate themselves with male teachers and girls saw themselves as being preferred to boys by both male and female teachers. Boys saw themselves as preferred only by male teachers. Boys and girls alike thought that their male teachers liked them better than their female teachers like them. It is apparent from data that male teachers in early childhood programs are beneficial to male pupils without presenting any undue problems for female pupils.

Furnell (1977) studied the relationship of career motivation and teacher effectiveness of female early childhood educators. She found that teacher effectiveness as determined by the principal's ranking had no relationship to the career motivation of the teacher, and that, furthermore, the principals' rankings of teachers were unrelated to their ages, years of teaching experience, or educational attainment.

The Teacher's Ability to Predict or Influence Pupil Behaviors

According to Humes (1975), teacher characteristics relevant to the development of divergent thought processes in day care and Head Start children favor teachers who exhibit moderate rather than rigid classroom behaviors. Even during periods of relative inactivity, the teacher's behavior is influencing the pupils' reactions. Daniels (1976) determined that the level of the teacher's cognitive functioning during free play affected the level of the children's cognitive functioning during free play periods in prekindergarten classes.

Are kindergarten teachers who are better at predicting pupils' behaviors also better at managing pupils' behaviors? In this case, pupil behavior refers to the task related behavior of preschool children in teacher-led small groups. In addressing this specific situation, Schweinhart's (1975) profile of the novice preschool teacher indicates that he or she talks less and lets the children talk more. The children are less likely to appear noninvolved, but they are more likely to misbehave. On the other hand, according to Schweinhart (1975), the experienced preschool teacher talks more and allows children fewer chances to talk. The experienced teacher who does let children talk more often has children who are more involved in classroom interaction. Misbehavior is less of a problem in the classroom of the experienced teachers, but children in their classrooms appear noninvolved more.

Sogard (1975) studied early childhood teacher judgments of educational objectives in the cognitive, affective, and psychomotor domains. Even among nursery school, kindergarten, and first-grade teachers there are marked differences in terms of emphasis as summarized by Sogard (1972):

1. Cognitive domain objectives differentiated among teacher expectations. Affective domain objectives revealed similar teacher expectations. Psychomotor domain objectives presented variations in teacher expectations between the curricular areas.

2. In the cognitive and psychomotor domains, early childhood teachers accorded more emphasis on the lower hierarchical classification levels and less emphasis on the higher hierarchical levels. Early childhood teachers tended to accord more emphasis on the hierarchical levels as the grade level increased. In the affective domain, early childhood teachers tended to follow the same patterns of emphasis for the hierarchical classification levels.

3. Between groups of teachers, the cognitive domain was emphasized the most by first grade teachers and the least by nursery school teachers. The affective domain was emphasized the most by nursery school teachers and the least by first grade teachers. The psychomotor domain was emphasized the most by kindergarten teachers and the least by first grade teachers.

4. Within groups of teachers, nursery school teachers emphasized the affective domain the most and the cognitive domain the least. Kindergarten and first grade teachers emphasized the cognitive domain the most and the psychomotor domain the least.[6]

[6] The dissertation titles and abstracts contained here are published with permission of University Microfilms International, publishers of *Dissertation Abstracts International* (Copyright © 1972 by University Microfilms International), and may not be reproduced without their prior permission.

By establishing specific instructional objectives for nursery school, kindergarten, and the primary grades, teachers ensure that the pupils' thinking, feeling, and acting behaviors are considered within the framework of the continuous educational process.

Another important consideration should be whether or not attitudes of kindergarten teachers toward preschool education affect their perceptions of a child's social–emotional adjustment to kindergarten. In her study which involved only female kindergarten teachers, Allan (1977) concluded that the teachers' attitudes had no significant bearing on their perceptions of a child's social–emotional adjustment to kindergarten. For illustration, kindergarten teachers did not perceive children from more structured or cognitively oriented preschools as having greater difficulty in adjusting to the kindergarten program than those children from less structured preschool backgrounds. In the case of at least female kindergarten teachers, the notion that teachers have preconceived attitudes about the prior schooling experiences of children and their ability to adjust socially and emotionally to kindergarten seems unfounded.

Relationships among Teachers, Paraprofessionals, and Parents

If there is one major area of agreement among early childhood educators, it is the universal commitment to unite the home, school, and community in working toward the aims of the respective early childhood program. However, how this task is to be accomplished is often another area of contention or at least debate.

The close cooperation among teachers and classroom aides is important in ensuring a successful early educational experience for children. Yet in Giboney's (1977) comparative study of teachers' and aides' perceptions of their ideal and actual roles, he discovered disagreements with serious implications for improving job descriptions, initiating needed in-service training, and enhancing communication among teachers and aides. Based on his findings, teachers and aides seemed to disagree in their perceptions as to what classroom tasks they should perform and do perform on a day-to-day basis with children enrolled in the program.

In a comparison of mother–child and teacher–child interaction, Leong (1977) found that children behave in different styles when interacting with mothers and preschool teachers. While children are more demanding, assertive, and active in their interaction with mothers, they are more indirect, and in a manner, more polite when interacting with the teacher. Leong (1977) submits that adult behavior has a different pattern or relationship to child behavior for mothers and preschool teachers. This is why on-going communication between the teacher and the parents is important. Effective teachers generally establish and maintain a very cooperative and mutually beneficial association with the parents of the children in the classroom.

Accountability is the watchword in education today. It conjures up in the minds of many teachers an image of control and that "Big Brother" is always watching. Horton and Bryan (1971) target their research at the concept of accountability. They studied the relationship of accountability and teacher satisfaction both in terms of teachers' perceptions of accountability and the concomitant effects. The subjects for their study were early childhood teachers and the study investigated (a) the extent of satisfaction with accountability, (b) teachers' perceptions of extent of accountability, (c) identification of source of pressures for accountability, (d) extent of pressures for accountability from adminstrators and parental sources, (e) extent of work created by level of accountability, (f) the effect of level of accountability upon teacher effectiveness and sense of professionalism, and (g) the satisfaction with in-service training, cooperation of supervisors, and supervisors evaluation process by level of accountability. The researchers concluded that greater accountability may actually increase teacher sense of effectiveness and professionalism, and in-service training along with positive assistance from supervisors may also increase satisfaction and teacher effectiveness.

While attempting to identify the appropriate training and work qualifications, day care teachers should possess prior to employment, Turock (1977) discovered that there was a significant difference in the perceptions of day care employees regarding the training and prior work experience qualifications teachers should possess. In his study, bachelor degree teachers strongly supported the criterion of formal training while nondegree teachers tended to support criteria closely aligned to their own employment model and educational background. There is a favorable mood for some type of differentiated staffing in most early childhood programs. But as Guith (1974), Jarrard (1974), and Smith (1974) agree there is also a great need to provide the necessary pre- and in-service training for paid and volunteer aides and paraprofessionals in the early childhood classrooms. Without a quality in-service program, it is difficult for any program to be successful regardless of the criteria used to evaluate the teachers and support staff.

SUMMARY

1. There are specific research methods usually associated with investigations designed to determine the specific traits and characteristics considered desirable in effective early childhood educators.

2. Although there has been in recent years a marked increase in the quantity of research studies related to teacher effectiveness and influence in the classroom, there still remain a great many questions which are unanswered, especially in preschool and primary grade learning environments.

3. Process–product research studies attempt to show the relationship between certain teacher behaviors and pupil behaviors in terms of attitude or achievement. Most research in this category has centered on pupil outcomes in arithmetic and reading achievement as measured by standardized tests. The "gain score" has been the primary criterion in determining if a significant increase in pupil achievement is possibly due to some specific teacher behavior or action.

4. What seems to be effective, as far as teacher behavior or methodology in the classroom, for low Socio-Economic Status (SES) pupils may not be effective or as effective in terms of achievement for high SES pupils enrolled in early childhood programs.

5. Effective early childhood teachers exhibit basically the same kinds of pupil-centered, positive reinforcement behaviors that effective teachers in higher grades tend to exhibit or demonstrate.

6. Effective early childhood teachers spend a significant amount of time engaged in individualized and one-to-one activities with pupils. The "quality" of time devoted to working with a pupil is more important than the amount of total time designated as individualized instruction or "seatwork" time in the classroom.

7. Successful early childhood teachers tend to be good organizers and aware of the importance of determining specific instructional goals.

8. Early childhood programs should involve all persons with a direct concern for the pupil including teachers, paraprofessionals, supervisors, caregivers, parents, and/or guardians. A community-based program is of paramount importance especially with preschool and Head Start programs.

9. Both male and female teachers and aides can serve as effective teachers in early childhood programs. There are very few serious arguments which reject the participation of males as teachers in preschool and primary grade programs.

10. There are many valid and reliable evaluation instruments available which measure certain aspects of an early childhood program. Accountability in early childhood educational enterprises tends to improve the quality of the program, and teachers are apparently more content in well-organized operations.

11. There is a definite need for increased and better preservice and in-service training for teachers and teacher aides serving in early childhood educational programs.

REFERENCES

Akers, G. M. A model physical education curriculum for Alabama first-grade students based on concepts of early childhood education, movement education, perceptual-motor development, and physical fitness. Unpublished doctoral dissertation, Auburn University, 1977.

Allan, N. E. Attitudes of female kindergarten teachers and their perceptions of adjustment problems of kindergarten children as related to preschool experience. Unpublished doctoral dissertation, Michigan State University, 1977.

Anderson, H. H. The measurement of domination and of socially integrative behavior in teachers' contacts with children. *Child Development*, June, 1939, *10*, 73–89.

Amidon, P. *Nonverbal interaction analysis*. Minneapolis, Minn.: Paul S. Amidon & Associates, 1971.

Amidon, E. J., & Hunter, E. *Improving teaching: Analyzing verbal interaction in the classroom*. New York: Holt, Rinehart, and Winston, 1966.

Banta, T. J. Is there really a Montessori method? Paper presented to the Ohio Psychological and Ohio Psychiatric Associations, 1966.

Beaty, J. J. Initial assessment of preschool teacher competencies for training purposes. Unpublished doctoral dissertation, Cornell University, 1975.

Beller, E. K. Teaching styles and their effects on problem-solving behavior in Headstart programs. In E. Grotberg (Ed.), *Critical issues in research related to disadvantaged children*. Princeton, N.J.: Educational Testing Service, 1969.

Bemis, K. A., & Luft, M. Relationships between teacher behavior, pupil behavior and pupil achievement. In A. Simon & E. G. Boyer (Eds.), *Mirrors for behavior: An anthology of observation instruments continued*. (1970 Suppl. Vol. A). Philadelphia: Research for Better Schools, 1970.

Brophy, J. E., & Evertson, C. M. *Process–product correlations in the Texas teacher effectiveness study: Final report*. Austin: University of Texas, June 1974.

Cogan, M. L. The relationship of the behavior of teachers to the productive behavior of their pupils. *Journal of Experimental Education*, 1958, *27*, 89–124.

Coker, H., Lorentz, J. L., & Coker, J. G. *Interim report on carroll county CBTC project, Fall, 1976*. This report covers procedures for major analysis of first year (1974–75) data, reliabilities and correlations. Reported to Georgia State Department of Education, 1976.

Dalton, E. L. Preparation programs of junior high school teachers. Unpublished doctoral dissertation, George Peabody College for Teachers, 1962.

Daniels, U. P. An analysis for the cognitive behaviors of preschool children and teachers during free play, Unpublished doctoral dissertation, New York University, 1976.

Fagot, B. I. Influence of teacher behavior in the preschool. *Developmental Psychology*, 1973, *9* (2), 198–206.

Falek, A. B. The development of a procedure for delineating attributes of a comprehensive early childhood development center, Unpublished doctoral dissertation, University of Pittsburgh, 1974.

Flanders, N. A. *Interaction analysis in the classroom: A manual for observers*. Ann Arbor: University of Michigan, 1960.

Flanders, N. A. Teacher influence, pupil attitudes and achievement. Cooperative Research Monograph No. 12, U.S. Department of Health, Education and Welfare, Office of Education, 1965.

Flanders, N. A. Knowledge about teacher effectiveness. Paper presented at the annual meeting of the American Educational Research Association, New Orleans, Louisiana, February 1973.

Furnell, M. H. Relationship of career motivation and teacher effectiveness of female early childhood education teachers, Unpublished doctoral dissertation, Florida State University, 1977.

Galloway, C. M. *Silent language in the classroom.* Bloomington, Ind.: The Phi Delta Kappa Educational Foundation, 1976.

Getzel, J. S., & Jackson, P. W., The teacher's personality and characteristics. In. N. C. Gage (Ed.), *Handbook of research on teaching.* Chicago: Rand McNally, 1963.

Giboney, T. T. A Comparison of selected Orange County early childhood education school teachers' and aides' perceptions of their ideal and actual roles. Unpublished doctoral dissertation, University of Southern California, 1977.

Good, T. L., & Grouws, D. A. *Process-product relationship in fourth grade mathematics classrooms.* Columbia: University of Missouri, October 1975. (Final Report to the National Institute of Education.)

Greenburg, M. The male early childhood teacher: An appraisal. *Young Children,* 1977, *32,* 34–47.

Guith, N. C. Differentiated staffing practices in selected early childhood education schools in California. Unpublished doctoral dissertation, University of Southern California, 1974.

Haramis, M. Technology in kindergarten. In *Industrial arts which way now?* Addresses and Proceedings of the 39th National and 6th International Meeting of the American Industrial Arts Association. Washington, D.C.: American Industrial Arts Association, April 1977.

Harris, A. J. & Serwer, B. L. *Comparison of reading approaches in first-grade teaching with disadvantaged children.* (The CRAFT project). Final Report, cooperative Research Project No. 2677. New York: Division of Teacher Education, The University of New York, 1966.

Harris, A. J., Morrison, C., Serwer, B. & Gold, L. *A continuation of the CRAFT project—comparing approaches with disadvantaged Negro children in primary grades.* New York: Division of Teacher Education, The City University of New York, 1968.

Herbert, J. A research base for accreditation of teacher preparation programs J. L. Burdin & M. T. Reagan, (Eds.), *Accreditation and research problems.* Washington, D.C.: ERIC Clearinghouse on Teacher Education, 1971.

Horton, R., & Bryan, C. *Accountability and teacher satisfaction.* Kalamazoo, Mich.: Western Michigan University, 1971. ED 063 270.

Hough, J. B. An observational system for the analysis of classroom instruction. Unpublished paper, Ohio State University, 1966.

Hough, J. B., & Amidon, E. J. The relationship of personality structure and training in interaction analysis to attitude change during student teaching. Paper presented at annual meeting of the American Educational Research Association, Chicago, 1965.

Humes, C. Z. Teacher characteristics relevant to the development of divergent thought processes in young children. Unpublished doctoral dissertation, Lehigh University, 1975.

Jarrard, R. D. Inservice education for the paraprofessional in early childhood education, Unpublished doctoral dissertation, University of Southern California, 1974.

Johnson, I., & Johnson, Y. M. An analysis of the relationship between attitude, teacher academic preparation and preschool student achievement. Unpublished doctoral dissertation, United States International University, 1975.

Jones, N. R. Attitudes of Palm Beach County, Florida kindergarten and first-grade teachers concerning selected issues in early childhood education. Unpublished doctoral dissertation, University of Utah, 1973.

Katz, L. G., Peters, D. L., & Stein, N. S. Observing behavior in kindergarten and preschool classes. *Childhood Education,* 1968, *44,* 400–405.

Kendall, E. We have men on the staff. *Young Children*, 1972, *27*, 358–362.

Kendall, M. E., Mallet, M., Sherwood, F., Zapisocky, M., & Nanji, M. *Summary of the early childhood services task force report on teacher competence.* Edmonton, Alberta, Canada: Alberta Department of Education, June 1976.

Klein, R. P. Multivariate comparison of two model preschool programs. Paper presented to the International Society for the Study of Behavioral Development, Ann Arbor, Mich., 1973.

Leong, D. J. A comparison of mother–child and teacher–child interaction in an unstructured game. Unpublished doctoral dissertation, Stanford University, 1977.

Lewin, K., Lippitt, R., & White, R. K. Patterns of aggressive behavior in experimentally created "social climates." *Journal of Social Psychology*, 1939, *10*, 271–299.

Medley, D. M. *Teacher competence and teacher effectiveness. A review of process–product research.* Wshington, D.C.: American Association of Colleges for Teacher Education, 1977.

Medley, D. M., & Mitzel, H. Technique for measuring classroom behavior. *Journal of Educational Psychology*, 1958, *49*, 86–92.

McDonald, F. J., & Elias, P. *The effects of teaching performance on pupil learning.* Beginning Teacher Evaluation Study: Phase II, 1973–74. Final Report: Vol. I. Princeton, N.J.: Educational Testing Service, 1976.

McGee, H. M. Measurement of authoritarianism and its relation to teachers' classroom behavior. *Genetic Psychology Monographs*, 1955, *52*, 89–146.

Miller, L. B. Situational determinants of behavior in preschool classrooms. Paper presented at the meeting of the International Society for the Study of Behavioral Development, Guilford, England, July, 1975.

Mischel, W. Toward a cognitive social learning reconceptualization of personality. *Psychological Review*, 1973, *80*(4), 252–283.

Mitzel, H. E., & Rabinowitz. Assessing social-emotional climate in the classroom by Withall's technique. Psychological Monograph, 1953, 67, No. 18. Washington, D.C.: American Psychological Association.

Mitzel, H. E. Teacher effectiveness. In C. W. Harris (Ed.) *Encyclopedia of educational research* (3rd ed.). New York: Macmillan, 1960.

Neale, D., Gill, N., & Tismer, W. Relationship between attitudes toward school subjects and school achievement. *The Journal of Educational research*, January 1970, *63*, 231–237.

Nottingham, B. The measurement of pupils' attitudes. *Educational Research* (June 1970) *12*, 247–249.

Peck, R. F., & Tucker, J. A., Research on teacher education. A State-of-the-Art Paper produced at the Research and Development Center for Teacher Education, The University of Texas at Austin, Copyright, July 1971. (Later published as Research on teacher education. In R. M. W. Travers (Ed.), *Second handbook of research on teaching.* Chicago: Rand McNally College Publishing Company, 1973.

Perham, B. H. A study of multiple relationships among teacher characteristics, teaching Behaviors and criterion-referenced student performance in mathematics. Unpublished doctoral dissertation, Northwestern University, 1973.

Prescott, E., Jones, E., & Kritchevsky, S. *Group day care as a childrearing environment.* Report to Children's Bureau, U.S. Department of Health, Education, and Welfare. Pasadena, Calif.: Pacific Oaks College, 1967. ED 024 453.

Remmers, H. H., Rating methods in research on teaching. In N.L. Gage (Ed.), *Handbook of research on teaching.* Chicago: Rand McNally, 1963.

Remmers, H. H., & Gage, N. L. *Educational measurement and evaluation* (Rev. ed.). New York: Harper and Brothers, 1955.

Ribble, R. B., & Schultz, C. B., The social substantive schedule: A language of congruence between operationally stated objectives and instructional implementation. In *Mirrors for behavior: An anthology of observation instruments continued* (Vol. 12). Philadelphia: Research for Better Schools, 1970.

Robinson, B. E. Sex-typed attitude, sex-typed contingency behaviors, and personality traits of male caregivers. Paper presented at the biennial meeting of the Society for Research in Child Development, New Orleans, March 1977. ED 063 270.

Rosenshine, B. Teaching behavior related to pupil achievement: A review of research. In I. Westbury & A. A. Bellack (Eds.), *Research into classroom processes*. New York: Teachers College Press, 1971. Pp. 51–98.

Ryans, D. G., *Characteristics of teachers*. Washington, D.C.: American Council on Education, 1960.

Sandefur, J. T. *An illustrated model for the evaluation of teacher education graduates*. Washington, D.C.: American Association of Colleges for Teacher Education, 1970.

Schweinhart, L. J. Kindergarten group management and teacher ability to predict children's behavior. Unpublished doctoral dissertation, Indiana University, 1975.

Shaw J. M. Teacher–pupil communication in selected nursery schools. Unpublished doctoral dissertation, Columbia University Teachers College, 1977.

Sheldon, M. S., Coale, J. M., & Copple, R. Concurrent validity of the warm teacher scales. *Journal of Educational Psychology*, 1959, *50*, 37–40.

Siegel, H. A., & Rosenshine, B. Teacher behavior and student achievement in the Bereiter–Engelmann Follow-Through program. Paper presented at the annual meeting of the American Educational Research Association, New Orleans, 1973.

Soar, R. S. *An integrative approach to classroom learning*. Philadelphia: Temple University, 1966.

Soar, R. S. *Follow Through classroom process measurement and pupil growth (1970–1971)*. Final Report. Gainesville: College of Education, University of Florida, 1973.

Soar, R. S., & Soar, R. M. An empirical analysis of selected Follow Through programs: An example of a process approach to evaluation. In Ira J. Gordon (Ed.), *Early Childhood Education* (Part II), *The Seventy-First Yearbook of the National Society for the Study of Education*. Chicago: NSSE, 1972.

Sogard, L. I. Early childhood education teacher judgments of educational objectives in the cognitive, affective, and psychomotor domains. Unpublished doctoral dissertation, University of Wisconsin at Madison, 1972.

Smith, H. I. A conceptual model for inservice education based on early childhood education objectives. Unpublished doctoral dissertation, University of Southern California, 1974.

Spaulding, R. L. *Achievement, Creativity, and self-concept correlates of teacher–pupil transactions in elementary school classrooms*. Hempstead, N.Y.: Hofstra University, 1965.

Stallings, J., & Kaskowitz, D. *Follow Through classroom observation evaluation 1972–1973: A study of implementation*. Menlo Park, Calif.: Stanford Research Institute, 1974.

Taba, H. *Thinking in elementary school children*. San Francisco: San Francisco State College, 1964.

Taylor, T. D., Chow, S. L., Hubner, J. J., & Stripp, S. P. Measurement of classroom versus written exam teacher performance: Should teachers show or tell? Research and Development, Paper presented at the annual meeting of the American Educational Research Association, San Francisco, April, 1976.

Thrower, R. G. (Ed.). *Industrial arts for the elementary school*. Twenty-third Yearbook of the American Industrial Arts Association. Bloomington, Ill.: McKnight, 1974.

Tsantis, L. A. An achievement test for the graduate special education/early childhood program at the George Washington University. Unpublished doctoral dissertation, George Washington University, 1974.

Veldman, D. J., Student evaluation of teaching. *Research Methodology Monograph No. 10*, Research and Development Center, University of Texas at Austin, 1970.

Verzaro, M. A. The relationship of teacher personality variables to models of early education. Unpublished doctoral dissertation, University of Wisconsin at Milwaukee, 1975.

Williams, B. M. A symposium: Men in young children's lives: Part I. *Childhood Education*, 1970, *47*, 139–143.

Withall, J. The development of a climate index. *The Journal of Educational Research* ,1951 , *45*, 93–99.

Wolinsky, A. P. Male and female teachers in early childhood settings. Unpublished doctoral dissertation, Columbia University, 1974.

Zamora, G. L. A comparison of the nonverbal communication patterns of bilingual early childhood teachers. Unpublished doctoral dissertation, University of Texas at Austin, 1974.

CHAPTER 7

Implications for Early Childhood Education Practices and Procedures

DALE G. RANGE
JAMES R. LAYTON
DARRELL L. ROUBINEK

When viewed simultaneously, the information in the preceding chapters may be interpreted to contain implications in terms of knowledge and practices for three major groups: (1) family members, (2) teachers in early childhood programs, and (3) designers of early childhood education pre- and in-service programs. The remainder of this chapter includes those implications. There will be some overlap contained in the implications as there should be. Until a solid, united effort is exerted to meet the needs of young children, then less than desirable results will be obtained. Also, until subsequent higher levels of education for children beyond 8 years of age are designed to accommodate and allow for children to progress smoothly in accordance with their ability levels, then early childhood education efforts may have been largely wasted. However, if the establishment of early childhood programs provides children with an opportunity for a smooth and continuous transition from home to school with several years of success within the school, then the efforts of early childhood education may be labeled as effective and worthwhile.

ASPECTS OF EARLY CHILDHOOD EDUCATION
Theory to Research to Practice

FAMILY AND PARENTING:
THE BASE FOR SUCCESSFUL
SCHOOL ACHIEVEMENT

Parents must come to understand that the initial success their children achieve in school may be more related to familial variables than school related or teacher variables. Although many teachers are well prepared and can provide individualized programs for a variety of linguistic, cultural, and handicapping conditions of young children, *many* are unable to do so. Often the ambitious efforts of those teachers will fail as a result of community and familial influences that may have affected the children's perceptions of themselves and their view of *their* world.

Parents who exert efforts to learn more about child growth and development and seek the aid of teachers to help them understand and learn their roles and responsibilities as parents will probably enhance their parenting roles. Early childhood educators should not reject parents with those desires. Once parents have learned that they are more effective and their children are more successful when they appropriately match their actions with their children's stages of growth and development, then chances for parent–teacher cooperation exist. However, the process is not a simple one.

Early childhood researchers have indicated that programs designed to include parents had the greatest impact on the children's success. But according to researchers, at least 2 years were required to affect significant changes. During a training program, parents must be presented general and specific information about themselves and about their children. Many parents may encounter difficulty accepting certain types of information and assimilating it into their present store of knowledge or learning to apply the knowledge to change themselves as well as their children.

Parents must be taught that their children's behaviors between 10 months and 3 years of age are largely a result of parenting and child-rearing practices. Prior to and after those years, parents must be brought to understand that they are solely responsible for the safety and economic security of their children. Many childhood physical, mental, emotional, language, and intellectual anomolies observed in young children, even at 1 year of age, can be traced directly to exogenous causes rather that indogenous ones.

Parents must also be educated to view modeling as one of the most potent teaching techniques available. However, parents must also come to know that genetic and societal variables will also affect children's behaviors and that children's temperaments and certain other behaviors cannot always be traced directly to modeling. Still, parents who become aware that their teaching styles (impulsive, compulsive, nondirective, and so forth) may be responsible for their children's learning styles, have a better opportunity to change, when necessary, than parents without that knowledge. Parents must learn that they are often likely to view their physically or mentally handicapped or physically unattractive children with disdain or be embarrassed by them. With this understanding, parents may be well on their way to overcoming many familial situations that may have direct bearing upon their children's school and home behaviors.

As teachers, parents must learn appropriate procedures for becoming effective models. Their efforts should be largely in the direction of developing their children's total growth and development rather than attending to only a few behaviors. Areas of safety, security, and language should be stressed with the knowledge that children will sometimes set higher goals for themselves than their parents will establish for them. Although external influences will alter the goals children establish, parents who learn to communicate openly with their children will be better able to aid children in establishing appropriate goals and in coping with frustration when ambitious goals are not realized.

Parents must learn not only to communicate openly with their children, but also to project warmth as they control and shape their children's behaviors, require relatively high standards of mature behavior, delegate responsibilities, and lead their children toward self-control and self-discipline. Parents who can perform those tasks effectively while at the same time provide a healthy balance of freedom and independence within set limits will, in most instances, rear well-adjusted children.

Parents who are overly rigid and lack warmth may not produce well-adjusted children. However, when parents resort to violent behaviors, they compound children's problems. Abused and neglected children enter formal schooling yearly. They have been characterized as listless, apathetic, noninteractive, and unattractive in personality. The characteristics of parents that have impact upon children's behaviors must be communicated to all parents who, through group efforts, could help eliminate the existence of such practices.

Looking broadly at the general responsibilities of parents toward their children, while at the same time considering the reasons for Head Start in 1964, there appears to be support for the criticism that the success of Head Start was evaluated solely upon the academic achievement of the pupils and not the positive impact of the social services, medical aid, and especially parent involvement. As parents do become involved in the education of their young children, they must receive correct and appropriate information that will lead to their success as teachers and their children's success as learners. Those successes are initiated in the home.

Home Environment

In addition to the specific roles and responsibilities that parents should accept liability for, in interacting with, and in their attitudes toward their children, several other areas of knowledge should be provided. Within the community and home are many persons, institutions, and figural objects that to unknown degrees will influence children's behaviors. In addition, those also may be sources for enhancing or diminishing various aspects of children's growth and development. But essentially, models provided by parents, peers, siblings, and other adults in the community will exert strong influences upon young children's overt and covert behaviors.

Three major areas that were extracted from the information presented in the foregoing chapters have direct bearing on young children's development. Those are linguistic stimulation, play, and television. Apparently, young children entering formal schooling will have developed cognitive, affective, psychomotor, and creative skills that have resulted from verbal and nonverbal forms of communication, playing, and watching television.

Parents should know techniques to stimulate their children's language development to enable the children to establish a linguistic coding system early in life. One of the best ways that an environment can be provided is through frequent and diverse opportunities for play. Parents must understand that young children will derive many more benefits from play than from formal teaching that parents may employ. Parents also need to know that one of the detriments to active play is the tendency of children to consume too much time watching television.

Television cannot be judged as either *good* or *bad*, but certainly when viewing habits interfere with verbal interaction with family members and friends, free active play, and learning in the home, then no one would argue the merits of television. The major knowledge and skills that parents should learn concerning television include the following.

1. Television productions may be categorized into three major types: (a) commercial (prime time shows, cartoons, etc.); (b) educational (Sesame Street, Electric Company, etc.); and (c) instructional (programs designed to be used in schools with teacher guidance); parents should learn to identify the types of programs children watch.

2. A linguistic gap may exist between the children's language level and that used on television; if the content of the video portion is dependent upon the audio portion to clarify concepts and explain happenings, the child's learning may be foreign to those intended; also, since the children did not understand the oral portion, few linguistic skills were gained.

3. Television commercials may be responsible for children's desires for foods and other material goods that are a source of conflict between the

parents and children; additionally children who cannot separate reality and fantasy may harm themselves emulating television personalities.

4. Emotional aspects of some television programs may cause unconscious anxieties and fears in young children unbeknown to their parents or the children.

Parents should learn to objectively and subjectively evaluate the television programs available for their children to view. Violent and nonviolent shows cannot be predicted based upon titles or the times they occur. Violent and emotional impact are found within many programs purported to be especially for children.

Children's emotional development can be fostered through play and through stories read or told to them. Appropriate sex roles can be established best by parent, peer, and sibling models. Attitudes toward responsibilities and work habits are established best through those same models. To unconsciously depend upon television viewing for those important learnings is illogical and erroneous. However, the major reason that televiewing may be harmful to children is that parents miss opportunities to teach important lessons and to shape their children's behaviors in ways that are considered essential if success in school is to be realized.

Shaping Behavior

Recent reports from many agencies have revealed that parents and teachers are concerned about discipline in the schools. Each group in one way or another likes to delegate the responsibility to the other or to the children themselves. It is true that at certain maturity levels children do exert their strengths to become independent. However, those desires and efforts do not accumulate overnight and appear the next morning. When parents of adolescent children suddenly discover that they have lost control of their children, it would be difficult to convince them that the source of the problem could have possibly begun during the formative 3-, 4-, or 5-year-old period.

Parents are responsible for many aspects of their children's development. Teaching specific concepts and developing attitudes cannot be separated from their responsibility to shape their children's behaviors in such a way as to provide the children with attributes that will allow them to learn efficiently and effectively.

Parents must learn that love alone will not suffice to provide for their children's learning needs. In fact, data are available to support the contention that parents who are overindulgent and permissive lessen their children's abilities to cope successfully in social and educational environments. Parents must also recognize that children will avoid an authority figure whose role is that of a dispenser of punishment and nothing more. Mothers or fathers who require children to wait to receive punishment from the other parent create more problems than are solved. Parents who ignore their children except when they are to be punished for unacceptable acts also violate basic principles of accepted behavior modification techniques, as established by social learning theorists. From the preceding chapters, the statements below appear pertinent for parents and teachers if children's behaviors are to be shaped. Although the statements are presented as guidelines for controlling, shaping, and changing behaviors, each is also closely related to teaching. Educational programs for parents designed to aid them in understanding and guiding children's behavior would include the following concepts.

1. Parents must learn to establish realistic standards for their children and also guide their children so that they learn to set realistic standards for themselves.

2. Parents must understand and be aware that through interaction with their children, the parents' behavior can change; if the parents' behavior change places the children in control, then an unhealthy situation exists.

3. Parents who behave in restrictive and rigid manners will likely produce compliant, obedient, conscientious, and relatively overinhibited children who will develop conforming and dependent-prone personalities.

4. Young children will copy or mimic specific behaviors of parents, other adults, peers, and siblings when those models are observed receiving rewards for the behaviors.

5. Parents should learn that attending to some undesirable behaviors exhibited by children will constitute a type of reward and the behavior may continue; praising other children who are not displaying the behavior, thus ignoring the misbehaving child, may produce better results.

6. Parents who can provide an adequate amount of warmth and discipline can predict children's immediate and future behaviors in most instances.

7. Parents must learn the differences between positive and negative incentives, how to apply each, and be made aware that a child's perception of either kind of incentive employed may be opposite of that intended.

8. Parents must learn that material, activity, social, verbal, and nonverbal incentives exist and that the overuse of any one may have diminishing effects; however, an important learning for parents is that incentives and bribes are not synonymous.

9. Parents must learn to employ inductive techniques in which children learn the negative consequences of their actions upon others;

parents should also learn that assertive techniques are not useful in guiding children toward mature, self-discipline.

10. Parents must learn to guide children to the level of self-punishment which, when internalized, will result in children's behaving in socially acceptable manners.

11. Parents who set limits for their children's behaviors and do not accept nagging, whining, and crying behaviors, will produce better adjusted children.

12. Parents will be better relaxed and able to provide a more favorable learning environment if their child's temperament is mild.

13. Parents may experience difficulty in shaping and controlling the behaviors of impulsive children and may require special counseling.

14. When parents resort to punishment to control behavior, the punishment and rationale should be commensurate with the child's level of understanding; the rationale should be in concrete terms rather than abstract ones.

15. Parents should learn that punishment is the least effective of all incentives and that results from it cannot be predicted; also, many times a restatement of a rule may suffice to terminate an unwanted behavior without punishment.

16. Parents who model aggressive behaviors may produce children who exhibit aggressive and antisocial behaviors.

17. Parents who use punishment without favorable results and subsequently continue to employ progressively stronger forms of punishment may reach a point of abusing their children.

18. Parents should learn that there is no one-to-one causative relationship between parents' actions and their children's reactions.

19. Parents must learn that punishment, especially physical punishment, is most effective when rarely used.

Learning to behave in specific manners is learned through a system of observation and imitation and is analagous to learning to talk. Linguistic and behavioral characteristics exhibited by children reflect the values, mores, culture, attitudes of community and home members. Upon entry into early childhood education programs, the amount of knowledge children have, their learning styles, and their problem-solving abilities will, to a large degree, also reflect environmental influences. Therefore, parents should be alerted to their roles and responsibilities as teachers.

Teaching

Techniques employed to shape behavior are also employed to teach children. As was stated earlier, teaching is a means to shape children's behaviors into desired forms. When parents enter a cooperative educational venture with school personnel, one major precaution should be taken. Parents, especially mothers, should not be delegated secondary roles in providing for the welfare of their children. Additionally, teachers must use information supplied by parents or gained during home visits to establish an appropriate educational climate for the child in school. Parents must learn to interact with teachers to explain their teaching styles and plan learning activities for the child especially in instances where the child has been identified as mildly or severely handicapped. Many of the principles and specific activities parents should learn appear below.

1. Parents must learn that their attitudes toward, performance in, and attention to intellectual pursuits in many instances will be reflected in their children's behaviors.

2. Parents must learn that their abilities to aid their children in building self-concepts, feelings of self-esteem, and learning to gain the self-esteem of others, is one of their major teaching responsibilities.

3. Parents must be taught techniques of interacting with young children in ways that will motivate the children to engage in appropriate, but vigorous physical, linguistic, and mental activities.

4. Parents must learn that children will be better adjusted and learn more if they are allowed to express themselves freely; adjustment and learning are enhanced if parents welcome such expressions with warmth and understanding.

5. Parents should be provided with information concerning aspects of language functions that serve as substructures to reading, listening, composition, and mathematics skills to be learned in school; parents should learn to provide activities that will stimulate growth in those substructure areas but not to teach the basic skills per se.

6. Parents should learn questioning techniques that will lead children through problem solving sequences and also lead to children's use of questioning.

7. Parents must learn that children cannot learn by observing only; some overt and covert, physical and congitive behaviors to be learned must be divided into small units, taught through figural contents and verbal explanations, then recombined or synthesized into wholes.

8. Parents must learn that appropriate modeling, verbal explanation, concrete examples in simplified steps, and verbal instructions at the child's level of understanding will enhance learning.

9. Parents must provide children with opportunities for practice and rehearsal of things learned, as well as guided practice if learning is to be complete.

10. Parents must be informed of the nature of young children who are

constantly changing interests and activities, and that undue, forced teaching may produce harmful effects.

The major teaching responsibility of parents is to provide environments for their children in which self-discipline and self-control are learned. The degree to which children can control their behavior will relate directly to their success in school. Parents can also be effective in providing information to teachers that may be used to reduce the cultural and linguistic gap between the teacher and the child. Parents and teachers can cooperate in providing children with optimum opportunities for rule learning, obedient behaviors, tolerance of delay, and persistence in performing tasks.

Summary

Parents' inclusion into early intervention programs is an absolute necessity if teachers are to be successful in their somewhat ambitious tasks to provide the least restrictive, most appropriate education for all children. Earlier it was stated that parent programs should span approximately 2 years. A review of the parental information presented above may lead to the thought that 2 years may be a minimum period. Teachers and other school officials are urged to develop parent programs even in view of the reports that many of the programs were ineffective.

Seemingly, in the final analysis, the bulk of the responsibility to provide adequate programs for young children lies with the classroom teacher. The information presented thus far in this chapter was related to parents' characteristics, behaviors, and roles as teachers but can be employed by teachers, as well as parents. However, those recommendations will not be repeated in the following section.

IMPLICATIONS FOR TEACHERS WHO DEVELOP EARLY CHILDHOOD EDUCATION PROGRAMS

Teachers should be taught to design and implement early childhood education programs based partly upon aspects of community and familial (societal) variables and specifically the teaching and behavioral management techniques of the adult models in the family. Also, teachers of young children must understand the nature of learning and techniques of providing activities that employ the most reputable research-supported ideas from the maturational, cognitive, and behavioral viewpoints. An earlier chapter directed teachers to design learning systems that would allow children from linguistically and culturally distinct groups to become bicognitive. Certainly such an ambitious task cannot be accomplished without the teachers' full knowledge of the philosophical, educational points of view found within the community and family units and also provisions to include family members into early childhood educational programming.

It may appear contradictory to demand that early childhood educational specialists design programs that are educationally sound then recommend that parents, especially those who are largely uneducated and socioculturally distinct, aid in the planning of those programs. Additionally, it may appear ridiculous also to recommend that the teaching techniques found in the home be utilized by teachers to allow children to continue learning in ways commensurate with the home style, while the children begin newer learning techniques that will result in their being bicognitive. But if teachers are to design programs that allow them to teach children to regulate their behaviors effectively and induce them to incorporate realistic standards of achievement and performance into their behaviors, then the total child must be studied. Additionally, as teachers pursue those tasks they must also insure that their own race, sex, cultural, and socioeconomic backgrounds do not interfere with their attitudes toward the children. Beyond the establishment of objectives and sequencing activities to achieve those objectives, teachers must also know methods of evaluation. Evaluation techniques must be employed to describe success in terms of the consequence behaviors of youngsters. Attempts to view successful growth in terms of academic or intellectual achievement only will be erroneous. The impact that early childhood teachers have upon young children should be much more encompassing and far reaching.

Teachers must incorporate the teaching and behavioral management techniques presented earlier in this chapter into their operational procedures as part of their plans to (a) reduce the linguistic gap and cultural division between teacher and child and (b) allow the child to transfer easily and comfortably from the home to the school. Teachers msut also establish purposes for the school's existence and design sequenced activities that will lead to the achievement of objectives that will satisfy the intents of those purposes. To accomplish those tasks, teachers will need to develop knowledge skills in (a) involving parents, (b) screening and diagnosis, (c) behavior management, and (d) teaching, as each relates to a well-balanced curriculum.

Parent-Teacher Communication

Teachers and parents must develop cooperative, reciprocal communicative systems that become mutually advantageous for each. Teachers learn from parents of the facilities and techniques in the community and home that led to the linguistic, cognitive, behavioral characteristics of the child. Parents are made aware of the purposes of the school, the methods employed to teach, and the expectations of the child. Through initial and continued interaction between teachers and parents adjustments are made for the child in both the home and the school. In that way, teachers can encorporate the mother's teaching style in the school and mothers can begin using certain teacher practices in the home.

Parents provide teachers with valuable information. Conversely, teachers supply parents with information related to child growth and development patterns and other aspects of the educational environment of the home. That information would include the following.

1. Health and safety precautions
2. Importance of adult models
3. Language stimulation activities
4. Social-learning theory teaching techniques
5. The importance of and provisions for free play
6. The importance of and activities for social and linguistic interaction
7. The role of television viewing in diminishing linguistic, emotional–social, and cognitive development
8. The use of television to stimulate and motivate children toward linguistic, cognitive, and emotional–social development
9. Techniques for using modeling, incentive, and punishment to change behavior.

As previously mentioned, an inherent danger in teacher–parent cooperation is that of diminishing the role of the mother in childrearing. Precautions must be taken to assure that mothers do not perceive their tasks as secondary. Also, the recommendations above cannot be allocated sporadically. Instead, they must be incorporated into a program for parents and dispensed in a combined ongoing guidance program with provisions for flexible dispensation as special needs arise. Programs so designed not only provide services to young children who are in school, but allow parents and teachers to monitor, through a process of continuous screening, the development of younger children who have not reached the age required for school entry.

Screening and Diagnosis

Many authorities, including Burton White, believe that children's mild learning problems can be identified by the second year and that severe problems can be observed by the first year of a child's life. Seemingly, if the anomolies or debilities discovered are correctable through medical, educational, or psychological treatment, it behooves all early childhood educators to learn techniques of screening, diagnosis, and remediation. The specialists must also be adept at analyzing disabilities and referring the parents to specialists in allied fields when it is determined that surface symptoms are caused possibly by conditions that cannot be corrected by educational techniques alone. Teachers' responsibilities in screening, diagnosis, and remediation include the following.

1. Developing a vast mental repertoire of children's characteristics and behaviors at various ages and be perceptive of children who appear to vary significantly from the norms
2. From the normative information available, utilizing and/or devising observational checklists used to record instances of developmental lag in physical development, linguistic proficiencies, cognitive and intellectual characteristics, perceptual development, and self-discipline and self-control as observed during free play and structured learning experiences
3. Developing screening techniques to identify children who have impulsive, compulsive, aggressive, passive, or work-avoidance behaviors that interfere with learning; subsequently, when warranted, diagnostic measures would be used by the teacher (or for referral) for in-depth diagnosis
4. Providing appropriate learning sequences for children who have mild handicaps, are linguistically or culturally distinct, or who exhibit behaviors within normal limits
5. Designing varied and specific activities and attending to teaching learning style matches for children with or without problems as specified above
6. Developing techniques for parent programs, parent conferences, and parental inclusion as relates to gaining permission for diagnosis, special placement, or the teacher–parent roles and responsibilities in aiding young children in overcoming their problems

Screening, diagnosis, and remediation procedures, in totality, should evolve into prescriptive techniques in which teachers employ varieties of appropriate teaching and behavioral change techniques. Those procedures based upon learning theories and knowledge of learners, should be the foremost responsibility of teachers. However, teaching academic skills is only one of the responsibilities of teachers. Children's behaviors, when separated from academic and intellectual variables, are also the responsibility of the teacher. Bright children in creative or gifted classes, children in special or handicapped classes, or children who are classified within the broad category of normal or average, fail at times to develop behaviors for social, educational, and other types of interactions. For that reason, early childhood specialists and parents must develop plans to foster the development of behaviors that will form the substructures of subsequent, acceptable behaviors in a variety of situations

Behavior Management

The reader is reminded that this chapter contains implications for the education of young children, for parents, teachers, and faculty members in departments or schools in institutions of higher education. The implications are drawn from the foregoing chapters with few references to the specific chapters. Hom and Hom, and Robinson in Chapters 3, 4, and 5 presented adequate information that can be employed by parents and teachers to control and shape children's behaviors. The other writers also presented cogent suggestions or recommendations to teachers' roles in modifying children's behaviors. In essence the writers contended that early childhood teachers would be more successful if they did the following.

1. Learn to be authoritative and not authoritarian in character
2. Employ inductive techniques to change young children's behaviors as opposed to assertive techniques which may lead to strong disciplinary measures
3. Set limits for children's behaviors, but have inherent flexibility in the rules
4. Utilize alternate forms of behavior shaping schemes to match models' behaviors, incentives, and punishment to the characteristics of the child
5. Be aware that misbehaviors may result from teaching techniques or models
6. Employ materials, activities, social, verbal, nonverbal, affection withdrawal, and physical incentives in proper proportions, matched to children's personalities, learning styles, and needs
7. Model effectively, whether involved in social, emotional, intellectual, physical, or achievement skill learning situations
8. Employ positive incentives rather than negative or punishment incentives
9. Know that the restatement of rule can suffice in many situations and preclude the need for punishment
10. Know that all punishment should be accompanied by concrete, not abstract, rationale

11. Employ verbal remarks and oral gestures that will indicate to the child that a specific behavior is unacceptable
12. Develop skills to ignore forms of children's inappropriate behaviors by shifting attention to a child or group by remarking about their appropriate behavior at the time the inappropriate behavior is occuring
13. Know that the same incentives or punishments used too frequently may diminish in affecting desired behaviors
14. Know that punishment should be the last resort and least used incentive
15. Develop programs in which adult control of children's behaviors guides the children to internalized self-punishment and control that surfaces in the form of socially acceptable behaviors

Teachers who design parental programs, and sequenced activities that lead to increased learning and behavior growth capabilities should incorporate those aspects of early childhood education into the total curriculum. Within the total curriculum, provisions must be made not only for children to learn substructures of and possibly basic skills in reading, writing, and mathematics, but also fine arts, social and physical sciences, literature, physical and social recreation, and other liberal arts disciplines. To provide less would be erroneous and disastrous for young children. All of the content or subject matter areas that children are to encounter during formal schooling and when formal learning has been terminated should be appropriately incorporated into the early childhood education curriculum.

Chapter 1 of this book contains the major beliefs of maturational, behavioral, and cognitive proponents toward the types of activities that would be contained in their early childhood programs. Chapter 2 contains specific programs that have been designed and implemented in accordance with those views. Chapter 5 contains social learning theory that is applicable for developing programs for young children. Finally, Chapter 6 contains research data that is used by Kohut to present beliefs about young learners and learning, teachers and teaching, and the environment that should be established for learning to occur. By combining the authors' views simultaneously, the following major points concerning teachers and curriculum appear relevant.

1. Early childhood education programs should be designed to be eclectic in nature and open-ended. But the programs should be highly structured (objectives and teachers' roles and responsibilities) in terms of outcomes for young children's learning behavior.
2. Children must be provided with appropriate activities in struc-

tured, sequential stages to allow teachers to instruct and monitor learning and behavior, but children should be allowed to progress naturally through the sequence and not forced unduly.

3. Learning sequences should not be designed to be narrow in scope; neither should the teacher focus upon only rote memory tasks and academic concepts; broader, more basic social and cognitive skills must be included in the curriculum design.

4. Objectives, properly sequenced, in a competency/performance based scheme, with accompanying activities that contain provisions for learning and teaching preferences and alternatives, will be superior to other designs.

5. Competency/performance programs should contain adequate provisions for structured and unstructured discovery learning and play.

6. Teachers must know that young children will set high goals for themselves but that their accomplishment of those goals may be altered by exogenous and endogenous variables.

7. Teachers must learn to model the behaviors (verbal, nonverbal, intellectual, academic, and so forth) they desire young children to adopt or emulate. Those models can be presented best through structured sequences in which observational learning is planned, not left to chance.

8. Children can learn to master many new learnings if the total is presented in smaller units or components, taught one step at a time, and later recombined or synthesized into the whole; the learning can be enhanced by using linguistic forms and terms that children can readily understand.

9. Breaking whole learning tasks into parts will enable children to learn certain skills; however, teachers must ascertain the necessity of the skill and if the time devoted to teaching/learning the skill should be allocated to other, more important learnings.

10. As teachers model specific behaviors and guide children in learning new concepts and skills, appropriate problem solving questions should be asked that will stimulate children to think; those questioning techniques should be presented in such a manner that children will learn to use them as they progress through various experiences or activities.

11. Formal reading and mathematics teaching/learning should be delayed until children have developed a desire to read and do arithmetic and have developed substructure skills, readiness, or prereading-mathematics skills sufficiently well that learning to read and perform in arithmetic will be easy.

12. The introduction of reading and mathematics into preschool programs should be initiated informally; parents and teachers should cooperate to shape instruction to the child's learning preferences, growth and development characteristics, and needs; employing predesigned, commercially prepared materials arbitrarily to large groups of children predestines many to failure.

13. The formal introduction of formal mathematical and reading skill development in the kindergarten or lower levels of early childhood education will require that the total curriculum in higher grades be revised and adjusted accordingly.

14. New learnings that are introduced should be accompanied by plans for adequate amounts of guided practice, time for rehearsal, and provisions for physical and emotional reinforcement and support, prior to introducing another learning that requires the newly learned skill.

15. Children, given the opportunity, will be able to learn in several separate and distinct areas during the same period of time.

16. Evaluation techniques must be designed to measure the consequence behaviors of children; the consequence behavior would be used to evaluate the appropriateness of the lesson, the teaching technique employed, the learning preference of the child, or the child's readiness for the learning.

17. Unstructured or informal discovery learning environments and accompanying teaching techniques will not be sufficient to allow teachers to teach young children all that they need to learn; however structured or unstructured discovery learning activities will provide children avenues for some cognitive, language, intellectual, social and emotional learning.

18. Free or structured play can provide children with opportunities to master certain aspects of their environment; however, as in the case of discovery learning, play cannot serve as the sole means for education even though much physical and mental vigor is generated.

19. Teachers can provide visual, auditory, kinesthetic, olfactory, tactile, and gustatory figural content aids as they model certain learnings; but random uncontrolled use of such devices only may be detrimental to learning.

20. Teachers must evaluate each goal, objective, learning activity, internal demand of the child, and external demand made upon the child to insure that none encroach upon the child's human rights or jeopardize physical, mental, and emotional safety and security.

Program Components

Early childhood education specialists will be expected to develop parent involvement in programs, early screening and diagnosis procedures, and design, as well as teach in programs for young children. With the advent of the enforcement of Public Law 94-142, those tasks are no longer viewed as *desirable*, but are for the most part *required*. The curriculum that is designed by early childhood education specialists could be no more than a collection of various predesigned, packaged programs through which the teacher and the children progress each day, whether learning occurs or not. The program could be quasi-eclectic, or a conglomeration of activities using various materials used in accordance with views of protagonists representing the various points of view presented in Chapter 1. A teacher may, however, establish a true eclectic program as described in Chapter 1 or employ one of the specific programs described by Day in Chapter 2. But whatever direction the early childhood education specialist chooses, the program that is designed should contain several components, carefully balanced, to insure that children's growth and development can be stimulated.

Aspects of the Curriculum

Essential or Basic Skills Aspect

Provisions must be made for children to develop the specific prerequisite skills, as each is able, to successfully encounter the tasks of learning to read, learning to solve arithmetical problems, and learning to write. Foremost among those skills will be the ability to (a) attend, (b) store, (c) recall, (d) discriminate between visual and auditory stimuli, (e) be directionally oriented, (f) be effective in oral presentations, and (g) follow oral directions. Although some children who do not have all those characteristics learn to read and do arithmetic, the presence of the abilities will enhance their abilities to learn well.

Application or Functional Skills Aspect

When children enter the early school program they should be afforded many opportunities to receive and express ideas and knowledge. The degree to which those modalities are utilized will have a reciprocal effect on the degree to which the essential or basic skills areas develop. Rather than attending to the essential skills per se, teachers should devise sequential lessons in all content and psychomotor (art, music, physical education) areas. The content and activities of those curriculum areas should be used as carriers to guide and direct children's development of essential skills, while at the same time used to develop their knowledge, skills, and abilities to question, identify problems, and solve problems inherent in functional areas of the curriculum. An integrated approach as described here will allow for the inclusion of children with varying levels and degrees of abilities, even though some will be able to perform better than others. Still, the behavioral and learning principles can be controlled better in integrated procedures rather than segregated ones. And too, debilitated learners will not be isolated or rejected from activities, if teachers can organize the learning sequences properly and attend to the special characteristics of all learners.

Relaxation or Recreational Skills Aspect

Without special provisions for relaxation or recreational skills many developers of early childhood programs may design activities void of providing children with time to rest, relax, and refresh themselves. To many authorities, free play, discovery learning periods, recess, and so forth, may serve to fulfill the children's need for relaxation or internally or externally motivated forms of entertainment. However, early childhood specialists should design programs in which teachers allow young children opportunities for unstructured play, and other forms of recreation. Also, teachers must provide for structured recreational activities. By providing structured recreational activities for children, teachers can open new avenues of interest for children to explore and evaluate, then accept or reject them. However, opportunities for free and structured relaxation and recreation must be provided and balanced carefully with other aspects of the total early childhood education curriculum. But building favorable attitudes, respect, and love for educational or intellectual endeavors cannot be left to chance.

Speaking and Listening Skills Aspect

Although it is intended by many curriculum planners that children will be allowed many opportunities for verbal interaction with the teacher and peers, such plans should not be left to chance. And too, many teachers assume that an activity that is presented orally, in which children are allowed to participate either spontaneously or after seeking permission to speak by raising their hands, will naturally develop listening skills and speaking skills. Listening comprehension, including auditory discrimination and following spoken directions, will provide children with at least part of the abilities required to learn to read and solve mathematical problems. The children's performances in listening and understanding and their ability to express themselves verbally in comprehensible thought patterns may be early indications of learning problems, creativeness, or giftedness. Listening and speaking skills should be included in integrated lessons, but should be designed separately when the curriculum areas for young children are being prepared.

Corrective/Remedial Aspect

The need for early childhood education specialists to become expert in observing, screening, diagnosing, and remediating has been presented. To dwell upon the issue is hardly necessary. However, when objectives are established and activities are designed in accordance with research findings related to learners and learning processes, and a child who is carefully placed in the activity performs at a lower level than expected, the event must be studied. Through analysis, the teacher may determine that the task was above the child's ability level; it may be discovered that the incorrect teaching/learning style was employed; or the problem may be an indication of a more serious learning problem. The purpose for writing this book was not to delve into corrective and remedial practices, but the exclusion of provisions for screening, diagnosis, and remediation in the design and implementation of early childhood education curriculum cannot be ignored.

The foregoing statements are applicable to any portion of early childhood education programs or curriculum development. The presentation thus far has included implications for parents and implications for teachers. Considered simultaneously, both may be interpreted to reflect the responsibilities of faculty members in departments or schools of early childhood education to educate prospective teachers or develop inservice education programs that will produce highly qualified early childhood specialists.

IMPLICATIONS FOR EDUCATORS OF EARLY CHILDHOOD EDUCATION SPECIALISTS

Early childhood education specialists play a vital role in the total educational personnel community. In fact, if children's initial attempts to learn in formal educational environments are as important as many educators, psychologists, and psycholinguists believe, then the early childhood educator may be the most important teacher a child will encounter. Seemingly, the programs for educating early childhood education specialists must be cleverly and scientifically designed to insure that their behaviors are as well-shaped as the children whom they will teach.

In Chapter 1 reference was made to Zigler's work in competency-based programs; later the ideas of Sever and Cartwright were presented. In Chapter 6, Kohut presented a wealth of data related to teaching and teacher characteristics. From among those ideas, two positional statements have been generated.

1. The education of early childhood specialists should be an integrated, on-going process in which teacher educators use a set of sequenced objectives to guide the cognitive, affective, and teaching skill development of early childhood education specialists.
2. To guide the cognitive, affective, and teaching skill development of early childhood educators, the objectives that are established and sequenced should be administered through competency/performance based programs rather than through traditional systems.

The major goals that would be used to guide the development of the specific objectives would include all those ideas and recommendations that were included in the chapters. To repeat them, at this point, would be anticlimatical. But for those readers who accept Seaver and Cartwright's ideas for teacher education as presented in Chapter 1, this book contains the necessary data for designing such a program.

Index

EDUCATIONAL PSYCHOLOGY

continued from page ii

Donald J. Treffinger, J. Kent Davis, and Richard E. Ripple (eds.). Handbook on Teaching Educational Psychology

Harry L. Hom, Jr. and Paul A. Robinson (eds.). Psychological Processes in Early Education

J. Nina Lieberman. Playfulness: Its Relationship to Imagination and Creativity

Samuel Ball (ed.). Motivation in Education

Erness Bright Brody and Nathan Brody. Intelligence: Nature, Determinants, and Consequences

António Simões (ed.). The Bilingual Child: Research and Analysis of Existing Educational Themes

Gilbert R. Austin. Early Childhood Education: An International Perspective

Vernon L. Allen (ed.). Children as Teachers: Theory and Research on Tutoring

Joel R. Levin and Vernon L. Allen (eds.). Cognitive Learning in Children: Theories and Strategies

Donald E. P. Smith and others. A Technology of Reading and Writing (in four volumes).

> *Vol. 1. Learning to Read and Write: A Task Analysis (by Donald E. P. Smith)*
> *Vol. 2. Criterion-Referenced Tests for Reading and Writing (by Judith M. Smith, Donald E. P. Smith, and James R. Brink)*
> *Vol. 3. The Adaptive Classroom (by Donald E. P. Smith)*
> *Vol. 4. Designing Instructional Tasks (by Judith M. Smith)*

Phillip S. Strain, Thomas P. Cooke, and Tony Apolloni. Teaching Exceptional Children: Assessing and Modifying Social Behavior